Caffé Magia

Ristorante Italiano

198 2nd Street San Francisco
546-6985

Lucio Fanni
Sergio Frigerio

THE
AMERICAN EXPRESS
POCKET GUIDE TO
LOS ANGELES
& SAN FRANCISCO

Brian Eads

PRENTICE HALL PRESS
NEW YORK

The Author

Brian Eads is a widely traveled foreign correspondent who has worked for *Newsweek*, *The Washington Post*, the London *Observer* and the BBC. He is now with Granada Television and lives in Derbyshire, England.

Acknowledgment

The author and publishers would like to thank Bob Thompson, author of the excellent *The American Express Guide to California*, to which this new volume owes a great deal.

General Editor   David Townsend Jones
Art Editor   Nigel O'Gorman
Designer   Christopher Howson
Illustrator   Karen Cochrane
Map Editor   David Haslam
Indexer   Hilary Bird

Edited and designed by
Mitchell Beazley International Limited,
Artists House, 14-15 Manette Street,
London W1V 5LB
for the American Express Pocket Travel
Guide Series

Published by Prentice Hall Trade
Division
A Division of Simon & Schuster, Inc.
Gulf & Western Building
One Gulf & Western Plaza
New York, New York 10023
PRENTICE HALL is a trademark of
Simon & Schuster, Inc.

**Library of Congress
Cataloging-in-Publication Data**
Eads, Brian
  The American Express pocket
  guide to Los Angeles and San
  Francisco / Brian Eads
    p.   cm.
  ISBN 0-13-025305-7 : $10.95
  1. Los Angeles (Calif.)—
  Description—1981- —Guide-books.
  2. San Francisco (Calif.)—
  Description—Guide-books.
  I. Title.
F869.L83E23 1990
917.94'610453—dc20   89-36975
                                  CIP

Maps in 2-color and 4-color by Lovell Johns Ltd, Oxford, England.
Typeset by Castle House Press, Llantrisant, Wales.
Typeset in Garamond and Univers.
Linotronic output through Microstar DTP Studio, Cardiff, Wales.
Produced by Mandarin Offset. Printed and bound in Malaysia.

Contents

Los Angeles

San Francisco

How to use this book

The *American Express Pocket Guide to Los Angeles and San Francisco* is an encyclopedia of travel information, organized in the sections listed on the previous page. There is also a comprehensive *Index* (pages 166-173) and *Street gazetteers* for both cities (pages 173-176), and there are full-color *Maps* at the end of the book.

For easy reference, all major sections (*Sights and places of interest*, *Hotels*, *Restaurants*), and other sections where possible, are arranged alphabetically. For the organization of the book as a whole, see *Contents*. For individual places that do not have separate entries in *Sights and places of interest*, look in the *Index*.

Abbreviations

As a rule only standard abbreviations have been used, such as days of the week and months, points of the compass (N, S, E and W), street names (Ave., Blvd., Pl., Sq., Dr., Rd., St.), Saint (St) rms (rooms), C for century, and measurements.

Bold type

Bold type is used mainly for emphasis, to highlight items of special interest or importance. It also picks out places — shops or minor museums, for example — that do not have full entries of their own. In such cases it is usually followed in brackets by the address, telephone number, details of opening times, etc., which are printed in *italics*.

Cross-references

A special type has been used for cross-references. Whenever a place or section title is printed in *sans serif italics* (for example *Alcatraz* or *Basic information*) in the text, this indicates that you can turn to the appropriate heading in the book for further information.

Cross-references in this typeface refer to (1) sections

How entries are organized

Hood House

1411 Lincoln Ave., Lincoln Green, Sherwood Forest
☎ *426-5960 (house), 426-5961 (group tour reservations).*
Map *8J11* 🗺 𝒦 *Open Apr-Sept 9am-5pm, rest of year 9am-4pm. Closed Christmas, New Year's Day. Metro: Bow & Arrow.*

Robin Hood (?1149-1205) was the leading spokesman for the poor and downtrodden in their struggle for freedom and justice under the Plantagenets. He lectured and wrote books about his own early life as a serf, campaigned endlessly for human rights, helped recruit peasants to the Civil Service, and finally settled down to a distinguished old age in Sherwood Forest. He lived first in A St. (see *National Museum of Outlawed Art*), then bought Sheriff Villa, which he renamed Hood House, a handsome white dwelling on a height overlooking the Trent Valley. All the furnishings, except for curtains and wallpaper, are original. Hood's library and other belongings are still *in situ*, and the whole house is redolent of the spirit of a very remarkable man. In the **Visitors' Centre** at the foot of the hill you can see a film about Hood's life.

of the book such as *Basic information* or *Ideas for children*; (2) individual entries in *Sights and places of interest* such as *Little Tokyo*; or (3) individual entries in *Environs and excursions* such as *Marin County*.

For easy reference, use the running heads printed at the top corner of the page. LA and SF prefixes denote the Los Angeles and San Francisco sections. See, for example, **LA Sights/Little Tokyo** on page 56 or **SF Hotels** on page 135.

Map references
Each of the full-color maps at the end of the book is divided into a grid of squares, identified vertically by letters (A, B, C, D, etc.) and horizontally by numbers (1, 2, 3, 4, etc.). A map reference identifies the page and square in which the street or place can be found — thus *Venice* is located in Map **2**C1.

Price categories
Price categories are denoted by the symbols ☐ ☐ ☐ ☐ and ☐, which signify cheap, inexpensive, moderately priced, expensive and very expensive, respectively. In the cases of hotels and restaurants these correspond approximately with the following actual prices, which give a guideline at the time of printing. Although actual prices will inevitably increase, in most cases the relative price category — for example expensive or cheap — is likely to remain more or less the same. Dollar amounts quoted below reflect prices in fall 1989.

Price categories	Corresponding to approximate prices	
	for **hotels** *double room with bath and breakfast; single not much cheaper)*	for **restaurants** *meal for one with service, tax and house wine*
☐ cheap	under $50	under $15
☐ inexpensive	$50-75	$15-25
☐ moderate	$75-125	$25-35
☐ expensive	$125-175	$35-50
☐ very expensive	over $175	over $50

— Bold blue type for entry headings.

— Blue italics for address, practical information and symbols.
For list of symbols see page 6 or back flap of jacket.

— Black text for description.

— Sans serif italics used for cross-references to other entries or sections.

— Bold type used for emphasis.

Entries for hotels, restaurants, shops, etc. follow the same organization, and are usually printed across a half column.
In hotels, symbols indicating special facilities appear at the end of the entry, in black.

Pullman
*2600 Express Ave., Orient City 20037 ☎ 299-4450 ⓕ 299-4460. Map 2F4 ☐ 238 rms ☞ ☞ ☒ ☒ ☒ ☒ ☒ Metro: High Standard.
Location: On a height overlooking the Universal Trade Center.* Part of a large conglomeration overlooking the seafront, this luxurious hotel is set in attractively landscaped grounds and is run with clockwork precision. Its restaurant, the **Simplon**, is highly regarded.
☒ ☒ ☒ ☒ ☒

Key to symbols

☎	Telephone	🚗	Secure garage
ⓕ	Facsimile (fax)	◠	Quiet hotel
★	Recommended sight	♨	Elevator
☆	Worth a visit	♿	Facilities for disabled people
♣	Good value (in its class)	▢	TV in each room
i	Tourist information	☎	Telephone in each room
�""	Parking	🐾	Dogs not allowed
🏛	Building of architectural interest	☘	Garden
†	Church or cathedral	⋘	Good view
💷	Free entrance	≋	Swimming pool
💰	Entrance fee payable	🏖	Good beach nearby
📷	Photography forbidden	♂	Tennis
⸱	Guided tour	👕	Gym/fitness facilities
■	Cafeteria	👥	Conference facilities
✻	Special interest for children	ⴼ	Bar
✿	Hotel	🍴	Restaurant
🏰	Luxury (hotel)	◉	Simple (restaurant)
▢	Cheap	◠	Luxury (restaurant)
▨	Inexpensive	⌑	A la carte available
▨▨	Moderately priced	▬	Set (fixed-price) menu available
▨▨▨	Expensive		
▨▨▨	Very expensive	🍷	Good wines
📧	Air conditioning	🍽	Open-air dining
⌂	Residential terms available	◉	Disco dancing
AE	American Express	🎵	Nightclub
CB	Carte Blanche	✿	Casino/gambling
◉	Diners Club	♪	Live music
●	MasterCard	✦	Dancing
VISA	Visa	✎	Revue
		✖	Adults only

A note from the General Editor

News of the October 1989 earthquake in North California reached us as we went to press — too late to amend most of our information. By the time this book is published, Californian optimism and efficiency will no doubt have ensured that much of the damage is made good. Readers are unlikely to be seriously inconvenienced, but we do regret any difficulties caused by events literally beyond our control.

No travel book can be completely free of errors and totally up to date. Telephone numbers and opening hours change without warning, and hotels and restaurants come under new management, which can affect standards. We make every effort to ensure that all information is accurate at the time we go to press, but are always delighted to receive corrections or suggestions for improvements from our readers, which if warranted will be incorporated in a future edition.

The publishers regret they cannot accept any consequences arising from the use of the book or from the information it contains.

The cities and the state

It could be the supposed eccentricity of the people, or envy excited by visions of perpetual sunshine and conspicuous consumption. Whatever, both Los Angeles and San Francisco stimulate the jokers and those who like their cities in a nutshell. There's Woody Allen's famous put-down of LA: that the only cultural advantage of living there is being able to turn right on a red light. Gertrude Stein could have had the city in mind with the remark, "There's no there, there." As others would have it, LA is "49 suburbs in search of a city." For San Francisco it's the city's self-satisfaction that invites the barbs: "A city in love with itself," or: "Parochial in its cosmopolitanism."

But the cities — and the "Golden State" they inhabit: El Dorado to the earliest Spanish explorers with their visions of gold and exotic spices — continue to excite both the senses and the imagination. Traversing the western slopes of the towering Sierra Nevada 120 years ago, Robert Louis Stevenson, "The Amateur Emigrant", felt the weariness of the arduous journey from his native Scotland slip from his shoulders. "At every turn we looked further into the land of our happy future. At every turn the cocks were tossing their clear notes into the golden air and crowing for the new day and the new country. For this indeed was our destination——this was 'the good country' we have been going to for so long." Much has changed since then. But the clichéd images of promise are demanding still. And, by and large, Los Angeles, San Francisco and the California they inhabit still deliver.

Rain does fall on Southern California; Los Angeles has been known to endure it for a week at a time. Then the sky clears to cloudless blue, and the even-tanned *jeunesse dorée* put on their string bikinis or shorts, toss the roller skates, frisbees and surf boards into the convertible, and head for the beaches; in February! That, or a two-hour drive into the snow-coated mountains, for a day's skiing under the same robin's-egg sky. True, six months later, in high summer, San Franciscans could be walking their long, sandy beach swathed in woolens against an 11°C (52°F) chill as shredded fog whirls past at 25mph. But they could as well be jogging in Golden Gate Park on President's Day. When either city is ready for a bite to eat it'll have more choice of cuisine and fresh produce than anywhere on earth. They can shop till they drop and, when the sun goes down, take in movies fresh off the nearby studio lots.

Yes, they can be wacky. The 70-year-old blue-rinsed matron in lycra jumpsuit slaloming her skateboard through traffic cones by Venice beach. The checkout boy at the Alpha Beta 24-hour supermarket jiving through his day like Michael Jackson on multivitamins. The store-front psychic advisors, the elderly man easing his Chevy down the freeway one-handed while playing a trumpet with the other, the man with dark glasses and white cane riding his bicycle down a rural highway. The Madonna wannabees who tell you their name is Tiffany, they're your waitress for this evening, and a whole lot more before serving up your hot pastrami on rye.

There are areas of both cities you'd be unwise to visit after dark: parts of East and South Central Los Angeles and the "Tenderloin" and Western Addition in San Francisco's Bay Area. Mostly, however, from the wild shenanigans of gold-rich 49ers on the 19thC "Barbary Coast" to today's between-jobs actors valet-parking at the pastel-pink Beverly Hills Hotel, we are talking life-enhancing optimists. Theirs is a Pacific culture, far from the leaden skies and inhibiting chills of the North Atlantic coasts. Through the centuries, the opportunities for work and play have attracted, and continue to attract, wave after wave of immigrants: Hispanic, Anglo Saxon, Southern and Eastern European, Armenian, Arab and Asian. And they work as hard, maybe harder, than they play. Adjacent to Los Angeles and San Francisco are powerhouses of the aerospace and computer industries. The world knows that Hollywood *is* the movies and that, as an agricultural and economic power, an independent California would rank in the world's top ten. Awesome, as they say in California!

It's likely to be even more so in the decades to come. To the east lie the natural barriers of deserts and mountains, and beyond them the memory of less sun-kissed lives. The physical and psychological orientations are to the west. LA and San Francisco are cities of the Pacific Rim. And, as economic pundits continually remind us, we are approaching the "Pacific century," with booming economies from Tokyo to Vancouver, Singapore to San Diego, accelerating a spiral of rising prosperity. Of course, there is a downside: pollution, drug-related crime, pockets of poverty. But the human traffic is still toward California, not away from it.

The stereotypes can be engaging, amusing and, sometimes, correct. But it is probably the contradictions that are most memorable. The glorious differences are legion — among the people, between the architectural styles, the flora and fauna, the shape and feel of the cities and the landscape. If the freeway-scored, sometimes tacky, low-rise sprawl of Los Angeles is the prototype of an urban giantism that could be our future, San Francisco is the very model of a small, user-friendly, old-fashioned, "European" city, complete with tasteful turn-of-the-century architecture. Were it not for the live-and-let-live tolerance common to both, the cities could be almost on different planets. Above all else, it has to do with history, climate and terrain. San Francisco was already a thriving city when Los Angeles was little more than a pioneer encampment. Los Angeles has wide skies and horizons, whereas San Francisco spends forever looking back upon itself up and down its hills. And while Los Angeles basks in (almost) year-long summer, San Francisco has four identifiable seasons reminiscent of Southern Europe.

Both entertain notions of utopia. Angelenos aspire to space, growth, property and the kind of personal mobility symbolized by the automobile. As befits the dream factory of the Western world, they reserve the right to re-invent themselves and their surroundings. The often flimsy architecture speaks of future possibilities. San Franciscans value continuity, care passionately for the natural environment, view their city as a western outpost of refinement and sophistication, pride themselves on civic devotion, and yet feel free to challenge conventional aspirations. Not for nothing did the "beat" generation, the hippies of Haight-Ashbury and the gays of the Castro district make their home there; though, very possibly, home would be nothing more radical than a gingerbread Victorian town house.

LA gave birth to Hollywood and the two-limo family, San Francisco to the United Nations and the topless dancer. In short, each city is a vivid tableau of the American Dream. They are glossy, de-luxe versions, in a land of exceptional opportunities free from East Coast constraints. As writer and environmentalist Wallace Stegner observes "America only more so". It is perhaps worth remembering that California's motto is, "Eureka"... "I have found it."

Before you go

Getting there

Almost all international airlines serve Los Angeles International (LAX) and San Francisco International (SFO) airports. Los Angeles is the world's third busiest airport, San Francisco the sixth. All major domestic airlines serve both these airports and one or more of eight smaller ones in California (see pages 14-15).

For drivers, five major interstate freeways ("I" routes) connect California to points S, E and N. The all-year routes leading to Los Angeles are I-8 running E-W along the Mexican border, I-10 running E-W from Arizona, and the I-15 running NE-SW through Las Vegas and the intermountain basin. The I-5, running from San Diego in the S through the length of California and up to the Pacific NW, is kept open all year, but drivers can be subject to winter delays when snowstorms blanket the Siskiyou Mountains on the California-Oregon border. The more northerly I-80 crosses some of the higher parts of both the Sierra Nevada and the Rocky Mountains before ending at San Francisco. Although it too is kept open all year, there can be snowstorms between Oct and Apr.

Amtrak, the subsidized passenger rail service, runs daily trains on three interstate routes. One daily train connects both Los Angeles and San Francisco with the Pacific NW. The second connects San Francisco with Chicago via Reno and Denver. The third connects Los Angeles with points NE and SE including Las Vegas, Phoenix, Houston and New Orleans.

Climate

California's climates are as varied as its people and its cuisines. Summers in Los Angeles and along the S coast are hot and dry and winters mild with plenty of sunshine. However, contrary to the songs, it does rain occasionally, and coastal areas can experience chilly winter fog. (Average temperatures midday are 28°C (83°F) from June-Oct and 18°C (65°F) from Nov-May.) In San Francisco and along N coastal areas warm summers are tempered by cool sea breezes and persistent fog, while winters are generally wet. (Average temperatures are 16°F (62°F) from Mar-Oct and 12°C (52°F) from Nov-Feb.)

Elsewhere in the state, inland areas have drier, hotter summers that are less oppressive on the hills than in the valleys. Winters are colder and drier than on the coast. Southern deserts are warm in winter but often intolerably hot in summer.

Mountain regions enjoy four distinct seasons: fine, cold winters; warm, sunny summers; and changeable springs and falls.

Clothes

Choice of clothing should be tailored to some extent by the climate of the particular region (see above). In general, dress tends to be functional and casual, although Los Angeles and San Francisco are intensely fashion-conscious cities. Some of the smarter clubs and restaurants insist on jackets, a few of the smartest insist on neckties, and many frown on "sneakers." Elsewhere, the not uncommon notice "No shoes, no shirt, no service" speaks for itself.

Mail

Visitors choosing not to receive mail care of their hotels can use US Postal Service General Delivery, addressed to any small town post office. In cities, only one post office, usually the main office downtown, is equipped to handle General Delivery. Outgoing mail can be sent from these and smaller post offices, and stamps can frequently be bought in hotels and drugstores.

Getting around

Public transportation
Between cities, flying and driving are the easiest ways to get around, although interstate buses offer a cut-price alternative. Within cities, driving is sometimes the only efficient means of transportation, particularly in Los Angeles. Buses, trains and taxis exist, but not always when and where they are wanted. In Greater Los Angeles, City Bus Services (RTD) provides infrequent services and runs specials to major attractions such as Disneyland (*information on services and routes from RTD Information* ☎ *(213) 626-4455; information for those with impaired hearing* ☎ *(800) 252-9040*). Taxi stands operate at Los Angeles International airport, at rail and bus stations and at major hotels. But, given LA's sprawl, taxis are almost invariably expensive.

San Francisco is more user-friendly thanks, in large part, to its Municipal Railway ("Muni"), which can be classed as a bargain. Cable cars, light rail vehicles and a rapid transit system crisscross the city. San Francisco taxis are pricier per mile than those in Los Angeles, but the distances are shorter.

Renting a car
The best way to travel.... Major car rental firms include Airway, Avis, Budget, Dollar, Econocar, Hertz, National and Thrifty. All have downtown offices, and depots near Los Angeles and San Francisco International airports; most have them at smaller airports too. Many have toll-free (**800**) numbers through which reservations can be made. It is wise to reserve in advance.

It pays to shop around even among the major firms; rates can vary and managers are often open to negotiation. Fly-drive packages, available through airlines, may offer the most favorable rates for renting a car. Rent-it-here/leave-it-there arrangements are available but can be expensive. In addition, major cities have cut-price firms such as Rent-a-wreck offering old but basically sound vehicles at relatively low prices.

Most firms offer insurance packages additional to those required by law. Given the high costs of medical care and the possibly astronomical costs of litigation, these are well worth considering. The especially cautious should consult their insurance broker before leaving home. Limousine services are widely available as a relaxing alternative.

Speed limits
Maximum speed limits are indicated on most California roads. Freeway and highway maximums are 55mph; on some busy highways, speed limits may be 50 or 45mph. In city and town centers and in residential areas, the maximum speed is 25mph; on main urban thoroughfares, 30 or 35mph. On roads that pass schools, there is a speed limit of 25mph during school hours. All of these are maximums: you can be charged with reckless driving at lower speeds when driving conditions are poor.

Getting around on foot
It is best in towns to cross only at pedestrian crossings — usually at traffic lights and intersections. When there are pedestrian signals, cross only when the light reads "Walk" or a small walking

figure appears. At crossings without traffic lights, traffic is supposed to but doesn't always stop for pedestrians. You are prohibited from walking along or across freeways. Walking alone at night should be avoided in some neighborhoods.

On-the-spot information

Public holidays
Jan 1; Martin Luther King Day, third Mon in Jan; President's Day, third Mon in Feb; Memorial Day, last Mon in May; Independence Day, July 4 (but businesses close on nearest Mon or Fri); Labor Day, first Mon in Sept; Columbus Day, second Mon in Oct; Veterans Day, Nov 11; Thanksgiving, last Thurs in Nov; Dec 25. Banks and almost all businesses are closed on these days, though stores frequently stay open for sales. Good Friday is a half-day holiday; many offices close on Easter Monday.

Time zones
All of California is within the Pacific Time Zone: 3hrs behind New York, 2hrs behind Chicago and 1hr behind Denver. California law establishes Daylight Saving Time from the first Sun in Apr through the last Sat in Oct.

Banks and currency exchange
Normal business hours for banks are Mon-Thurs 10am-3pm and Fri 10am-5pm. An increasing number of banks in Los Angeles and San Francisco keep later weekday hours; fewer open on Sat. Travel service firms typically open Mon-Fri 9am-5pm and Sat 10am-noon. Banks vary in their policies on cashing travelers cheques; some will provide the services only for regular customers, some charge commission, other provide the service free. Travel service offices are more consistent and reliable.

Shopping and business hours
Department stores and clothes and sports equipment stores generally open between 9 and 10am and close at 5.30 or 6pm. Late-night shopping, particularly in the malls, is usually until 9pm on Thurs. The larger supermarket chains and drugstores are open 24hrs seven days a week. Coffee shops and fast-food restaurants may open as early as 6am and close as late as midnight; some stay open around the clock. More formal restaurants open from about noon-3pm and 6-11pm, with last orders an hour earlier. Bars and cocktail lounges do not have to close until 2am.

Rush hours
In Los Angeles, morning freeway rush hours begin at 6am, peak between 7 and 8am, then ebb by 9.30am; the evening rush begins by 4pm, peaks by 5pm, and ebbs at major intersections after 7pm. Around San Francisco Bay the hours are slightly shorter, in other cities shorter still.

Telephone area codes and 800 numbers
California is divided into ten telephone area codes – especially important in Los Angeles and San Francisco where boundaries fall across populous areas in a seemingly arbitrary manner.

Area codes are dialed before the local number **only** when calling from one area to another. Note that from some areas a preliminary **1** is required for any trunk call; check the telephone directory or consult a local person before dialing.

Basic information

Public telephones are numerous and are usually in working order. Pay telephones accept 5¢, 10¢ and 25¢ coins. Local calls cost between 15¢ and 25¢. Trunk charges are paid as the call progresses, so arm yourself with a heap of coins. Helpful operators will give guidance on how much you need. Trunk rates reduce sharply between 6pm and 8am and are lowest on Sat.

In addition to their regular numbers, airlines, car rental firms and hotels often have no-charge (toll-free) numbers with an **800** prefix. Numerous hotel, tourist information and other listings in this book have toll-free 800 numbers. Often these are valid only for calls within California — and calls outside the state commonly require a different number after the 800 prefix. Before dialing national hotel chains or other nationwide service companies from out-of-state, check the local Yellow Pages to verify 800 numbers. Remember to prefix **800** with a **1**.

Public rest rooms
On interstate and US highways, California maintains excellent public rest rooms in roadside miniparks called "rest areas." Many gas stations maintain facilities for their customers. In cities, rest rooms are commonplace in shopping malls, department stores, restaurants, fast-food chains and hotels. Public rest rooms are less common and often best avoided.

Laws and regulations
Smoking is prohibited in elevators and buses, theaters and movie theaters. Restaurants and public rooms allow it only in specified areas. Laws prohibit jaywalking and littering but are unevenly enforced. Hitchhiking is also illegal, and although seldom punished it is strongly discouraged on freeways.

Parking violations are not taken lightly, so pay attention to color-coded curbing. Red means no stopping or parking, Yellow means a maximum half-hour loading time for vehicles with commercial plates, Blue is reserved for disabled people, Green allows 10mins' parking for all vehicles, and White gives a 5min limit during business hours. Do not park at bus stops or fire hydrants. Violation can incur a fine of up to $20, and charges rise dramatically if you park in a space reserved for disabled people or your vehicle is towed away.

Persons must be 21yrs or older to buy, serve or consume alcoholic beverages in California, and proof of age can be required. Liquor may not be purchased, served or consumed in public eating places and bars between 2 and 6am. The consumption of "controlled substances" (narcotic drugs) is prohibited by law; far more severe laws prohibit their sale.

Customs and etiquette
Although they are unfailingly polite, as a rule Californians do not stand on formality. But there are certain conventions. It is customary to shake hands on meeting. Once people have been introduced, first names are used in all but the most formal circumstances. They can be erratic about lining up; they form orderly lines outside movie theaters and intercity bus stations, but not for sporting events or for buses in the cities themselves. Courtesy is important: on buses men still give up seats for women, and everyone urges everyone else to "have a good day."

Tipping
Waiters expect a tip of 15 percent of the check before tax, although you may feel inclined to tip more if service has been

especially good, less if it has been poor. Barmen and hairdressers should also receive 15 percent. Doormen and staff who valet park your car expect $1, bellhops 75¢ to $1 per bag, and rest room attendants (rarely encountered) 50¢. When there is no fixed charge for leaving coats and parcels, give 50¢ per item.

Disabled travelers
California law requires new hotels, restaurants and other public buildings to be accessible to wheelchairs and to have wheelchair rest rooms. Older hotels and restaurants have converted rooms. Many cities reserve curbside parking for handicapped people, as do major banks, supermarkets and drugstores. Some companies operate buses with motorized platforms.

Publications
Both cities are rich in newspapers and magazines, as indeed is the entire State of California. In the *Los Angeles Times* and the *San Francisco Chronicle* it boasts two of the nation's most authoritative papers; both publish comprehensive entertainment sections, notably in Fri editions for the weekend and in Sun editions for the week ahead. In addition, monthly glossies such as *Los Angeles Magazine* and weekly freesheets such as *LA Weekly* offer up-to-date information on the hot spots from everything to eating out, shopping and the arts. Newsstands in both cities offer a wealth of local, national and international publications. Most hotels provide magazines that can be useful, although full of advertisements. The LA Visitors and Convention Bureau (☎ *213-624-7300*) and the San Francisco Convention and Visitors Bureau (☎ *415-391-2000*) publish frequently updated booklets detailing what's on offer.

Useful addresses

Tourist information
American Express Travel Service Office (*723 West 7th St., Los Angeles* ☎ *(213) 488-1301 and 237 Post St., San Francisco* ☎ *(415) 981-5533*), a valuable source of information for any traveler in need of help, advice or emergency services.

Department of Motor Vehicles (*Los Angeles* ☎ *(213) 744-2000, San Francisco* ☎ *(415) 557-1191*), for *California Driver's Handbook*, summarizing traffic regulations. Parking violations are dealt with by the local police department.

Department of Fish and Game (*1416 9th St., 12th Floor, Sacramento 95814* ☎ *(916) 445-3306*), for fishing and hunting license requirements, seasons, and game limits.

California State Park System (*PO Box 2390, Sacramento 95811* ☎ *(916) 445-6477*), for camping reservations forms and list of parks. In Los Angeles ☎(213) 485-5515 and (213) 485-4853; in San Francisco ☎(415) 556-0560 and (1-800) 444-7275.

US Forest Service (*630 Sansome St, San Francisco 94111* ☎ *(415) 556-0122*), for camping reservations forms and information on national forests.

Ticketron (*PO Box 26430, San Francisco 94126* ☎ *(800) 622-0904*), for a computerized reservations agency for all state and national park campgrounds. For entertainment, see *Nightlife* and *Performing arts* sections of individual cities.

Redwood Empire Association (*One Market Plaza, San Francisco 94104* ☎ *(415) 543-8334*), for information on the coastal region from San Francisco N to the Oregon border.

Direct air routes within California

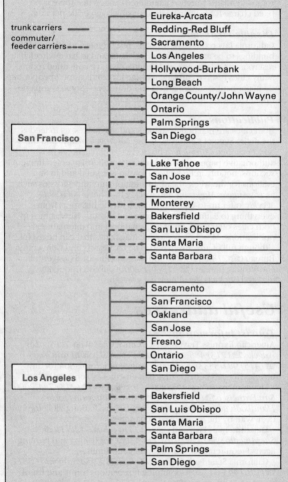

trunk carriers ———
commuter/
feeder carriers ----

San Francisco
- Eureka-Arcata
- Redding-Red Bluff
- Sacramento
- Los Angeles
- Hollywood-Burbank
- Long Beach
- Orange County/John Wayne
- Ontario
- Palm Springs
- San Diego

- Lake Tahoe
- San Jose
- Fresno
- Monterey
- Bakersfield
- San Luis Obispo
- Santa Maria
- Santa Barbara

Los Angeles
- Sacramento
- San Francisco
- Oakland
- San Jose
- Fresno
- Ontario
- San Diego

- Bakersfield
- San Luis Obispo
- Santa Maria
- Santa Barbara
- Palm Springs
- San Diego

Airport Codes

Los Angeles International LAX
San Francisco International SFO
San Diego International SAN
Sacramento SMF
Oakland OAK
San Jose SJC
Hollywood-Burbank BUR
Orange County/John Wayne SNA

Long Beach LGB
Ontario ONT
Palm Springs PSP
Fresno FAT
Monterey Peninsula MRV
Santa Barbara SBA
Eureka-Arcata ACV
Redding-Red Bluff RDD

Commercial airports without codes served by feeders:
Bakersfield, Visalia, Santa Maria, San Luis Obispo,
Lake Tahoe, Crescent City

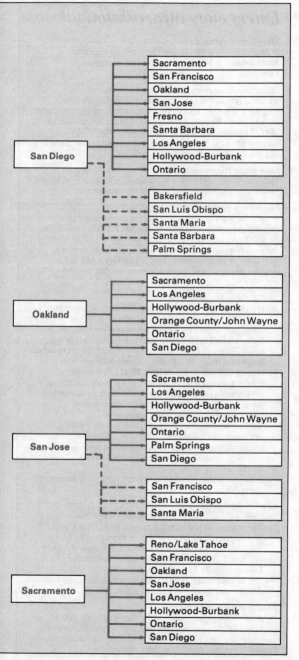

Emergency information

Emergency services

Police
Ambulance
Fire
} ☎911; ask operator to connect you with the appropriate emergency service

Other medical emergencies

To find a private doctor, consult the Yellow Pages of the telephone directory under *Physician*. Or in Los Angeles, contact the LA County Medical Association Physician Referral Service (☎ *(213) 484-6122*), and in San Francisco, the SF Medical Society (☎ *(415) 567-6230*). Dentists are listed under *Dentist*. If in a hotel, ask the reception desk for help.

Late-night pharmacies

They can be difficult to find in cities, and seldom exist in smaller towns. Consult Yellow Pages under *Pharmacies*.

Help lines (crisis lines)

Some crisis intervention organizations are quasi-official; many are private; all are local or narrowly regional. For help consult the Yellow Pages under: *Crisis Intervention Service, Drug Abuse Information and Treatment Centers,* or *Suicide Prevention Counselor*. A useful contact point is **Traveler's Aid**: in Los Angeles ☎ (213) 625-2501, in San Francisco ☎(415) 781-6738.

Automobile accidents

— Call the police immediately.
— **On city streets**, call municipal police at emergency number, which is universally **911**. Nonemergency numbers are in local telephone directories. **On all freeways** (even within city limits) and **all highways and roads** outside municipal boundaries, call California Highway Patrol (CHP). **On urban freeways**, roadside call boxes automatically connect to the nearest CHP office. **Elsewhere ☎911** in emergency.
— If a car is rented, call the number in the rental agreement. (You should carry this, and your license, at all times when driving. Failure to do so can complicate matters.)
— Never admit liability or incriminate yourself.
— Ask eyewitnesses to stay, and take down their names, addresses and statements.
— Exchange names, addresses, car details, driver's license numbers, insurance companies' names and policy code numbers.
— Remain at the scene of the accident to give your statement to the police.

Car breakdowns

Call one of the following from the nearest telephone.
— The number indicated in the car rental agreement.
— The local office of AAA if you are a member. The AAA is listed as California State Automobile Association (CSAA) in northern California, or Automobile Club of Southern California (ACSC) in southern California.
— The nearest garage with towing service (listed under *Towing-Automotive* in Yellow Pages).

Lost travelers cheques

Notify the local police immediately, then follow the instructions provided with your travelers cheques, or contact the issuing company's nearest office. Contact your consulate or American Express if you are stranded without money.

City people

Los Angeles County has a population of more than 8 million. There are so many "illegals" that it is hard to be precise. The official city accounts for a little more than 3 million, and in population and area (465 sq. miles) is California's largest.

But the distinction between county and city is almost irrelevant. Some "Westside" people might do most of their living, working and playing around, say, Beverly Hills. Glendale's Armenians or Mid-Wilshire's Koreans might have their own tight communities in their own parts of town. But transportation and communications systems, the freeway, the phone and, lately, the fax, have made LA into one huge intermingling supercommunity.

Things do divide people — money, interests, even language — but geography is not one of them. Angelenos will drive 50 miles for a good beach, a good doubles match with friends or a memorable lunch. Certainly, *they'll* be aware when they've crossed from LA County into Orange County or San Bernardino. Confronted by a seemingly endless urban sprawl, the bewildered visitor may not. But the locals consider themselves, and Greater LA, as being distinct from its neighbors.

Los Angeles lacks the focus of conventional cities. The downtown area, dating back to 1781 when the city was founded near Olvera Street, is the center for civic and commercial activity, and by day up to 250,000 people work there. But they commute. The resident population is only around 20,000 and, despite efforts to invigorate the area's cultural and community life, its nighttime streets can be deserted. Rather the notional "49 suburbs in search of a city" each create their own focus closer to home: in the valleys and canyons, on the beaches, the plains and the foothills.

The City of San Francisco, sitting like a thimble on the thumb of its peninsula, has a population of just 713,000, making it only the fourth largest of California's cities. But the figure is misleading; the population of the Bay Area is approaching 5 million, and many commute into the city proper to work and play. And what diversity they encounter within its intimate scale! If LA's distinctive communities are separated by miles, in San Francisco the distances are measured in the width of streets; the journey from Chinatown to Little Italy is a matter of crossing Columbus Avenue. The distances and shapes of the city are easily comprehended and managed. In Los Angeles people drive. In San Francisco they also walk, take buses and trains. Angelenos would probably say it's because there's nowhere to park and their northern neighbors have only just begun to discover the liberating joys of valet-parking. In large part this may be true; but San Francisco does afford an intimacy and human scale that LA sometimes lacks. "San Francisco has only one drawback," lamented Rudyard Kipling, "... 'tis hard to leave." And Kipling wasn't talking about the traffic jams.

What the cities have in common is diversity. It is said that a hundred different languages are spoken among their citizens. That could be an exaggeration, but only slightly. Basques, Filipinos, Russians, Iranians, Japanese, Irish, Khmers, Ethiopians etc., etc., etc. — the list of ethnic groups reads like the UN General Assembly. And, for the most part, they enjoy a more relaxed co-existence than the diplomatic delegates.

Of the other cities and towns within striking distance of LA and San Francisco, San Diego is the most populous; around 1 million people make it California's second city. It was at San Diego in 1542 that Juan Rodriguez Cabrillo claimed what is now California for the Spanish Crown, and many regard it as the state's birthplace. Like LA, its

17

northern neighbor, San Diego sprawls — 20 miles to north, south and east. A relaxed mix of US naval base, fishing port and beach resort, its closeness to Mexico gives it an even more marked Hispanic flavor.

Other towns, inland and along the coast, are small in comparison. Palm Springs (40,000), Santa Barbara (80,000), Carmel (5,000) and Monterey (30,000) are a mixture of elegantly polished retreat and gift-wrapped tourist attraction sustained by visitors and wealthy residents. Each has its celebrities — John Steinbeck, Clint Eastwood, Bob Hope, Sonny Bono — and a unique, if predictable, charm.

Nature

From the earliest years the economic riches of California and its principal cities were derived from the land: gold in the north, oil in the south, and an agriculturalist's Eden along the length of its Central Valley. They are matched by the esthetic richness of setting.

It is no accident that one of LA's best-known thoroughfares is named "Sunset Boulevard," or that the street runs east-west, following the sun to the Pacific Ocean. Between Malibu and Balboa, LA's white sandy beaches run almost unbroken for 70 miles. Only the beaches of Rio de Janeiro come close, and they don't have the Pacific sunset — often so beautiful one suspects it's been manufactured by a major studio. And San Francisco Bay, 450 square miles of water entered through the Golden Gates, is among the world's finest and most visually pleasing natural harbors. The city itself, draped over tumbling hillsides and surrounded by water on three sides, offers an almost inexhaustible range of vistas. Its flora is equally compelling, and in the 1,017-acre Golden Gate Park, complete with lakes, meadows, waterfalls, English country-estate-style landscaping and Japanese Garden, San Francisco has an inner-city recreation area second to none. LA's subtropical climate lends itself to the cultivation of just about anything that can be irrigated, as best evidenced in the 200-acre gardens of the Huntington Library Botanical Gardens with its desert garden, roses, camellias and azaleas. And the weather allows the private gardener to indulge in a botanical anarchism that would be doomed to failure elsewhere.

Beyond the cities is a comparable diversity — mountains, deserts, lakes, fertile valleys, cathedral-high coastlines and rugged offshore islands. From the northeast corner of the state the Sierra Nevada mountain range runs south for some 400 miles, a solid granite barrier reaching a height of 14,495ft at Mount Whitney. Lower down its slopes are forests of giant sequoia, pine fir and cedar. From the northwest the gentler Coastal ranges, with elevations of between 2,000 and 7,000ft, extend almost to Los Angeles, with northern evergreens giving way to oaks and finally a chaparral of stunted shrubs. Between the two lies the fertile Central Valley, between 40 and 50 miles wide.

One third of California is desert. But it is seldom desert characterized by the monotony of sand dunes. The High Desert or Mojave, most of which falls within San Bernardino County, and the Low Desert or Colorado in the southeast of the state can both be as unforgiving. Joshua trees, cacti, scrub and man-made oases aside, their flora offers little excitement. Visible fauna seems limited to an occasional coyote. Nonetheless, the landscape serves up an artist's palette of colors and shapes that might have been formed by whimsical giants. Death Valley offers a tranquility that's hard to duplicate. Most of the lakes are in the north, and Tahoe, the biggest, ranks as one of the world's great alpine lakes. Farther south, the high, man-made Arrowhead and Big Bear Lakes provide easily accessible playgrounds for LA. Along much of the coast, particularly south of Monterey and north of San Francisco, the Pacific Coast Highway hairpins above majestic cliffs. The views, like the drive along Highway 1, can be literally breathtaking — especially if they include the sight of migrating whales.

Although it is all Pacific Ocean as far as China, it might almost be two oceans. South of Santa Barbara the Pacific waters are warm and the waves ruler-straight, making it a swimmer's and surfer's paradise. North, the colder waters are more suited to well-kitted-out sailors or fishermen. Early sailors, less well equipped, believed California to be an island. We know better, but islands there are: the four Catalinas, the four Santa Barbaras, and a dozen smaller ones. Much of Santa Catalina, 27 miles southwest of LA's harbor at Wilmington, is preserved largely unscathed as "open land." Indeed, although transforming California into the richest and most populous state in the United States has involved considerable violence to the natural environment, much of it remains generally unspoiled, having proved too big, uncompromising and remarkable.

History

The earliest known inhabitants were seminomadic Indians (known nowadays as "Native Americans"), maybe numbering 150,000 at their peak, with a score of distinct language groups and more than a hundred regional dialects. They fared badly after the arrival of European settlers. Their population was ravaged by alien diseases, land-grabbing by Europeans, and Indian "wars." By the early years of the 20thC the total Indian population was put at 16,000.

The European explorations gathered pace in the 16thC with Spanish explorers seeking to expand their king's Mexican dominion ever farther north and west. They were seeking a land of legend called "Califomia," described as being "...very near to the Terrestrial Paradise." In 1525 Hernando Cortez discovered a land he named California. But the first white man known to have seen the place was Juan Rodriguez Cabrillo, a Portuguese navigator in the service of Spain. Cabrillo National Monument in San Diego marks his landing there in 1542. In the same year he sighted San Pedro harbor and named it "Bay of Smokes"; legend has it that he saw the campfire smoke of Indian villages within the present LA County.

Then Spanish interest flagged. It was almost 40 years before it revived with news that the Englishman Sir Francis Drake had anchored his *Golden Hinde* near what is now San Francisco and claimed the new land for England. More thorough Spanish explorations of the coast followed, and in 1602 Sebastian Vizcaino reasserted his monarch's claim. But it was not until 1697 that Jesuits received royal warrants to enter the territory, and it was another 70 years before the first permanent colony was established at San Diego. With Jesuits out of favor by then, it was left to Franciscan friars and the army to extend the northward penetration. Between them, the Cross and the sword had by 1823 established a chain of 21 missions along 600 miles of the Camino Real or King's Highway. In 1776 a mission, Dolores, and a small military fortress had been founded at San Francisco. One of the first civilian settlements, in 1781, was Los Angeles, established with 44 settlers.

Earnest development began in the 19thC. First, in 1821, Mexico won its independence from Spain and retained California as a colony. Relations between the Californios and their Mexican governors were strained, sometimes violent. But the watershed came

in the early 1840s with a quickening influx of American settlers.
The Californios welcomed them; Mexico banned their further
immigration. Finally, in 1846, a small group of yanquis staged the
"Bear Flag Revolt" declaring the California Republic. Then, 23
days later, Commodore John D. Sloat raised the American flag
over Monterey and claimed California for the US.

The next surge of immigration followed almost immediately. News
of James Wilson Marshall's discovery of gold in January 1848
prompted what has been described as the greatest mass movement
of people since the Crusades. The year before, the population was
put at 15,000. By 1850, when California became the 31st state, it was
nudging 100,000. A decade later it was close to 400,000. Many were
'49ers, and much of the growth was in and around San Francisco,
which fast emerged as the dominant city on the west coast. It was a
city confident enough to humor a man such as Joshua Abraham
Norton, a failed English businessman and eccentric, who in 1859
declared himself Emperor of the United States, and commanded his
San Franciscan subjects to build bridges. In due course they did and,
at the end of his 21-year "reign," 30,000 people attended his funeral.

By comparison Los Angeles was a sleepy pueblo. The
transcontinental railroads, with the South Pacific completed in 1876
and the Santa Fe in 1885, signaled the changes. The Mid-West soon
began boarding trains and heading for Los Angeles and the newly
irrigated farmlands around it. By the 1880s LA was the center of an
hysterical property boom. By the end of the decade its population
had grown from 11,000 to 50,000. An even more profound change in
its economic fortunes came on either side of 1900 with the discovery
and commercial exploitation of oil.

San Francisco, with its cable cars, enclaves of wealth and style and
cosmopolitan sophistication continued to overshadow the southern
city. Indeed San Francisco was know as "The City." Two things
changed that: LA's quickening momentum of population and
economic growth and, on April 18, 1906, the San Francisco
earthquake and the fire that followed. 500 were dead or missing and
5 square miles of the city were destroyed. Reconstruction plans were
being drawn even as the ruins smoked, and within three years 20,000
new buildings were constructed. But by then Los Angeles was
reaching for pole position. In 1906 the first motion picture studio was
opened in LA. The rest, as they say, is history.

Oil, the movies, the increasingly busy port of San Pedro, and
agriculture fed by the astounding engineering feats of William
Mulholland, all accelerated LA's growth. By the end of the 1920s the
population stood at 1.2 million, and already the city sprawled.
Motion pictures became a billion-dollar industry. Post-quake San
Francisco, meanwhile, did its best to bounce back. The opening of
the Panama Canal in 1914 boosted trade and manufacturing
industries, and the city's recovery was celebrated a year later with the
Panama-Pacific International Exposition.

Immigrants continued to arrive — in the 1930s, refugees from the
Midwest Dustbowl, many traveling down the famous Route 66; in the
1940s, Europeans fleeing war and tyranny, and tens of thousands of
servicemen demobilized on the West Coast after World War II; in the
1950s, Blacks from the south and northeast; and, through the
decades, a rainbow of races, people from the "rustbelt states," from
Eastern Europe, Indochina, the Middle East, Central America, seeking
the better life so temptingly portrayed by Hollywood. Every wave fed
the cities' and the state's greatest resource — ambitious, enthusiastic,
innovative, enterprising minds.

In the process came Henry Huntington's Pacific Electric Railway
Company and its "Red Cars," giving LA the finest interurban railroad

network in the world; the unprecedented irrigation scheme of the Central Valley Project (1935); the Golden Gate Bridge (1937); the Manhattanization of downtown San Francisco as it grew into the West Coast's Wall Street; Disneyland (1955); the aerospace industry embodied in Lockheed, Northrop and Douglas; Silicon Valley; and an array of new high-tech industries. In 1980 Ronald Reagan, former Hollywood movie star and Governor of California from 1967-73, was elected to the first of two terms as US President. It seemed to set the political seal on what West Coast people already knew; California and its great cities had not only arrived, they were the vanguard of the nation's economic and cultural life, with their front door on the Pacific, the ocean of the future. Now they *must* be taken seriously.

Time chart

1510	"California" received its first mention, in Montalvo's fiction *Las Sergas de Esplandian.*
1542	Sailing from New Spain (Mexico), Juan Rodriguez Cabrillo discovered San Diego Bay and claimed it for Spain.
1579	Sir Francis Drake landed near San Francisco, named what he saw "New Albion" and claimed it for England.
1769	Father Junipero Serra established Spain's first California colony at San Diego. Gaspar de Portola's expedition reached San Francisco Bay.
1776	As the American colonies declared independence from Great Britain, a Spanish mission and *presidio* (fortress) were founded at San Francisco.
1777	Felipe de Neve made Monterey capital of California.
1781	Pueblo (civilian settlement) founded at Los Angeles.
1796	First US ship, Ebenezer Dorr's *Otter,* anchored in a California port.
1812	As the US fought the War of 1812, Russian fur traders established a colony at Fort Ross on Sonoma coast.
1821	Mexico achieved independence from Spain, keeping California as a colony.
1828	Jedediah Smith became the first white man to cross the Sierra Nevadas.
1845	Mexico ineffectually banned immigration of American settlers into California. Mary Peterson and James Williams became the first Americans to marry in California.
1846	American settlers who overthrew the Mexican Government of General Mariano Vallejo in Bear Flag Revolt at Sonoma were put out of power within weeks as US declared war on Mexico and seized California. Yerba Buena became San Francisco.
1848	John Marshall discovered gold in American River at Coloma, setting off the Gold Rush of '49.
1850	California became the 31st American state.
1854	Sacramento became the state's permanent capital.
1861	As the US was consumed by Civil War, California remained little more than a bystander, its sympathies divided between Union and Confederacy. The state's first vineyards were planted with 1,400 varieties of vines shipped in from Europe.
1868	University of California established at Berkeley.
1869	The first transcontinental railroad was completed at Promontory Point, Utah, linking California with the E and ending the era of Pony Express and clipper ships around

Cape Horn. "Emperor" Norton commanded bridges built across San Francisco Bay.

1872 End of the Modoc War, the last major confrontation with the Indians of California.

1873 The first San Francisco cable car began operating.

1881 The *Los Angeles Times* was founded, and State Normal School, the forerunner of UCLA, began in LA.

1891 California's first golf course was opened.

1900 Major oil discoveries in Los Angeles produced an economic boom there.

1904 A.P. Giannini created the Bank of Italy in San Francisco. Eventually it would become the Bank of America.

1906 The Great Earthquake and Fire leveled much of San Francisco. Rebuilding began almost immediately. Beverly Hills founded, along with the first motion picture studio.

1908 The first commercial motion picture was filmed in Los Angeles, beginning the phenomenon of Hollywood.

1913 The 250-mile Los Angeles Aqueduct, bringing water from the distant Owens Valley, was completed. It allowed LA to annex the entire San Fernando Valley.

1915 Panama-Pacific International Exhibition held in San Francisco. First transcontinental telephone call.

1928 Daily LA-San Francisco passenger flights began.

1932 Los Angeles staged the summer Olympic Games, and San Francisco opened its Opera House.

1935 Donald Douglas' great airplane, the DC-3, introduced the age of air travel and launched California as a center of aerospace technology. Construction of the Central Valley Project begun.

1937 The Golden Gate Bridge was opened.

1940 The Arroyo Seco Parkway, LA's first section of freeway, was completed.

1945 As World War II drew to a close, the United Nations founding assembly was held in San Francisco.

1955 Disneyland opened, the forerunner of a host of theme parks and symbol of California's playfulness.

1958 Planar technique of producing transistors devised by Fairchild Semiconductor, an electronics company in Santa Clara Valley SE of San Francisco. This paved the way for the silicon chip, cornerstone of the microelectronics revolution. Major league baseball arrived with the San Francisco Giants and the Los Angeles Dodgers.

1960 Winter Olympics were held at Squaw Valley.

1964 California surpassed New York as the most populous US state. John Steinbeck won the Nobel Prize for Literature.

1967 Ronald Reagan was elected State Governor, the *Queen Mary* was moored at Long Beach, and *Rolling Stone* magazine began publication in San Francisco.

1968 The Summer of Love: hippies discovered sex and drugs and rock 'n' roll.

1971 Earthquake in the San Fernando Valley killed 64 people and caused more than $1 billion in damage.

1981 The Mediterranean fruit fly (Medfly) infested Santa Clara County and neighboring areas, ushering in tight agricultural controls on the state's borders.

1984 LA staged the summer Olympic Games for a second time, matching the record of Athens, Paris and London.

1989 Ronald and Nancy Reagan retired to Bel Air. The USA's second worst earthquake hit the Bay area. More than 270 dead, thousands homeless, more than $2 billion in damage.

The arts

Los Angeles is home to the world's wealthiest cultural institution, the J. Paul Getty Museum at Malibu. Fitting perhaps for the world's most conspicuously wealthy society; but the museum, housed in a replica of a Herculaneum villa, owes little to the city. Arguably it could have been sited just about anywhere.

Not so the movies. The motion picture industry is quintessential LA. The earliest movie-makers came to escape the monopolistic stranglehold of the east's Motion Pictures Patent Co. Among the bonuses were the light and a seemingly inexhaustible choice of locations. The talented, and the not so talented, followed. If the city sometimes has a shaky hold on reality, then the movies are to blame. The first commercial picture produced there was *The Count of Monte Cristo* (1908), fiction with a vengeance. The earliest passions for a good drama, thrill-packed action, and $10,000-a-week stars such as Charlie Chaplin and Mary Pickford, spilled off the movie sets and into everyday expectations. And such is the irrationality of the industry that, 90 years on, stars are still discovered parking cars or serving hamburgers, albeit rarely.

In recent years, parts of the industry have fled LA; costs are lower and trade unions less troublesome in places such as Canada and Florida. But the deals are still done in LA and, through film and TV, Hollywood continues to set a cultural agenda, not only for California, but for much of the world.

To millions the city and its locations are as familiar as their home town. The consequence for LA is paradoxical. Noel Coward's observation that "there is always something so delightfully real about what is phoney here, and something so phoney about what is real" still holds true. Some would argue that the city's enduring legacy to 20thC culture was born of the ultimate masquerade: the Technicolor illusions of Walt Disney's animation. 30 miles south of downtown just off the Santa Ana freeway is Disneyland, which with typical south California hyperbole bills itself the "Happiest Place on Earth." In places to call something "Mickey Mouse" is a considered insult, implying shoddy workmanship, shallowness and unreliability. But Mickey is a billion dollar industry. Talk-show host Johnny Carson says that the only culture in LA is yogurt; and as a "cultural" experience Disneyland is about as nutritional as junk food. But Disneyland is also about as popular as popular culture can be. "The Magic Kingdom," with its idealized "Main Street, USA," fast food, technical sophistication, thrilling rides into the past and the future, and wholesome fun for all the family, serves as mythology for modern America in general and LA in particular.

Not unlike New York in its European notions of what constitutes "culture," San Francisco takes itself more seriously. San Franciscans read books, and if they have a cultural mecca it is the City Lights bookstore at North Beach. The Columbus Ave. shop, owned by poet Lawrence Ferlinghetti, took off in the 1950s and '60s, publishing the works of Jack Kerouac and Allen Ginsberg. It became unofficial HQ for the San Francisco "Renaissance," an anti-establishment movement of poets, writers, jazz musicians and artists. The beatniks are long gone, but Ferlinghetti is still there, and the cluttered shop carries an eclectic mix of literary, political and spiritual books and periodicals. In the mainstream performing arts also, the city is probably as well served as its much larger southern neighbor. San Francisco has fewer theaters than LA. But those there are attract audiences large and enthusiastic enough to rival LA's first-run movie theaters, and local historians like to recall that even in 1850, amid the bordellos of the Barbary Coast, the city boasted at least 15 legitimate theaters. Today's

23

choices range wide, from classical performances at the American Conservatory Theater (ACT) to the wild iconoclasm of Club Fugazi, and the highly regarded San Francisco Ballet.

None of which is to say that Tinsel Town is entirely without non-movie glitter. The Los Angeles Philharmonic, whose summer season is staged in the 18,000-seat Hollywood Bowl auditorium, is world class. The galleries and museums, including the Getty, LA County Museum of Art, downtown's Museum of Contemporary Art (MOCA), the Norton Simon with its marvelous collection of Impressionists, and the Huntington with its *Blue Boy*, testify to an enthusiasm for the visual arts and to patrons with the wherewithal to acquire the best. Anyone interested in debunking the suggestion that the West Coast's premier cities are cultural wastelands need only spend an hour or three leafing through their newspapers' arts and entertainments supplements.

Movies

The true literature of California is probably in motion pictures. From D.W. Griffith's *The Birth of a Nation*, through Orson Wells' *Citizen Kane*, Mike Nichols' *The Graduate* and Roman Polanski's *Chinatown* to Robert Towne's *Tequila Sunrise*, they and scores of other movies tell a vivid story of each generation's distractions and preoccupations. Whether it be sexual mores, the violent struggle for control of water, or cocaine trafficking and the latest trends in designer pasta, nowhere has had its social and cultural history more closely, creatively and entertainingly documented on film.

Movies to see

The Barbary Coast, 1935 — Edward G. Robinson costume drama of San Francisco's wildest days.

A Star is Born, 1937 and 1954 — vintage movie landmarks.

The Maltese Falcon, 1941 — Bogart stars as Hammett's hard-boiled private detective with an office on Van Ness Ave.

Snow White & the Seven Dwarfs, 1943 — Walt Disney's first feature-length animated cartoon.

The Big Sleep, 1946 — Bogart again, this time as Chandler's Philip Marlowe in LA.

Sunset Boulevard, 1950 — high drama of fading actress and young screenwriter.

Rebel Without a Cause, 1955 — James Dean works out his frustrations in Griffiths Park.

Vertigo, 1958 — Hitchcock's psychological thriller taking in some of San Francisco's best-loved locations.

The Loved One, 1965 — Evelyn Waugh's biting satire on LA as entombed in the Forest Lawn Cemetery.

Bullit, 1968 — Steve McQueen in classic car-chase cop movie.

Zabriski Point, 1970 — Antonioni explores LA and Death Valley.

Dirty Harry, 1971 — Carmel's favorite son Clint Eastwood plays merciless detective prowling San Francisco.

What's up Doc, 1972 — classic comedy remake of *Bringing up Baby*, with Barbara Streisand being wacky in San Francisco.

The Long Goodbye, 1973 — Elliot Gould plays Chandler's Philip Marlowe in contemporary LA.

Chinatown, 1974 — jaded Jack Nicholson uncovers LA's corrupt battles for water in the atmospheric 1930s.

Shampoo, 1975 — Warren Beatty as a Beverly Hills hairdresser on the make.

Annie Hall, 1977 — I Love New Yorker Woody Allen hates LA.

Invasion of the Body Snatchers, 1978 — aliens target San Francisco.

Bladerunner, 1982 — futuristic story of lunatic LA circa 2019.

E.T., 1982 — Steven Spielberg's cuddly creature from outer space visits the San Fernando Valley.

Books

Movies are supremely important, but there is no shortage of significant literature preceding and paralleling the movies. Richard Henry Dana's *Two Years Before the Mast* contains excellent descriptions of southern California in the years before it was settled. Mark Twain's *The Celebrated Jumping Frog of Calaveras County* is only one example of his brilliant reporting of the Gold Country and early San Francisco. Robert Louis Stevenson's essays, collected as *From Scotland to Silverado*, tell wonderfully evocative tales of life in 1879-80, from crossing the Atlantic in steerage to the beginnings of the Napa Valley wine country. Even more romantic is Helen Hunt Jackson's *Ramona*, a sentimental novel that in its day captivated millions of Americans.

Among the first California-born writers to command more than local attention was Jack London. His early works *Tales of the Fish Patrol* and *John Barleycorn*, set in his native San Francisco Bay area, contradict Stevenson's idyllic descriptions. John Steinbeck goes even further in *Grapes of Wrath*, and his story of the San Joaquin Valley establishment resisting an influx of impoverished farmers in *East of Eden* is one of the grimmest views of California on record. Steinbeck offers a more comic view of Monterey in two books, *Tortilla Flat* and *Cannery Row*. Nathanael West's *Day of the Locust* and Evelyn Waugh's *The Loved One* each provides in its different way a sharp-eyed, sharp-tongued exploration of southern California, in West's case through Hollywood, in Waugh's, inimitably, through the funeral industry.

However, the literature of LA and San Francisco probably reached its apogee in two writers who perfected a home-grown genre — that of the hard-boiled private eye. Dashiell Hammett's *Maltese Falcon* and Raymond Chandler's *The Long Goodbye, Farewell My Lovely* and *The Big Sleep* are unequaled in their evocation of the moods, styles, geography and underlying realities of the cities. Inevitably perhaps, their works were turned into memorable movies.

More recently Tom Wolfe's *Electric Kool-Aid Acid Test* and *The Pump House Gang* chronicle the Flower Power era in much the same kind of personal journalism that Mark Twain practiced on an earlier California society in upheaval. Ray Bradbury captures the essence of the sun-kissed society in one of his Martian tales *Dark They Were and Golden Eyed*. Gore Vidal's *Myra Brekinridge*, for all its rather heavy-handed symbolism, is an entertaining romp through multilayered Californian illusion. And Joan Didion's *The White Album* and *Play It As It Lays* offer penetrating insights.

Among many nonfiction works on the cities and their state, the British architect Reyner Banham's *Los Angeles: the Architecture of Four Ecologies* is probably the most intelligent and thought-provoking along with California historian Carey McWilliams' politically conscious *Southern California: An Island on the Land*.

Pictures

In California, photographs are to paintings what motion pictures are to plays. Thus photographs by Ansel Adams from the 1930s on have given the world more powerful and memorable images of the landscape (most notably of Yosemite National Park and Death Valley) than Albert Bierstadt, the state's most celebrated landscape painter. Photography began in California with the Gold Rush and provides a wonderful historical record. Interest in photography as an art form is such that outstanding prints can command prices comparable with those for paintings and drawings.

Among contemporary artists, the British painter David Hockney has done something to redress the balance. His seemingly clichéd paintings of deep-blue swimming pools, flanked by palm trees, and cube-shaped buildings in desert colors capture a unique reality that is at once both commonplace and central to the experience of southern California. Also prominent on the extremely fertile art scene are internationally acclaimed artists such as Robert Graham, Richard Diebenkorn, Ed Ruscha, Billy Al Bengston and Charles Arnolds.

Architecture

Again the two cities are very different in style: Los Angeles an essentially horizontal, sometimes quirky mishmash of borrowings and idiosyncrasies, San Francisco a more vertical, more considered attempt at permanence and preservation. While the southern city celebrates Arata Isozaki's geometric Museum of Contemporary Art (MOCA), the minimalist works of Richard Neutra and Rudolph Schindler, Frank Gehry's sometimes mischievous innovation and the unique cluster of Watts Towers, the northern rejoices in its baroque City Hall and Colonial Revival-style terraces. There is, of course, merit in both enthusiasms. And they are far from being the whole story. Few cities are so rich in architectural interest. There is an impressive body of literature on the subject, and what follows attempts only a broad-brush look at what's on view.

Los Angeles Mission

For the southland in general, and Los Angeles in particular, the most widespread, enduring and characteristic style is Spanish/Mexican. The Mission style, derived from the chain of missions established by Franciscan friars, involves thick undecorated masonry walls with simple wooden detail. Ironically, the popularity of the style at the turn of the 20thC prompted the restoration of original missions fallen into disrepair after their lands were secularized in the 1820s.

Subsequent variations on the Hispanic theme include Spanish

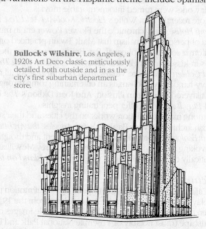

Bullock's Wilshire, Los Angeles, a 1920s Art Deco classic meticulously detailed both outside and in as the city's first suburban department store.

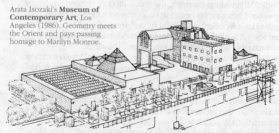

Arata Isozaki's **Museum of Contemporary Art**, Los Angeles (1986). Geometry meets the Orient and pays passing homage to Marilyn Monroe.

Colonial Revival, with thick white walls and low-pitched, tiled roofs, Spanish Baroque, with more flamboyant Churrigueresque decoration, and Hispanic Modern, with earlier influences informed by contemporary European ideas of line and integration with natural surroundings. The Hispanic/Mediterranean tradition continues today; in the southern California climate, with ample space for horizontal growth, it makes good sense.

Los Angeles high-rise

The same could not be said of the host of relatively high-rise Neoclassical, Beaux Arts designs to be found downtown. Similar buildings can be found throughout the United States. However, LA's city fathers decided that the center of a major metropolis needed monumental structures. The thinking is best typified in the 1920s-built City Hall, a 27-story stepped tower that mixes Greek, Roman and Renaissance influences.

But there are enough flights of fancy elsewhere to redress such conservatism. They range from Egyptian revival sparked by the discovery of the tomb of Tutankhamun in 1922, through pre-Columbian, to Art Deco, English Tudor, French Provincial, Hollywood Regency, Zigzag Moderne, "less is more" Modernism, High Tech, Industrial and, most recently, Post Modernism as seen in the recently opened Ma Maison-Sofitel Hotel. More often than not they have been designed with the automobile, as much as people, in mind: appropriately for a city that lives by the car, Bullock's Wilshire, a delightful 1928 Art Deco department store,

The 1928 **Los Angeles City Hall**, with 27 stepped stories, is an amalgam of Greek, Roman, Byzantine and Renaissance influences.

Primary-colored glass monsters like moon-colony hangars: Cesar Pelli's starkly elegant **Pacific Design Center**, West Hollywood, dating from 1975, has been fondly nicknamed the "Blue Whale" by Angelenos. A Green Whale adjoins it, and a Red Whale is expected soon.

27

was the nation's pioneer in providing car-parking for shoppers.

Efforts to revive downtown and invest the financial district with a degree of corporate grandeur have scored some architectural successes. The 1978 Westin Bonaventure Hotel with its five glass-sided tubes sets a futuristic tone, but many of its neighboring buildings are bland. Less easy to ignore in West Hollywood is the 1975 Pacific Design Center, an aircraft-hangar-sized hulk wrapped in cobalt blue glass designed by Yale Architecture Dean Caesar Pelli. Nicknamed the "Blue Whale" and described by one critic as a "metaphor for a place long known as a city of illusion," a green giant and, eventually, a red behemoth have been conceived to keep it company.

Los Angeles residential

Within its own context much of the architecture soon becomes recognizable. California Ranch, for example (the name says it all), predominates in post-World War II residential suburbs. Some of what is visible can seem almost like temporary structures of no historical or artistic consequence. Along the way, however, LA's size and exuberance have found space not only for the tackiest, the wackiest and the most self-indulgent, but also for the most sublime.

Arguably, the most fascinating structures have come after older influences have been shaken off. Best of all, in southern California, more than anywhere else, the architecture of family residences candidly reveals the personal idiosyncrasies of the people within and their myriad responses to their environment.

San Francisco's pagoda-style **Bank of Canton** once housed Chinatown's telephone operators.

Vedanta House, San Francisco: Joseph Leonard's tribute to Hindu tolerance. A rook and turban top the towers.

The Baroque **San Francisco City Hall** (1915) by Arthur Brown Jr and John Bakewell Jr was built as part of the superb Civic Center following the 1906 earthquake and fire. The Civic Center is regarded as the finest grouping of Beaux Arts architecture in the US.

San Francisco residential

San Francisco is more staid and urbane. Although a whiff of the Mediterranean remains, there is scant architectural evidence that this city also was once part of Spanish/Mexican California. The climate, of course, is less benign and more fitting to the New England and European styles that the boatloads of Gold Rush emigrants brought with them. Nor does San Francisco, just 49 square miles bounded by water on three sides, enjoy the luxury of limitless space in which to sprawl. As a consequence it is a more traditional, vertical urban environment. Among the earliest buildings were prefabricated kits shipped from the east, and the styles, if not many of the structures, survived the 1906 Earthquake. Thus residential architecture is typified by the "Victorian" row house, with bay windows and entrance portal.

Inevitably in such a cosmopolitan city, where money and imagination have allowed, other influences are to be seen. In Washington Sq. stands the imposing Church of St Peter and St Paul, looking like a transplant from southern Italy. Elsewhere there are fine Italianate houses from the 19thC, once-stately Georgian houses built London-style around a square, Roman Revival monoliths and, here and there, architectural imports acknowledging the city's large population of Asian origin, notably the three-tiered pagoda housing the Bank of Canton.

In the city proper only the wealthy are able to afford houses nowadays; most people live in apartment blocks. Generally they are low-rise, running the gamut of styles, from Art Deco to

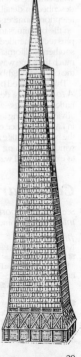

The **Transamerica Pyramid**, the unmissable needle of an LA-designed skyscraper that San Franciscans either love or hate.

Roddia's Watts Towers, in the Watts district of Los Angeles, a lifetime's work and folk-art masterpiece constructed from the affluent city's scraps. Once threatened by demolition, the towers are now being restored.

Mediterranean revival, to Edwardian brownstone, to sleek Modernist cubes. Almost invariably, they are lovingly cared for, with period details intact.

San Francisco public and corporate

The grandiose public buildings of the Civic Center fit easily into this context. Standing astride Van Ness Ave., regarded as San Francisco's Champs-Élysées, City Hall was designed in 1915 by Arthur Brown Jr and John Bakewell Jr, two Americans educated at the École des Beaux Arts in Paris. The complex is regarded with justification as one of the most successful examples of public architecture in the United States.

Corporate architecture has been more cautious. There are rare surviving examples of the imposing Chicago school and the Neo-Gothic, but the more recent flat-topped skyscrapers of the financial district are built mostly in the International Style of glass, stone and marble. One hard-to-miss and controversial exception is the 1972 Transamerica Pyramid — designed by a Los Angeles firm. But here too the latest trend is toward Post Modernism, and the new Nordstrom department store on Market St. is a fine example.

Los Angeles

This section is designed to help plan visits to Los Angeles and adjacent areas of California. It gives ideas and information, addresses and telephone numbers, and contains a calendar of the most notable events, which are cross-referenced to the entries in the *A to Z*, where they are described in detail. (Up-to-the-minute information is available at the telephone numbers given with each calendar entry.) There is also advice on the best times to go, the places to visit, the best ways to get around, plus recommended tours. The potentially bewildering sprawl of LA and southern California is broken down into more manageable areas — in much the same way that Angelenos themselves understand and inhabit the city and neighboring areas.

This is followed by introductory guides to the information given in the *A to Z* sections; descriptions of sights and places of interest including parks, buildings, amusements and museums; types of hotels, with advice on finding and reserving accommodations; a guide to eating out in LA, with advice on restaurant types and where to find the best food; the best in nightlife and the performing arts; pointers on shopping, both window-shopping and the real thing; and details on when and where to exercise, and watch and participate in sports.

Calendar of events

See also *LA Sports and recreation*, and *Public holidays* in *Basic information*. Some dates vary yearly, so best check beforehand.

January

Tournament of Roses Parade, Pasadena ☎(818) 449-4100.

Rose Bowl Collegiate Football game, Pasadena ☎(818) 793-7191.

World of Wheels, LA ☎(213) 587-5100.

Thoroughbred horse racing, Santa Anita ☎(818) 574-7223.

Japanese New Year Celebrations, Little Tokyo ☎(213) 628-2725.

Whale migration watching, s California coast ☎(213) 548-7562.

Basketball season begins ☎(213) 412-5000.

Ice hockey season begins ☎(213) 412-5000.

Annual dog-sled races, Palm Springs (weather permitting) ☎(619) 327-8411.

February

Mardi Gras, Olvera St., LA ☎(213) 680-2525/(213) 744-4210.

Chinese New Year Celebrations and Golden Dragon Parade, LA ☎(213) 628-1828.

South California Boat Show, LA Convention Center ☎(213) 741-1151.

Laguna Beach Winter Festival, with arts and crafts fair ☎(714) 494-1018.

Bob Hope Desert Golf Classic, Palm Springs ☎(619) 325-1577.

Riverside County National Date Festival, Indio ☎(619) 347-0676.

Pismo Beach Clam Festival, with jazz, parade and fair ☎(805) 773-4382.

March

Long Beach Grand Prix, Long Beach ☎(213) 436-7727.

Los Angeles Marathon, LA ☎(213) 624-7300.

Annual Academy Awards, LA ☎(213) 278-8990.

Kite Festivals, Santa Monica and Redondo Beach ☎(213) 392-9631.

Fiesta de las Golondrinas, celebrating swallows' return, San Juan Capistrano ☎(714) 493-1111.

International Film Festival, Santa Barbara ☎(805) 963-0023.

April

National Mime Week, LA ☎(213) 242-9163.

International Folk Dance Festival, LA ☎(213) 273-5539.

Easter Sunrise Services, Hollywood Bowl ☎(213) 850-2000.

Filmex, the LA film exposition ☎(213) 856-7700.

Cherry Blossom Festival, Little Tokyo ☎(213) 628-2725.

International Orchid Show, Santa Barbara ☎(805) 687-0766.

Baseball season begins ☎(213) 224-1500.

Toyota Grand Prix, Long Beach ☎(213) 436-3645.

Hollywood Park thoroughbred racing, Inglewood ☎(213) 419-1500.

Blessing of the Animals, a traditional Mexican parade, Olvera St. ☎(213) 624-7300.

May

Cinco de Mayo Celebrations marking Mexican Independence ☎(213) 680-2525, (213) 273-744-4210.

UCLA Mardi Gras, Spaulding Field ☎(213) 825-4321.

Pacific Southwest Tennis Championship, LA Tennis Club ☎(213) 464-3195.

Bullfight seasons opens, Tijuana ☎(619) 565-9949.

June

Grand Irish Fare and Music Festival, Burbank ☎(213) 624-7300.

Highland Games, Santa Monica Scottish festival ☎(213) 393-9825.

National Shakespeare Festival, Old Globe Theatre, San Diego ☎(619) 239-2255.

Playboy Jazz Festival, Hollywood Bowl ☎(213) 850-2000.

Dragon Boat Festival, Chinatown ☎(213) 624-7300.

Gay Pride Week, West Hollywood.

July

Hollywood Bowl Summer Festival/LA Philharmonic season opens, Hollywood Bowl ☎(213) 850-2000.

4th July Celebrations/Fireworks, Catalina and elsewhere.

Watts Jazz Festival, LA ☎(213) 624-7300.

Grand Prix Bicycle Race, Manhattan Beach ☎(213) 545-5313.

August

International Surf Festival, Hermosa, Manhattan and Redondo beaches ☎(213) 545-5042.

Beach Volleyball Championship, Laguna Beach ☎(714) 494-1018.

Old Miners Day, with races, parades and dances, Big Bear Lake ☎(714) 866-4601.

San Diego National Air Show, San Diego ☎(619) 232-3101.

Old Spanish Days, rodeo, Santa Barbara ☎815) 965-3021.

Nisei Week, celebration of Japanese-American culture, Little Tokyo ☎(213) 687-7193.

September

LA City Birthday and Mexican Independence celebrations, Olvera St. ☎(213) 680-2525.

LA County Fair, the nation's largest, Pomona ☎(714) 623-3111.

Pro Beach Volleyball Championships, Redondo Beach ☎(213) 245-3778.

National Football League season begins ☎(213) 322-5901/(714) 277-4700.

Hollywood Bowl season ends, with fireworks finale ☎(213) 850-2000.

October

Discovery of California/Cabrillo Landing Pageant, Cabrillo Marine Museum ☎(213) 548-7562.

Festival of Masks, Hancock County Park ☎(213) 937-5544.

LA Philharmonic season opens ☎(213) 972-7211.

Oak Tree Meeting, Santa Anita ☎(818) 574-7223.

Grand National Irish Fair, Northridge ☎(818) 885-2519.

Sandcastle building contest, Corona del Mar ☎(714) 644-8211.

November

Hollywood Christmas Parade, Hollywood ☎(213) 469-8311.

Dia de los Meurtos, Olvera St., LA.

Death Valley Days, Furnace Creek and Stovepipe Wells ☎(714) 786-2331.

Annual "Doo Dah" parade, Pasadena ☎(818) 795-3355.

December

Annual 10k and Waiters/Waitresses 5K race, Beverly Hills ☎(213) 624-7300.

Christmas Boat Parade, Marina del Rey ☎(213) 822-0119.

Las Posadas, Mexican candlelit parade, Olvera St., LA.

31

When and where to go

For many non-Californians the classic image of LA weather is New Year's Day on a sun-drenched beach. The notion of an all-year playground is most appropriate for the coastal areas s from Santa Barbara. Mild, sunny days come to this region in rows throughout Jan and Feb; summer is simply warmer and drier, and ocean breezes act as nature's air conditioning.

The sun shines 75 percent of the time. Sept-Oct are hottest, Dec-Jan coolest; in LA the difference is between an average of 75˚F (24˚C) and 50˚F (10˚C). The San Fernando Valley is generally a few degrees warmer than areas s of the Hollywood Hills. In the fall Santa Ana winds blow out of the desert, intensifying the heat and increasing the danger of fires. The "rainy season," such as it is, comes between Nov and Mar, with the heaviest showers from Dec to Feb. LA averages about 15ins a year. Smog is most severe in Aug and Sept. Visitors are thickest on the ground in the summer months, when major attractions can be oversubscribed and crowded.

Elsewhere, expectations, and wardrobe, must be a little more flexible. Palm Springs and other desert communities only a few score miles inland from the s coast are delightfully warm from Thanksgiving to Easter, but grow so hot in summer that many resorts close down from June to the end of Sept. Death Valley, which has one of the world's hottest summer climates, throttles back to half speed from May to Oct. Desert variations between day and night temperatures can be as wide as 40˚F (22˚C).

Mountainous areas have a more conventional cycle of seasons. Summers are warm and dry. Skiers' snows may come as early as Nov but are most predictable in Jan-Feb. In most seasons, enough late storms keep the high slopes open until Easter. Spring and fall are as erratic in these mountains as in England, Olde or New. But broadly speaking the mountains are cold in winter, cool in spring and fall, and very warm in summer.

Weather is not the only factor to consider in scheduling an LA vacation: events crowd the calendar. A summary of some outstanding events may be found on p30. Others are noted in the *A to Z*. Problems in deciding how to spend a vacation in California are caused by the state's embarrassment of riches. The sensible approach would be to tackle either southern or northern California from a base in either LA or San Francisco. However, for those on a once-in-a-lifetime visit this advice will hold little appeal, and with planning and energy just about everything is possible. Dividing the major cities and the state into its natural regions helps the visitor define the practical possibilities in terms of time as well as seasons and attractions. LA and San Francisco not only count for themselves; they provide natural anchor points for drawing most of the regional boundaries. ▣

Getting there

Los Angeles International Airport (LAX) (☎ *(213) 646-5252*), on the w side of the city, 22 miles from downtown, is the world's third busiest airport, served daily by nearly all national and international airlines. There are four E-W runways, and the central complex comprises eight separate terminals around a two-level loop. In addition there is the nearby West Imperial Terminal to the s handling charter aircraft and unscheduled flights.

Free **Airline Connection** buses, colored blue, green and white, run between the different terminals at both levels. **Handicapped Connections** has special free minibuses to cope with wheelchairs (☎ *(213) 645-8021*). Departures are at the upper level, arrivals at the lower. There are the usual restaurants, bars, gift stores and newsstands. At the arrival level are to be found baggage claim, greeting areas, foreign currency exchange counters, information desks and courtesy phones for transportation and accommodations information. The new Tom Bradley International Terminal also offers **Skytel**, where travelers can shower and sleep.

LAX has its own multilingual information service, and inside the airport yellow telephones link directly to Airport Information Aides from 7am-11.30pm daily. For telephone numbers of individual airlines see the Yellow Pages.

From the airport to the city

Ground transportation between the airport (off the San Diego Freeway 405 at Florence/Century exits) and other districts of Los Angeles is excellent. Still, with so many buses and taxis circling the airport the system can appear haphazard and confusing. Shuttle services, like those listed below, will generally want to fill their vans before leaving the airport. So using them could involve a wait and dropping off other passengers en route to your destination. However, they are cheaper than taxis and limousines unless there are three or more people traveling together. Vans and buses load from the center islands outside baggage claim areas, but baggage capacities can be limited. Car rental agencies with LAX operations operate shuttle services to their depots. For information on all buses, taxis, limousines and other transportation ☎ (213) 247-7678. Advanced reservations are recommended for limousines and rentals. Among the choices are those listed below.

Buses
Airlink To downtown LA hotels ☎ (800) 962-1976.
Airport Service Bus To major hotels throughout LA ☎ (213) 723-4636, (213) 855-1727, (714) 778-3141.
Flightline To downtown, Hollywood, Westside, Santa Monica, Marina del Rey ☎ (213) 971-8265.
Flyaway To Van Nuys Airport in the E San Fernando Valley ☎ (213) 994-5554, (213) 781-5554.
Fun Bus Systems Nonstop express service from LAX to Disneyland every ½hr ☎ (800) 962-1976.
Great American Stage Lines To w San Fernando Valley and Ventura ☎ (805) 499-1995.
Prime Time Shuttle Links all LA area airports ☎ (213) 558-1606.
RTD Airport Services Regular buses to most parts of town, and regular 24hr shuttle to its Airport Transfer Terminal ☎ (213) 723-4636.
Super Shuttle Door-to-door service throughout LA and Orange County ☎ (800) 325-3948, (213) 777-8000, (818) 244-2700, (213) 417-8988.

Taxis
Airport Taxi Service From and to LAX ☎ (213) 837-7252.
Blue & Yellow Cab From and to LAX ☎ (213) 204-4833.
Independent Cab Company 24hr driver-owned cabs ☎ (213) 385-8294.
LA Taxi Air-conditioned cabs with uniformed drivers ☎ (213) 627-7000, (213) 412-8000.
United Independent Taxi Throughout LA County, major credit cards accepted ☎ (213) 653-5050.

Limousines
Dunhill Limousine Service Cadillac and Lincoln stretch limos with bars, phones, color TV, moon roofs etc ☎ (213) 770-4383.
Music Express Limousine Sedans, Cadillac and "Presidential"

stretch limos ☎(800) 255-4444.
Prime Time Limousine   Chauffeured sedans, limos: cellphones available ☎(213) 463-3435.
Prince Transportation Services   Chauffeured sedans, stretch limos ☎(213) 378-9292.
Sedan by Michael's Inc.   24hr chauffeured sedans for tours, conventions, seminars ☎(213) 460-2429.

Car rental

Ace Rent-a-Car   From vans to Mustang convertibles ☎(213) 417-2220, (800) 223-3457.
Alamo Rent a Car   Competitive rates, 24hr LAX pick-up ☎(213) 649-2245.
AutoExotica   Top-name sports and luxury cars ☎(213) 652-2834.
Avis Rent a Car   75 locations in s California ☎(213) 646-5600, (800) 331-1212.
Budget Rent-a-Car   American and prestige European cars, convertibles ☎(213) 645-4500, (800) 527-0700.
Dollar Rent-a-Car   Late-model economy and luxury American and Japanese cars ☎(213) 645-9333, (800) 421-6868.
Hertz Corporation   Ford cars, with special group and convention rates ☎(213) 646-4861, (800) 654-3131.
Regency Exotic Car Rental   Sports and luxury cars including Rolls-Royce, Porsche, Jaguar, Corvette ☎(800) 545-1020.
Rent-A-Wreck   No airport pick-up, but used cars, vans, trucks at rates up to 50 percent below competitors ☎(818) 762-3628, (818) 343-0047, (213) 478-0676.
Thrifty Rent a Car   Convention rates ☎(213) 645-1880, (800) 367-2277.

Recreational vehicles

Budget Rent a Car and Truck   Economy and luxury motorhomes, airport pick-up ☎(800) 446-7368, (213) 670-1744.
Cruise America-RV Rentals   Motorhomes and custom vans, LAX pick-up ☎(800) 327-7778, (714) 772-9030.
El Monte Rents/LA Motor Home Rental Center   Motorhomes and trailers, multilingual service ☎(800) 367-3687, (818) 443-6158.

Alternative airports

Los Angeles International is the biggest but not the only airport in the LA area. There are smaller airports that could be a more convenient alternative for flights within the US.
Burbank-Glendale-Pasadena Airport   2627 N Hollywood Way ☎(818) 840-8847.
John Wayne Airport   MacArthur Blvd., Orange County ☎(714) 745-6500.
Long Beach Airport   4100 Douglas Dr., Long Beach ☎(213) 421-8293.
Ontario International Airport   Mission Blvd., Ontario ☎(714) 983-8282.

Other transportation

Los Angeles is also served by **Amtrak** (*Union Passenger Station N of downtown, at 800 N Almeda St.*), **Greyhound Lines** (*downtown depot at 208 E 6th St.*) and **Trailways** (*depot at 1501 S Central Ave.*).

Once arrived, attempting LA without a car, save for the briefest of visits, is to invite frustration and/or unnecessary expense. The **Automobile Club of Southern California** (*2601 S Figueroa St.*) is a superb source of motoring information — but alas only for members (*for membership details* ☎ *(213) 741-4880*).

However, there are local bus services. **Southern California Rapid Transit District** (*write to: RTD Los Angeles 90001*) operates buses throughout the Los Angeles Basin and Orange County, with more than 200 buses covering 2,200sq. miles (☎ *(213) 626-4455 Mon-Fri 6am-midnight, Sat-Sun 6am-6pm, no information service on major hols except Jan 1; impaired hearing ☎ (800) 252-9040; information and rover ticket sales kiosk on Underground Level B, ARCO Plaza, 5th St. and Flower St., Mon-Fri 9am-5pm, closed Sat-Sun and major hols; RTD's free "Rider's Kit" gives information on fares and routes*). Culver City, Santa Monica and several other independent cities within RTD's service area operate a supplementary local service.

Tours

Agentours Inc.   11321 Iowa St., LA 90025 ☎(213) 473-2456, scheduled sightseeing tours, multilingual services, hotel pick-up.
Air LA   3000 N Clybourn Ave. Burbank 91505 ☎(800) 225-9843, (818) 843-2713, one-day air and ground tours of Grand Canyon, Las Vegas.
Judith Benjamin   2210 Wilshire Blvd., Suite 754, Santa Monica 90403 ☎(213) 476-3659, luxury personal limousine tours.
Blue Line Tour and Charter Inc.   PO Box 25 "B" 17, LA 90025 ☎(213) 312-3326, scheduled local tours including beaches and Getty Museum.
The California Native   6701 W 87th Pl., LA 90045 ☎(213) 642-1140, one-day visits to mountains, desert, San Andreas Fault, Old West historical sites.
California Parlor Car Tours   515 S Olive St., LA 90017 ☎(800) 227-4250, (213) 624-1889, 3-6 day tours including Hearst Castle, Monterey, Yosemite, San Diego.
California Wine Tours   2554 Lincoln Blvd., Suite 525, Marina Del Rey 90291 ☎(213) 305-1475, guided tours of s California wine-growing areas with tastings and lunch.
Casablanca Tours   6362 Hollywood Blvd., Hollywood 90028 ☎(213) 461-0156, 4hr tours of stars' homes, Chinese Theater, Sunset Strip, Rodeo Drive, Farmers Market.
Grave Line Tours   PO Box 931694, Hollywood 90093 ☎(213) 392-5501, macabre tour around sites of Hollywood's famous murders, suicides, scandals and crimes, in a renovated hearse.
Gray Line Tours Co.   1207 W 3rd St., LA 90017 ☎(800) 538-5050, (213) 481-2121, standard bus tours.
Hollywood Fantasy Tours   1721 N Highland Ave., Hollywood 90028 ☎(800) 782-7287, (213) 469-8184, stars' homes, movie studios and landmarks, in double-decker and open buses.
Piuma Aircraft   PO Box 1201, Malibu 90265 ☎(818) 888-0576, hot-air balloon flights plus champagne lunch: reserve ahead.
River Mountain Action   5916 W 77th Pl., LA 90045 ☎(800) 762-7238, (818) 348-3727, 2-day ski trips to Mammoth Jan-Apr, American River Raft trips May-Sept.
Starline Tours   6845 Hollywood Blvd., Hollywood 90028 ☎(800) 451-3131, (213) 463-3131, stars' homes, Hollywood, Beverly Hills.
Tour Elegante   15446 Sherman Way, Suite 3-118, Van Nuys 91406 ☎(818) 786-8466, city tours, 6hr beach tour, plus wine country and coastal tours as far as San Francisco.
The Wilderness Institute Inc.   23018 Ventura Blvd., Suite 202, Woodland Hills 91364 ☎(818) 887-7831, naturalist-led tours of scenic spots.

Driving
Like it or not, you'll almost certainly need to; taxis don't cruise the

streets as in other cities, and public transportation leaves much to be desired. The freeway system can be unforgiving, but it is understandable. Interchanges and exit roads are signaled well in advance, and it is essential to heed the signs overhanging the freeway and be in the correct lane at the correct time; a mistake can involve miles of needless driving before there's an opportunity to rectify it. Lane discipline is of a different order from what some visitors might be used to. There isn't a slow, fast and faster lane. Rather drivers choose lanes according to speed, intentions and the progress of other vehicles. Expect to be passed on the inside.

Freeways also change name and number; thus the 134 Ventura becomes the 210 Foothill; the 5 is variously the Golden State, Santa Ana and San Diego. The solution is to study the map and plan ahead, making a note of proposed routes. Disabled vehicles should be parked on the shoulder along which there are yellow phone booths at frequent intervals. Wait for assistance with closed windows and locked doors. For updated traffic information listen to local radio stations or ☎(213) 626-7231.

Whatever their shortcomings, the freeways are usually the best way to travel any significant distance. When traveling the major boulevards and smaller roads expect to move more slowly and have your progress interrupted by stop signs, traffic lights and turning vehicles. Don't rely only on a street name and number to find addresses; streets run for miles, numbers run into the ten-thousands, and different cities have different systems. Find out the nearest intersection and take it from there.

Walking

Mostly people don't. Angelenos and their cars are like cowboys and their horses: almost inseparable. Except in the glossier recreational and shopping areas of downtown, Beverly Hills, Hollywood and Santa Monica, walkers are regarded as mad or bad or possibly both. However, where walking is relatively risk-free, for example along much of trendy Melrose Ave., it can be a pleasure. The land is flat and the Mediterranean weather perfect. But remember that LA blocks are huge. What appears on a map to be a manageable six-block walk may be anything but easy.

Useful information

American Express Travel Service Office　327 N Beverly Dr., Beverly Hills 90210 ☎(213) 274-8277; 723 W 7th St., LA 90017 ☎(213) 488-1301; 251 S Lake Ave., Suite 102, Pasadena 91101 ☎(213) 449-2281.

i *Greater Los Angeles Visitor and Convention Bureau*　ManuLife Plaza 515, S Figueroa St., 11th floor, LA 90071 ☎(213) 624-7300 ✆(213) 624-9746.

i *Bureau-operated visitor information centers*　Downtown at ARCO Plaza, Underground Level B, Mon-Fri 8.30am-5pm ☎(213) 689-8822, and at LAX arrival and departure levels of Bradley International Terminal, daily 8.30am-9pm ☎(213) 215-0606.

Travelers Aid Society of LA　☎(213) 625-2501.

Weather　☎(213) 554-1212.

Beach conditions　☎(213) 378-8471.

Highway conditions　☎(213) 626-7231.

Post Office　☎(213) 586-1467.

Emergency information

Los Angeles Police Dept. (LAPD)　Emergency ☎911, nonemergency ☎(213) 485-2121.

California Highway Patrol　Emergency ☎911 and ask for

Highway Patrol, nonemergency ☎ (213) 736-3374.
Fire ☎ 911.
Coast Guard ☎ (213) 499-5380.
Ambulance ☎ 911.
Paramedics ☎ 911, nonemergency ☎ (213) 483-6721.
Medical Society referrals ☎ (213) 483-6122.
Dental Society referrals ☎ (213) 481-2133.
Suicide Prevention ☎ (213) 381-5111.
Drug Hotline ☎ (213) 463-6851.

Late-night

Pharmacies: **Thrifty Drugstore** *(1533 N Vermont Ave., LA ☎ (213) 666-5083, open 24hrs)*; **Horton & Converse Pharmacy** *(6625 Van Nuys Blvd., Van Nuys ☎ (818) 782-6251, open 24hrs)*; **Bel-Air Pharmacy** *(820 Moraga Dr., Bel-Air ☎ (213) 472-9593, on call 24hrs)*; **Robert Burns Pharmacy** *(9049 Burton Way, LA ☎ (213) 271-5126, on call 24hrs)*; **Family Pharmacy Service** *(8314 Wilshire Blvd., LA ☎ 653-4070, on call 24hrs)*.

Locksmiths: **US Lock** *(☎ (213) 463-1982, 24hr service)*; **Wilshire Lock and Key** *(☎ (213) 389-8433, 24hr service)*.

Baby-sitters: **Baby Sitters Guild** *(☎ (213) 469-8246, on call 24hrs)*.

Foreign exchange

Banks can sometimes be a problem. Often they will change foreign currency and travelers' cheques only for regular customers or with a hefty service charge. There are, in addition to the **American Express Travel Service Office** listed above, **LA Currency Exchange** *(International Terminal, LAX ☎ (213) 646-9346)*, **Bank of America** *(International Terminal, LAX ☎ (213) 568-8064, and 525 S Flower St., LA ☎ (213) 228-2721, (800) 233-3760)*, **Deak-Perera** *(452 N Bedford Dr., Beverly Hills ☎ (213) 274-9176, and 677 S Figueroa St., LA ☎ (213) 624-4221)*.

Maps and publications

Guidebooks and maps from bookstores: *LA/Access* (Access Press); *Gault Millau The Best of Los Angeles* (Prentice Hall); *Flashmaps Instant Guide to Los Angeles* (Random House); *Thomas Brothers Road Atlas and Driver's Guide to Los Angeles* (Thomas Bros Maps).

Local newspapers and magazines: morning *LA Times*, evening *Herald-Examiner*, especially Fri editions for weekend events, and Sun editions for coming week; the free *LA Weekly*, offering probably the most comprehensive what's on; *LA Magazine*, a glossy monthly on chic LA living; *GuestInformant* and *Key*, advertiser-oriented magazines available free in hotel rooms.

Los Angeles area planner

Los Angeles fits no traditional notion of a city. To think of LA County as 82 towns, with 1,500 miles of freeway and 12,500 miles of paved streets, or of the city of LA as the country's second largest with a land area of 464 sq. miles is almost inevitably to be overawed and overwhelmed. That is not the way Angelenos look at the place. Rather they break it down, geographically and psychologically. Freeways replace conventional thoroughfares as the only manageable links between neighborhoods that were two days apart before cars replaced horses. Seemingly endless commercial strips run alongside or beneath the freeways, making it possible to spend what *seems* like two days crossing a city more than 52 miles across at one point, but barely half a mile wide on another axis. These bizarre boundaries exist because Los Angeles flowed around what it could not flow over in its heyday of growth. Beverly Hills, Pasadena, Santa Monica and other incorporated cities were drawn in largely because to stay outside was to be denied water.

But few outsiders would claim to understand the complexity of today's local politics. It is probably best not to dwell too long on the detailed patchwork. The city can be understood more easily as six adjacent districts: **Downtown**, **Hollywood**, **Westside**, **Coastal**, **Valleys** and **Central**. Neighboring areas of interest are: **Mountains**, **Desert**, **Central Coast**, **Orange County** and **San Diego**.

Downtown (map 7 D9)

12 miles E of the Pacific Ocean, within the area described by the wobbly trapezoid of the Harbor (SR-11), Hollywood (US-101) and Santa Monica (I-10) freeways, is the daytime center for business and civic activity. But it is not only that. As well as the **Civic Center** and the **commercial district**, it encompasses **Chinatown**, **Little Tokyo** and the historic Hispanic heart of the city, **El Pueblo de Los Angeles**. The heart of the heart is the **Plaza** (N Main St. and Paseo de la Plaza) the tree-shaded venue for annual Mexican festivities such as Cinco de Mayo (see *Calendar of events*). Running into the Plaza is **Olvera St.**, re-created in 1930 as a Mexican marketplace/theme park.

The surrounding area is rich in historically and architecturally significant buildings such as the Renaissance-style **Masonic Temple**, the Victorian **Old Firehouse** and Mission-style **Union Passenger Station**. The contemporary hub of downtown Hispanic life is **Broadway**, which in its colorful, slightly seedy bustle is reminiscent of Tijuana, the Mexican border town to the S. Around N Broadway, **Chinatown** is an equally coherent ethnic minority enclave, with Chinese shops, restaurants and homes. To the S, **Little Tokyo**, around Central Ave. and 1st St., is a more orderly and contrived attraction, although no less culturally authentic. The **financial district** lies to the S and W, centered around Flower St. It boasts some top-class hotels, several fine shopping arcades and restaurants, and is conveniently placed for the **Music Center**, the **Museum of Contemporary Art** and the **Temporary Contemporary**. But after dark its streets are somewhat desolate.

Farther S and W the terrain becomes more commercial, with the garment district, the wholesale flower market and manufacturing premises. Probably of most interest to visitors are a number of notable architectural landmarks, plus **Exposition Park** with its great museums, and, as venues for sports and the arts, the **Memorial Coliseum** and the **Shrine Auditorium**.

Hollywood (map 5 B5)

As you would expect, Hollywood straddles the Hollywood Freeway, 101, taking in flatland in the S and foothills in the N. The Hollywood sign is still there on the S slopes of Mt. Lee, but Hollywood is no longer physically the movie capital of the world. Most of the big studios have moved to Burbank, the stars to Beverly Hills and Malibu, and the fabled intersection of Hollywood and Vine ranges between tawdry and sleazy.

But while there is some truth in the wisecrack that "Hollywood is the place that people from Iowa mistake each other for stars," the district is still rich in movie nostalgia. The heart of **Hollywood Blvd.**, roughly between Vine and Sycamore, is designated a National Historic District, and much of its 1920s and '30s architecture is intact, along with the **Chinese Theater** and the **Walk of Fame**. Movie studios, labs and agents are still in residence, as is the music industry, most visibly in the **Capitol Records Tower**.

In recent years efforts to clean up the tarnished image of the area have been partially successful. The four parallel E-W boulevards, **Hollywood**, **Sunset**, **Santa Monica** and **Melrose**, apart from their daytime commercial activity, have become centers of vivid nightlife, with more than their fair share of fashionable hotels, restaurants, nightclubs, bookstores and galleries. Perhaps surprisingly Hollywood is now the center of legitimate theater in LA, and the **Hollywood Bowl** remains one of the world's great natural amphitheaters.

The hills to the N, cut through by **Laurel and Nichols Canyons** and **Mulholland Dr.**, are much more prosperous but less interesting, save for their scenic beauty and the sometimes bizarre architectural taste of the literary and artistic inhabitants.

Westside (*map 2 B2*)

In a lop-sided rectangle w of Hollywood, s of Mulholland Dr., E of the San Diego Freeway 405, N of the Santa Monica Freeway 10 and bisected by Wilshire Blvd. running E-W, is the Westside, the area containing LA's ritziest, most affluent communities: **Beverly Hills**, **Bel Air**, **Westwood** and **Brentwood**. N of Wilshire they have the cleanest streets, the most perfectly manicured lawns, the lowest crime rate, the shiniest imported luxury cars, the best schools, the costliest stores, some of the finest restaurants, and hotels with a broad range of prices, beginning with expensive. But don't be daunted; there's no visa required or entry fee into this Monaco-like enclave of wealth and extravagance. s of Wilshire things are more modest and restrained, becoming less polished to the s and E.

Among the residential communities, Beverly Hills, Bel Air and Brentwood lead in the mansion, swimming pool and exclusive country club stakes. The infrastructure reflects that; commercial activity is of the white-collar, nonpolluting kind, and everything is tightly regulated, even the dimensions of signs. Consuming, and watching the sleek inhabitants consume, is the main leisure activity.

The stretch of Wilshire Blvd. running E-W into Beverly Hills from downtown is an interesting and important example of the type of connective tissue that unifies LA. Toward the downtown end, the focal points for visitors are the hotels; near Beverly Hills, the museums, such as the **LA County Museum of Art**, and the restaurants. At the sw corner of Beverly Hills, **Century City** used to be 20th Century Fox's back lot. 1960s developers threw up clusters of high-rise condominiums, making it a rather soulless place. More recent high-rise office buildings have done little to humanize it, though a new movie theater/restaurant complex has enlivened its nightlife; other redeeming features are a pleasant enough shopping mall with some good restaurants, and a handful of theaters.

Westwood Village, near the **University of California, Los Angeles (UCLA)**, has fared equally poorly at the hands of developers. But it boasts the highest concentration of first-run movie theaters, and the nearby campus adds a frisson of youthful energy, useful restaurants with prices students can afford and a good choice of stores selling sports equipment, books and collegiate fashions.

Coastal (*map 2 D2*)

Between the exclusive Malibu colony in the NW and the major port city of Long Beach in the SE is "surfurbia," the coastal communities that make LA an extra special city. Traveling from N to S, they are **Malibu**, **Pacific Palisades**, **Santa Monica**, **Venice**, **Marina del Rey**, **Manhattan Beach**, **Hermosa Beach**, **Redondo Beach** and **Palos Verdes**. Although they all nuzzle the Pacific, and most are accessible along the Pacific Coast Highway, all are quite evidently different.

Forget the bogus maps sold along Hollywood Blvd. Malibu is where the movie stars really live. However, there isn't much to interest the visitor at the so-called Malibu Colony; the beach is private, screened from the highway by often nondescript homes tightly packed together townhouse-style. The likelihood of seeing a Hollywood idol is about the same as seeing one of the luxury homes fall down a crumbling cliff. It happens occasionally but not often. Few of the restaurants are good enough to warrant a special journey, but there are other attractions. The drive down from **Woodland Hills** along winding **Topanga Canyon Blvd.**, a 1960s hippie haven, is delightful; the **J. Paul Getty Museum** is at the s edge of the town; Will Rogers' old house also is now a museum within the 187-acre **Will Rogers State Historic Park**; and the public beach is a good one with excellent surfing. To the E and high above the highway is **Pacific Palisades**, the district with the highest average income in LA. Apart from the wealth, the most noteworthy fact about the area is that it was originally founded as a community by the Methodist Church, and many of the streets are named after its bishops.

To the s, **Santa Monica** is a different story. One of the most engaging places in LA, it is easily reached from the E via the Santa Monica Freeway 10 and the Wilshire and Santa Monica Blvds. Efforts by residents and the city council to keep down rents earned it the nickname "The People's Republic of Santa Monica." The people seem to be running Santa Monica pretty well. Just a stone's throw from the original downtown is one of the finest beaches in all of s California. On a fine day, up to a million people will descend upon it. **Santa Monica Pier** is slightly worn at the edges but is everything a pier should be, with all the familiar diversions from popcorn to carousels. There are good hotels, with a welcome range of affordable prices, near but not on the beach, excellent to extraordinary restaurants throughout town, and good shopping both downtown and along recently gentrified Main St. Clean sea breezes and an easy-going atmosphere continue to attract a population of wealthy families and upwardly mobile young professionals.

To the s is **Venice**, begun as a sincere attempt to imitate the best of the original. In the early years of the century 16 miles of canals were built, but somewhere along the way Venice took a wrong turn, or maybe a right turn, and decided that the counter-culture was probably more fun than medieval culture. Ever since, it has attracted the eccentric and the exhibitionist, most of whom seem to turn out for the amusement of visitors and each other along **Ocean Front Walk**. Apart from this street theater, Venice has some excellent restaurants, noteworthy buildings, pleasant narrow streets, countless artists and a few surviving canals.

Marina del Rey, s of Venice, is yet another part of LA where what ought to be fantasy functions as opulent reality. Sited around a man-made marina with moorings for 10,000 pleasure craft, the area has good hotels and motels, excellent beaches and water sports and is supremely convenient for LAX to the s and downtown to the E. The only drawback is that everything seems too good to be true.

Beyond LAX is **Manhattan Beach**, along with its two neighbors to the s, **Hermosa Beach** and **Redondo Beach**, the spiritual home of beach culture. There are beautiful homes, beautiful beaches and beautiful people intent on enjoying themselves to the utmost, along with relaxing, reasonably priced hotels and a few notable restaurants.

Farther s is the **Palos Verdes Peninsula**, an exclusive dormitory community set precariously on terraced hills above steep coastal cliffs. The audacity of the civil engineering and the physical drama of the place warrant a visit. In addition there is Lloyd Wright's **Wayfarer's Chapel**, a monument to Swedish theologian and mystic

BRAZILIAN FRUIT BASKET
107 7TH STREET
SAN FRANCISCO, CA. 94103
(415) 626-6432
CAMELOT FINANCIAL SYSTEMS
STATION # TEST1

FRI, OCT 01, 1993 00=43 AM

CREDIT CARD

CCT NO: 378263368881023
XP DATE: 9405
R TYPE: PURCHASE
MOUNT: $ 29.95
PP CODE: 000034
IC NO: 001

ERVER NO: 1
ICKET NUMBER:
B TOTAL = $ 29.95

P = $ 5.—

TAL = $ 34.95

GN _A. E. Belter_
SE BELTER
THANK YOU FOR YOUR PATRONAGE
WE HOPE TO SEE YOU SOON

Emanuel Swedenbor — and some splendid whale-watching spots.

Around the peninsula, reached by either the Pacific Coast Highway or the Harbor Freeway 110, **San Pedro** is what one expects of a major international port. But amid the docks and cargo containers there are some interesting relics of the 19thC, an intriguing fishing pier and good fresh seafood right off the boats. Many of the fishermen are of Greek, Portuguese or Yugoslav origin, and their cultural input enlivens the town. San Pedro also has an embarkation pier for ferry cruises to **Catalina Island**, directly beneath the Vincent Thomas Bridge to Terminal Island and Long Beach, reached by taking the Harbor Blvd. exit from the Harbor Freeway.

Finally, at the s tip of LA County down Freeway 710, is **Long Beach**, a major city in its own right, with much to recommend it to the visitor. At its s end is **Naples**, a human-scale, Italianate community crisscrossed with canals. The downtown area is an unappetizing study in high-rise building, but there are good hotels, and elsewhere there are notable museums, such as the **Long Beach Museum of Art**, some historic landmarks and the two biggest tourist attractions: the retired luxury liner **Queen Mary** and Howard Hughes' extraordinary airplane **Spruce Goose**. Equally unusual are the offshore oil wells cunningly disguised as tropical islands.

Valleys (map 15 16)

North of the Santa Monica Mountains, running w-e between Ventura Freeway 101 and the Simi Valley 118 and Foothill 210 Freeways, is the **San Fernando Valley**. To the e, bounded by mountains to the n and hills to the s, and encircled by the Glendale Freeway 2, Foothill 210 and Santa Monica 10 Freeways, is the **San Gabriel Valley**. These are the Valleys, with dozens of overlapping communities whose inhabitants have created Middle America with palm trees.

What characterizes the Valleys above all is that even by LA standards they are big; they make Hollywood seem almost dinky in comparison. When LA annexed the San Fernando Valley in 1915 it more than doubled its size. Parts of the 4,000-acre **Griffiths Park** overlook the Fernando Valley floor. Both valleys are predominantly white, middle-class and residential, with pockets of entertainment and high-tech industries, and their main thoroughfares, such as Ventura and Colorado Blvds., serve as the axis for a giant grid sprawling for miles in all directions.

Residents would not agree, but there is little to help the visitor distinguish between the various merged-together towns. Strung out e-w along Ventura Blvd., **Studio City**, **Sherman Oaks**, **Encino**, **Tarzana** (named for Edgar Rice Burroughs' jungle hero) and **Woodland Hills** have similar tracts of homes, similar shopping malls, similar choices of restaurants and motels. Much the same is true of other nearby districts such as **Van Nuys** and **N Hollywood**.

It is less true farther e. The characters of **Universal City** and **Burbank** are colored by the highly visible presence of major movie and TV studios, notably Burbank, Disney, NBC and Universal. **Glendale**, meanwhile, has at least two claims to fame: the biggest community of Armenians outside Armenia, and the rolling acres of **Forest Lawn**, the one-of-a-kind cemetery that at times seems like a theme park for the deceased. In addition, there are some goodish restaurants patronized by locals and the media folk, and a few outstanding hotels. But apart from the tours of the studios, the main attraction of this part of the Valley is that it is a less costly base than Westside and less nerve-wracking than Hollywood but, thanks to Highways 101, 134 and 405, within reach of just about anywhere.

East down the Freeway 134/210 are the communities of the San Gabriel Valley, once famed for its groves of oranges, lemons and walnuts. **Pasadena** is the most well established and defined: old money, attractive homes and gardens, a sedate, cultured atmosphere, with some of LA's best museums and botanic gardens, the best theater company in the **Pasadena Playhouse**, many interesting buildings and good restaurants, but, strangely, few notable hotels. Last but not least, every year on New Year's Day Pasadena plays host to the stunning **Tournament of Roses**.

To the SE, and even wealthier, is **San Marino**, once the fiefdom of tycoon Henry E. Huntington whose enduring legacy is the magnificent **Huntington Library**, **Art Galleries** and **Botanical Gardens**. Almost due S is **Monterey Park**, sometimes know as "Little Taiwan." The area is the most favored destination for middle-class Chinese immigrants, and the restaurants and shops reflect this. Of interest elsewhere in the San Gabriel Valley is **Santa Anita racetrack**, E of Pasadena in Arcadia, and the **LA State and County Arboretum**, also in Arcadia.

Central Los Angeles (map 2 C3)

South of the Santa Monica Freeway 10, E and N of the San Diego Freeway 405, is **Central Los Angeles**, taking in **East LA** and **South Central LA**. The former, with Whittier Blvd. as its main artery, has a population 90 percent Hispanic in origin. The latter, running S from **Watts**, birthplace of Eldridge Cleaver, has LA's largest African-American community. Sadly both areas have crime rates well above the average and, while most citizens are as law-abiding as anyone in LA, visitors are often deterred by reports of drug-related killings and gang warfare. Although sometimes exaggerated, the reports are usually true. But it would be wrong to characterize Central LA as a war zone; as a rule the violence is localized and selective.

And there are good reasons to visit. Watts is home to the extraordinary **Watts Towers**, and to the W is **Hollywood Park**, venue for horse-racing and site of the 17,000-seat **Great Western Forum** where, in season, the LA Lakers and the LA Kings play basketball and ice hockey respectively. Hispanic East LA has good fresh-food markets, inexpensive restaurants, *mariachis* and splendid murals bringing even more color to its streets. East of Whittier Blvd. is the town of **Whittier**, birthplace of former President Richard Nixon. The local Chamber of Commerce can provide a map of Nixonian sights. Farther E in **La Puente** is one of the city's priceless, vulgar, only-in-LA architectural landmarks, the **Donut Hole**, a snack-bar where customers drive through two gigantic donuts to place and collect their orders.

Mountains (map 15 I6)

Two mountain ranges contain Los Angeles: the **San Gabriels** to the N and E and the **Santa Monicas** to the NW. The Santa Monicas run E-W for about 50 miles right through the city, from the Los Angeles River to the Oxnard plain, and are easily accessed via Mulholland Dr. Ranging up to 2,000ft, the chaparral-clad hills are largely uninhabited, are administered by the National Park Service and offer stunning views and excellent trekking. However, creeping residential development makes them something less than pristine wilderness. Near the junction of Freeways 5 and 14 are a number of man-made attractions, notably the 260-acre **Six Flags Magic Mountain** amusement park with its breathtaking rides.

The San Gabriels to the E are wilder, higher (up to 10,000ft), and less accessible. The major routes from the S are the Angeles Crest Highway, the Angeles Forest Highway and San Gabriel Canyon. There are excellent campgrounds, and hiking through vast unspoiled areas. From the 5,710ft summit of **Mt. Wilson** it is possible to overlook LA as far as the Pacific. Farther E are even higher peaks, such as 10,080ft **Mt. Baldy,** offering exciting skiing in winter and climbing at other times.

Desert (map 15 I7)

Barely 100yrs ago much of what is now lush Los Angeles was desert. Today the city's hinterlands to the E, SE and NE, in fact one-third of California, and almost all of neighboring Nevada, remains just that — desert. Of most interest are the **Colorado**, low desert; the **Mojave**, high desert; and the **Trans Sierra**, a mix of mountains and basins including **Death Valley**.

Some areas are little more than relentless badlands: flat, arid and with little charm beyond their possible novelty. But the high desert of **Antelope Valley**, above the San Gabriel Mountains in N LA County, has some attractive parks and a 2,000-acre poppy reserve where the state's official flower grows wild. Farther E in the San Bernardino Mountains are two of LA's most popular playgrounds, exclusive **Lake Arrowhead** and less exclusive **Big Bear Lake**. The Mojave, to the E and NE, is overlooked by the ragged peaks of the Sierra Nevada. Highway 15, running N and E from San Bernardino to **Las Vegas**, gives a taste of the desert's stark realities, and encounters with them by pioneers are fossilized in the ghost town of Calico. Due N of Route 15 is **Death Valley**, which in the cooler months is a not-to-be-missed experience. To the S, straddling the high and low deserts, is the **Joshua Tree National Monument**, an 870sq. mile reserve populated almost exclusively by the giant, curiously-shaped yucca trees named "Joshua" by Mormon pioneers.

South of the Joshua Tree, just off the San Bernardino Freeway 10 and roughly 2hrs' drive from downtown LA, is the opulent oasis resort of **Palm Springs** (see *LA Environs*), dubbed by enthusiasts "Golf capital of the world." Californian hyperbole notwithstanding, they could be right; Palm Springs hosts over 100 tournaments a year. It is, all in all, a case of Beverly Hills in the desert, with the bonuses of clean air, hot springs, innumerable tennis courts and a swimming pool for every five residents. In keeping with the town's upscale image, restaurants, shopping and cultural diversions are all topnotch. 1960s pop star and one-time husband of Cher, Sonny Bono, is mayor. High season is Nov-Mar; Apr-May and Sept-Oct are the next most popular to visit. 30 miles S of Palm Springs in San Diego County is the **Anza-Borrego Desert State Park**, ½ million acres notable for striking rock formations. To the E lies the **Salton Sea**, at 30 miles in length California's largest lake and, at 235ft below sea level, probably its saltiest. Fishing, bird-watching and boating are the principal attractions.

Central Coast (map 15 I5)

From the N extremity of LA as far as newspaper tycoon William Randolph Hearst's magnificent folly at **San Simeon** runs the Central Coast. Easily accessible via Highway 101 and the Pacific Coast Highway 1, the coast is characterized by wonderful beaches, dramatic cliff-top drives and mile after mile of unspoiled countryside.

Of the major towns from S to N, picture-postcard pretty **Santa Barbara** (see *LA Environs*), fronting a 5-mile-long sandy beach and fringed by the Santa Ynez mountains, is a well-heeled study in Mission-style architecture and the laid-back California way of life. The town has just about everything by way of outdoor pursuits, attractive lodgings and restaurants and a lively cultural life.

Santa Barbara's own historic Spanish mission is attractive enough, but some 50 miles NE, along Highway 1, is **La Purísima**, possibly the most beautiful of California's 21 missions. Between the two in the

Santa Ynez Valley is the surprise of **Solvang**, translated as "sunny field," a quaint Danish village of startling architectural and atmospheric authenticity founded by immigrants from Denmark in the early years of the century. Farther N, set against the steep coastal hills of the Santa Lucia Mountains and at an intersection of Highways 1 and 101, is **San Luis Obispo**, local center for the nearby ranching country and some fine wineries developed within the past decade. The town is a pleasant half-way house on the drive between LA and San Francisco, and a good base for exploring Avila Beach, Morro Bay, San Simeon and other shoreside places.

Seven miles S of San Luis Obispo, **Avila Beach** is an unusually compact resort town, with fishing from the pier, charter boats, golf and volleyball on the white sandy beach. **Morro Bay**, 12 miles NW, is a working fishing port noted for its clams and the 576ft volcanic rock formation known as **Morro Rock**. Nearby are two state parks with camping, hiking and golf. **Hearst Castle**, to the NW, contrasts sharply with such wholesome recreations. Newspaper baron William Randolph Hearst's massive hilltop retreat serves primarily to show what colossal amounts of money can achieve when married to supreme bad taste. But there is nothing quite like it anywhere (save perhaps "Xanadu" in the movie *Citizen Kane*, a thinly-veiled fiction on Hearst's life and times), and it is now **The Hearst San Simeon State Historical Monument**, open to the public. Visitors will be able to dine out on a day spent there for years to come.

Orange County (map 15J6)

South of LA County, running N-S along the coast between Seal Beach and San Clemente, and E as far inland as the Santa Ana Mountains, Orange County is the second most populous county in California, and often cited as its most conservative. Most of the fragrant orange groves were torn up between 1955 and 1965 to make way for residential and industrial development, and nowadays the county is best known for its wealth, its exclusive beach communities, and Disneyland, its top attraction and the catalyst for Orange County's recent spectacular growth. The entire county has a web of freeways and major boulevards, and is within easy reach of LA via the Pacific Coast Highway 1 and the two N-S freeways, San Diego 405 and Santa Ana 5. It is also well served both by bus services and Amtrak. Around the I-5 between Buena Park and Anaheim, **Disneyland** and **Knott's Berry Farm** anchor a series of parks and entertainments. However, apart from these, the industrial-residential towns of Orange County's flat northern interior are of limited interest to visitors.

To the SW via Harbor Blvd., **Newport Beach** is the most fashionable playground in Orange County. Marinas, beachside homes, shops and restaurants are crowded onto a long, low-lying peninsula, which is said to be the most affluent concentration of boat people anywhere on the Pacific coast. The mainland shore and man-made islands inside the small bay have more of the same. Adjoining **Corona del Mar** is the tennis and golf suburb. The beach and the seafood at Newport Beach are first rate, there are comfortable hotels and motels, and the area is within easy reach of Disneyland and John Wayne-Orange County Airport.

Farther S down the coast and more remote, **Laguna Beach** began as an artists' colony and, although few artists can now afford to live there, it retains some of the flavor — not least in the **Laguna Museum of Art**. Shopping streets lined with galleries and craft studios and a coastline of coves, rocky promontories and sandy beaches give it the feel of a small southern European seaside town. The **Laguna Hills** behind the town offer some marvelous views. Other beach towns N and S beg not to be overlooked: **Huntington**

Beach for surfing; **Capistrano** for its beach; **Dana Point** (named for 19thC sailor-author Richard Dana) for beaches and boating; and **San Clemente** (best known from the days of Richard Nixon's Western White House) also for its beach.

Just off the I-5, E of Dana Point, is **San Juan Capistrano** and its mission, famed for returning swallows, tranquility and ruggedly beautiful buildings dating from 1777. It is said to be California's oldest. The commercial possibilities are not lost on the heritage industry, and the area around the mission is swamped with gift stores. Nevertheless, San Juan Capistrano is generally thought to be a must for visitors keen on exploring California's past.

San Diego

Down the Golden State Freeway 5, 120 miles s of LA, San Diego is too often regarded as the big city on the right that visitors pass en route to **Tijuana**, 20 miles farther s. If it comes to a case of either-or, most would be better advised to skip the rather tacky Mexican border town and turn right instead. For San Diego, seldom if ever mentioned ahead of its northern neighbors, has a Riviera climate, chic beach resorts, fine lodgings and shopping, a lively gastronomic and cultural life and some major attractions, while suffering neither from the smugness of San Francisco nor the congestions of Los Angeles. True, large parts of the city are likely to be of little interest; the huge military port; the major tuna fishing harbor; the industrial and commercial sprawl; and the hundreds of square miles of suburbs.

What *is* almost sure to attract are the world-famous **zoo** in **Balboa Park** near the city center, the **Sea World** oceanarium with its performing killer whales, a revived **downtown** area rich in architectural interest, the innovative **San Diego Opera**, highly regarded in the US, and superb year-round beach resorts.

These four, **La Jolla** (pronounced La Hoya), **Pacific Beach**, **Mission Bay** and **Coronado**, have entirely different characters. **La Jolla Village**, relaxing along a 7-mile stretch of beaches and cliffs, has a Monaco-like feel about it, or so the locals like to think. Certainly, it has the chic touches, and smells even more of money than it does of salt water. Tom Wolfe found The Pump House Gang of surfers at **Windansea** at La Jolla in the early 1960s. Today surfers still reign from Windansea s through Pacific and Mission Beaches, although the atmosphere is no longer quite so vehemently ageist as when senior citizenship was thought to begin at 30. The great recreation area of Mission Bay has no permanent population, only hotel guests, while Coronado is a peaceful, quiet, low-key community of people who delight in their isolation on the sandy peninsula that forms the outer side of San Diego.

Sights and places of interest

The following A to Z pages list an extensive selection of LA's sights: the most fascinating, revealing, unmissable, whatever.... What isn't individually listed here will very likely be described in another entry. For example, the **Los Angeles County Museum of Art** is a subentry of *Hancock Park*, and **Château Marmont** is described in the *Sunset Strip* entry. Look in the *Index* for these and other sights.

ABC Entertainment Center

Ave. of the Stars, Century City (directly s of Beverly Hills, between Santa Monica Blvd. and Pico Blvd.). Map 4D2.
The center contains the **Shubert Theater**, movie theaters, nightclubs, fine restaurants, an astonishing car dealership and other

commercial enterprises. ABC's television studios are elsewhere (see *Television shows*).

Academy of Motion Picture Arts and Sciences
8949 Wilshire Blvd. (Wilshire Blvd. E of Doheny Dr.) ☎ *(213) 652-8526. Map 4D4. Library open Mon-Tues, Thurs-Fri 9am-5pm. Closed Wed, weekends, major hols.*

Los Angeles' most important Academy — the one that awards the annual Oscars that can make or break careers in motion pictures. In addition, the superb 1,000-seat theater stages occasional public screenings, and the Academy library is unequaled in movie literature.

Gene Autry Western Heritage Museum
4700 Zook Dr., Griffith Park (via Zook Dr. exit from Ventura Freeway/SR-134 or Golden State Freeway/I-5) ☎ *(213) 460-5698. Map 2B2* 🔲 *&. 🗡 (☎ (213) 667-2000)* ▇ *Open Tues-Sun 10am-5pm. Closed Mon, Thanksgiving, Dec 25, Jan 1.*

One of the latest additions to Los Angeles' heritage industry, the museum explores the history of the West with exhibits, designed by Walt Disney Imagineering, organized into separate "spirits" — of discovery; of opportunity; of conquest; of community; of the cowboy; of romance; of imagination. Films and presentations, with dazzling special effects, are offered at the museum's two theaters.

Barnsdall Park
4800 Hollywood Blvd. (NW of downtown, two blocks W of Vermont Ave.). Map 6B7.

There are two points of artistic interest in the park. **Hollyhock House** (☎ *(213) 662-7272* 🔲 *🗡* *open Tues, Thurs 10am-1pm, first and third Sat and first Sun of each month noon-3pm)* was Frank Lloyd Wright's first (1921) Los Angeles private building. It has been restored to its original state and is used as a residence and cultural center. The **Los Angeles Municipal Art Gallery** (☎ *(213) 485-4581* 🔲 *🗡* *open Tues-Sun 12.30-5pm, closed Mon, major hols)* has a program of changing exhibitions of contemporary art and films by southern Californians.

Bradbury Building 🏛
Downtown at 304 S Broadway ☎ *(213) 489-1411. Map 6E8* 🔲 *Open Mon-Sat 10am-6pm. Closed Sun.*

The building's plain exterior hides a magnificently detailed, 5-story central court with a skylight. Designed by George Herbert Wyman in 1893, it is often used as a location in movies.

Burbank Studios
4000 Warner Blvd., Burbank (four blocks S of Ventura Freeway/ SR-134 via Olive Ave.) ☎ *(818) 954-1744. Map 2B2* 🔲 *🗡 compulsory, by appointment only, limited to 12 people: Mon-Fri 10am, 10.30am, 2pm, 2.30pm in summer, 10am, 2pm in winter* *Closed weekends, major hols.*

Warner Bros. and Columbia Pictures Ent. offer highly instructive 2hr tours showing day-to-day work on a movie set and sound stage at their shared premises. For an extra fee, and by separate appointment, visitors may eat with actors and technicians in a company restaurant.

California Afro-American Museum
600 State Dr., Exposition Park ☎ *(213) 744-7432. Map 6F7* 🔲 *🗡* *Open 10am-5pm. Closed major hols.*

Changing exhibitions on the history, art and culture of Afro-Americans, plus research library and museum shop.

Capital Records Building

*1750 Vine St., Hollywood (just N of legendary Hollywood and Vine intersection). Map **6B6**.*

Not open to the public, but visitors are likely to notice and wonder about this 14-story building, especially in Dec when it is lit up like a Christmas tree. Built in 1954, the world's first circular office building looks like a stack of 45rpm records with a stylus on top. It was meant to: what could be more appropriate for a record company's HQ?

Chinatown(s)

*New Chinatown: centered around 700-1000 N Broadway in between N Alameda, Yale, Bernard and Ord Sts. Map **7D9**.*

Southern California's Chinese community dates back to gold rush days, but "Old" Chinatown on Alameda was displaced in 1930 by the construction of Union Station. The "New" saw the tourist potential of chinoiserie, and the exaggerated architectural forms — all sweeping tiled roofs, elaborate decoration and pagoda-style telephone booths — reflect those early theme-park decisions. **Gin Ling Way** pedestrian mall running between Broadway and Hill St. has the best examples.

However, Chinatown is much more than that; it is the cultural and commercial center for some 20,000 people of Chinese ancestry who live and work in the area, and many more throughout southern California. The shops, markets, restaurants and recreational facilities aim first and foremost to serve them. Which is not to say that visitors are not welcome to wander, browse, eat and shop, or take in the colorful celebrations that mark Chinese New Year.

"Even Newer" Chinatown

*Monterey Park, around Atlantic Blvd., bounded by San Bernadino Freeway/I-10 to N, Pomona Freeway/I-60 to S and Long Beach Freeway/I-710 to W. Map **2C3**.*

Although by no means such a uniform or concentrated community as downtown's Chinatown, in recent years Monterey Park has won the sobriquet "Little Taipei" as a result of its popularity with immigrants from Taiwan. As in Chinatown, the area's shops, restaurants, even video rental outlets and newsstands, reflect the population shift. Less visually interesting than Chinatown, but some excellent eating.

Chinese Theater 🏛 ★

*6925 Hollywood Blvd., Hollywood (one block W of Highland Ave.) ☎ (213) 464-8111. Map **6A5** 🚗 Open daily.*

Originally Grauman's Chinese Theater, now **Mann's**, it has the famous courtyard with handprints and footprints of 150 movie stars pressed into concrete. The courtyard is open to passers-by without charge; the building, a functioning movie theater, is a real Hollywood-style fantasy of Chinese architectural themes.

City Hall

*200 N Spring St. (downtown, between 1st St. and Temple St.) ☎ (213) 485-2121. Map **7D9** 🎫 ⋘ ✗ by reservation only. Observation deck open Mon-Fri 8am-1pm, Bridge Gallery open Mon-Fri 8am-5pm.*

From its completion in 1928 until height restrictions were lifted in 1957 this monumental building's 28-story tower was the city's tallest. Today it is dwarfed by taller modern buildings but retains its architectural and symbolic importance. Such is the amalgam of styles, its architectural progenitors are hard to pin down: Greek here, Romanesque there, a Byzantine rotunda, adding up to pure American Civic. The symbolism began at the beginning, with construction materials drawn from throughout California, and Los

Angeles Police Department badges carry the building's image. On a clear day the view from the 27th-floor observation deck is spectacular.

Descanso Gardens
1418 Descanso Dr., La Canada (via Verdugo Blvd. from either Glendale Freeway/SR-2 or Foothill Freeway/I-210) ☎ *(818) 790-5571. Map 2B3* 📷 ✗ *weekend afternoons* 🚗 *Open 9am-5pm. Closed Dec 25.*

165 acres of oak-shaded gardens famed for 100,000 camellia plants representing some 600 varieties. The camellias bloom from late Dec to early Mar. There is also a Japanese garden and teahouse. Streetcar tours around the grounds depart on the hour.

Dodger Stadium
1000 Elysian Park Ave. (directly N of downtown in the angle formed by the Pasadena Freeway/SR-11 and Golden State Freeway/I-5 and accessible from either via Stadium Way) ☎ *(213) 224-1400. Map 7C9* 🚗 *Ticket office in parking lot open Mon-Sat 8.30am-5.30pm.*

The 56,000-seat cantilevered stadium on the s edge of **Elysian Park**, home to the Los Angeles Dodgers baseball team, occasionally hosts special events. Hot dogs and merchandise are sold during games.

Donut Hole
15300 Amar Rd., La Puente (on E corner of Elliot Ave. one block W of Hacienda Blvd., N of Pomona Freeway). Map 3C4.

Typical Los Angeles: Pop Art, symbolism and functionalism at its best/worst in the form of giant, drive-through fiberglass donuts. Needless to say, Donut Hole sells donuts in hundreds of different varieties. Drive through anytime, day or night.

Echo Park
Glendale Blvd. and Park Ave. (via Hollywood Freeway/US-101, Alvarado St. exit, then E) ☎ *(213) 250-3578. Map 7C8.*

The 26-acre park is one of the city's oldest and most attractive. Donated in 1891, it comprises landscaped and forested areas, a lotus pond, and a 15-acre palm-fringed lake with paddle boats for rental by the hour. At the NW end of the park is the 5,000-seat **Angelus Temple** (*1100 Glendale Blvd.* ☎ *(213) 484-1100*), where evangelist Aimee Semple McPherson preached in the 1920s and '30s.

Elysian Park
1880 Academy Dr. (near the intersection of Golden State Freeway/I-5 and Pasadena Freeway/SR-110) ☎ *(213) 225-2044. Map 7C9* 🍴 🛍 💻

At 575 acres the city's second largest park, this was originally established during the 1880s, taking in rolling hills and several valleys. Much of it has been preserved in its natural state, with numerous nature trails across the chaparral-covered slopes. **Chavez Ravine Arboretum** is noted for its rare trees, and there are picnic areas. *Dodger Stadium* is on the s edge of the park.

Exposition Park
Bounded by Exposition Blvd., Figueroa St., Santa Barbara Ave. and Menlo St. (one block W of Harbor Freeway/SR-11, Exposition Blvd. exit). Map 6F7.

The park contains major museums, a theater, athletics facilities and a 7-acre rose garden.
California State Museum of Science and Industry ✩
700 State Dr. ☎ *(213) 744-7400. Map 6F7* 📷 ✱ 💻 🚗 *Open 10am-5pm.*

Closed Jan 1, Thanksgiving, Dec 25.

Here are 14 halls of touchable displays, many of them elegantly mounted by major industrial companies, all of them designed for pleasurable learning. Bilingual computers use speech to explain their own history and capacities. Soap bubbles teach lessons in mathematics. Electricity, internal combustion, communications (especially film) and animal husbandry are subjects covered in surprising ways in the main museum building. Two other buildings contain equally engaging exhibits on health and the human body. The fourth, the **Aerospace Building**, is a vast hangar designed by top LA architect Frank Gehry (**🏛**) and has planes, rockets and aerospace exhibits, including a Gemini 11 space capsule. Next door to here is the 430-seat, large-screen **Mitsubishi Imax Theater** (**☎** *(213) 744-2014*).

Los Angeles County Museum of Natural History
900 Exposition Blvd. **☎** *(213) 744-3414, recorded information (213) 744-3411. Map 6F7* ▩ *(* 🖸 *first Tues of each month noon-9pm)* ♿ ▆
Open Tues-Sun 10am-5pm (summer Sat-Sun 10am-6pm). Closed Mon, Jan 1, Thanksgiving, Dec 25.

The museum takes an uncommonly broad view of natural history. In addition to major halls dealing with mammals (outstanding), paleontology, living mammals, insects and birds, there are exhibits of South Pacific ethnology, Indians, and American and Californian history. The latter section, in **Lando Hall**, covers the era 1540-1940 in strict chronology. Displays include a stage-coach, a superb turn-of-the-century fire engine, and a model of downtown Los Angeles as it was in 1940.

The museum shows free travel films (*each Sat at 2pm*) and holds free chamber music concerts (*each Sun at 2pm*).

See also **George C. Page Museum** under *Hancock Park*.

Memorial Coliseum
☎ *(213) 747-7111. Map 6F7.*

A 91,000-seat stadium, it was the major site for track and field events at the 1932 and 1984 Olympic Games. The **Olympic Arch** in front of the Coliseum is a permanent reminder of the 1984 games.

Memorial Sports Arena
Next to the Memorial Coliseum **☎** *(213) 748-6131.*

Its 17,000-seat main hall is the home base of the Los Angeles Clipper and USC basketball teams. It also hosts ice shows, concerts, rodeos and conventions, and is used for a variety of sports and entertainment events.

Farmers' Market
6333 W Third St. (at Fairfax Ave.) **☎** *(213) 933-9211. Map 5C5*
♣ 🍴 ☕ *Open 9am-8pm summer, 9am-6.30pm winter.*

Opened in 1934 as a genuine farmers' market, it is now an improvised center of 160 stalls and stores dealing especially in food, from produce to fast food, but also in general merchandise. Excellent butchers, pastry stores and green grocers, along with al fresco dining at a range of food stalls, from Cajun to Japanese.

Forest Lawn Memorial Park
1712 S Glendale Ave., Glendale (E of I-5 via Los Feliz Ave.)
☎ *(818) 254-3131. Map 2B3* 🖸 ✗ ☕ *Open 9am-5pm.*

This is the cemetery that provoked Evelyn Waugh to write *The Loved One*. In the well-manicured park are copies of Michelangelo statues and famous churches. The world's largest religious painting, 195ft by 45ft, is in the **Hall of Crucifixion-Resurrection**, where it is displayed on the hour every hour. But Forest Lawn refuses to reveal the exact sites of its more famous graves.

Gamble House 🏛 ★

*4 Westmoreland Pl., Pasadena (Ventura Freeway/SR-134 to
Colorado Blvd. exit, then N on Orange Grove Blvd.)* ☎ *(818)
793-3334. Map 2B3* ▣ *ⵋ Open Tues, Thurs 10am-3pm, Sun
noon-3pm. Closed Mon, Wed, Fri-Sat.*

Built in 1908 for David B. Gamble, heir to the fortune of Cincinnati
company Proctor & Gamble, but now owned by the University of
Southern California, the house is an immaculate legacy of the
Craftsman Movement in California. Lovingly finished teak, Tiffany
glass, overhanging roofs, low ceilings, cleverly articulated interior
and exterior spaces, and much of the original furniture and fittings
may be seen. The overall effect can be viewed as the refinement of a
host of influences, from northern Europe to Japan, on the architects
Charles and Henry Greene.

Gehry House 🏛

*1002 22nd St., Santa Monica (s corner of Washington Ave.).
Map 2C1. Private residence only viewable from street.*

This is an important shrine on any architectural pilgrimage. Frank
Gehry is one of California's most highly regarded architects,
responsible for, among others, the Aerospace Building (see
Exposition Park), the **Temporary Contemporary** museum and
the Loyola University Law School. His own house began life as an
ordinary Dutch Colonial-style cottage. Gehry has torn bits down,

J. PAUL GETTY MUSEUM FLOOR PLAN, LOS ANGELES

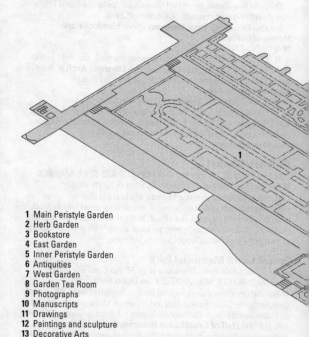

1 Main Peristyle Garden
2 Herb Garden
3 Bookstore
4 East Garden
5 Inner Peristyle Garden
6 Antiquities
7 West Garden
8 Garden Tea Room
9 Photographs
10 Manuscripts
11 Drawings
12 Paintings and sculpture
13 Decorative Arts
14 Maiolica and glass

uncovered things that were hidden, and created a new shell using materials he likes, such as exposed two-by-four studs, corrugated metal, chain-links, lots of glass, and an asphalt floor in the kitchen.

J. Paul Getty Museum 🏛 ☆
17985 Pacific Coast Highway, Malibu (w of intersection with Sunset Blvd.) ☎ *(213) 458-2003* ® *(213) 454-6633. Map 15l6* 🅿 ▣ ✗ ᵼ ♨ 🚗 *by reservation only for visitors arriving by car with admission to museum, dependent on parking space. RTD bus 434 will drop visitors at the gate: passes are available from drivers. Open Tues-Sun 10am-5pm. Closed Mon, major hols.*

On a remote shelf overlooking the Pacific, oil millionaire Paul Getty built in 1974 a copy of the Villa dei Papiri, a 1stC Roman seaside villa and its gardens, to house his extensive art collection. The museum has seven departments devoted mainly to European art from before 1900: Antiquities, Paintings, Decorative Arts, Drawings, Manuscripts,

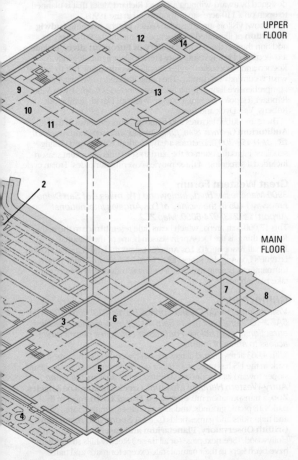

Photographs, and Sculpture and Works of Art. The 38 galleries are
filled with Greek and Roman antiquities from 2000BC to AD300; Old,
Renaissance and 19thC masters, with French, Dutch and Italian
Schools well represented; impressive collections of drawings,
especially by modern masters, illuminated manuscripts including
important Italian, French, German, Flemish, English, Polish,
Byzantine and Armenian works, and photographs from the early
1840s to the 1950s; fine furniture, tapestries, rugs, ceramics and gilt
bronzes, all from the mid-17thC to the early 19thC; silver, especially
French work from the 17th and 18thC; and porcelain.

The museum is the world's wealthiest, with an endowment of $2.2
billion, of which 4.2 percent must be spent each year. One
consequence is that it is not always possible to predict with
confidence precisely what will be hauled out of the ever-expanding
Aladdin's cave for public display. The museum stages what it calls
"changing exhibitions from the permanent collection." It might be
easier after inevitable expansion into new galleries in a complex
designed by award-winning architect Richard Meier that is planned
to open on a 110-acre site in Brentwood in the 1990s.

For now, visitors are advised to search out the stunning **Ludwig
collection** of illustrated manuscripts spanning the 8th-20thC. In
addition there is the splendid **gallery of European silver**, including
a collection of pre-revolutionary French silver in the Regency,
Rococo and Neoclassical styles. It is also worth calling first to inquire
what is currently on display. The range is so extensive that it defies a
comprehensive listing. But a brief taster includes works by da Vinci,
Raphael, Tiepolo, Bernini, Poussin, Watteau, David, Rembrandt,
Rubens, Van Dyck and Ensor.

There are public lectures and films on Thurs evenings in the
Auditorium (*lectures 8pm, films 7pm* 🕑 *but reservations essential*
🕿 *(213) 458-2003*). Lectures are by resident experts and visiting
scholars. Films are often of the hard-to-see variety: a recent season
included a screening of three movies covering Euripides' Trojan cycle.

Great Western Forum

*3900 Manchester Blvd., Inglewood (1½ miles E of San Diego
Freeway/I-405 in the vicinity of Los Angeles International
Airport)* 🕿 *(213) 674-6000. Map 2C2.*
This 17,000-seat arena, which bears little resemblance to the real
Roman thing, is the Oct-Apr in-season home of the National
Basketball Association's Los Angeles Lakers and the National Hockey
League's Los Angeles Kings (🕿 *(213) 673-1300 for both*). Tennis
tournaments, boxing matches, ice shows, rodeos and concerts also
take place here.

Griffith Park

Visitor Center, 4730 Crystal Springs Rd. 🕿 *(213) 665-5188. Map
6A7* 🌢 *General park hours 5am-10.30pm; hours for specific
attractions noted below. Four major entrances permit direct
access to areas of interest.*
With 4,063 acres draped across the Hollywood Hills, the largest city
park in the US has most of its major development on relatively gentle
slopes toward its E boundary. Located in this area are the *Gene
Autry Western Heritage Museum,* **Greek Theater,** **Los Angeles
Zoo,** a transportation museum called **Travel Town,** most of the
park's 18 picnic grounds, and its golf courses, tennis courts, pony
and train rides and games fields (see *LA Sports and recreation*).
Griffith Observatory, Planetarium and Laserium is high on Mt.
Hollywood. (See next page for all these.) Steeper hills still farther w
have been kept in their natural state except for roads and trails.

Greek Theater
2700 N Vermont Ave. ☎ (213) 410-1062. Map 6A7 🖼️
This has picnic tables and 6,000 seats in a natural amphitheater facing an open-air stage used during June-Oct for pop, rock and classical music and dance programs. Picnics, wine and beer may be bought at the site or brought along.

Griffith Observatory, Planetarium and Laserium 🏛️
2800 E Observatory Rd., at the N end of N Vermont Ave. ☎ (213) 664-1191. Map 6A7 🔢 ◀€ ⇔ *Open summer Sun-Fri 1-10pm, Sat 11.30am-10pm, winter Tues-Fri 2-10pm, Sat 11.30am-10pm. Closed Thanksgiving, Dec 24-25, Mon in winter.*
Inside the copper-domed 1935 building are conventional star shows, as well as simulated eclipses, auroras and space voyages three or four times daily between 1-8pm. The **Hall of Science** has a weather satellite, a Foucault pendulum and other displays on meteorology and astronomy. Visitors may look through the telescope when weather permits. Late-evening laser shows accompanied by sci-fi rock music follow the star shows (🖼️ ☎ *(213) 997-3624 for schedules and programs).*

Los Angeles Zoo
5333 Zook Dr., via Zook Dr. exit from the Ventura Freeway/SR-134, directly w of its intersection with I-5 ☎ (213) 664-1100. Map 2B2 🖼️ 𝒦 🍽️ ✹ ⇔ *Open 10am-6pm summer, 10am-5pm winter. Closed Dec 25.*
Built in 1966, the zoo follows the modern trend toward natural enclosures without bars for its 2,000 animals, including 78 endangered species, which are grouped according to continent of origin. The main zoo, including the picnic area, covers about 80 acres. A streetcar tour is available for an extra fee. There is also a new Children's Zoo called **Adventure Island**, which uses high-tech participatory exhibits to teach about animals and their habitats, and an Animal Nursery for newly-born animal babies.

Travel Town
5730 Crystal Springs Dr., via the same freeway exit as for the zoo, then w ☎ (213) 662-5874. Map 2B2 🔢 ✹ ⇔ *Open 9am-5.30pm. Closed Dec 25.*
An open-air museum of transportation with antique airplanes and locomotives as its primary treasures. Train rides are inexpensive.

Hancock Park
At the 5900 block of Wilshire Blvd., E of Fairfax Ave. Map 5D5.
A modest picnic park, but it also contains **Los Angeles County Museum of Art**, the **Rancho La Brea fossil pits** and the **George C. Page Museum of La Brea Discoveries**.

Los Angeles County Museum of Art ☆ 🏛️
5905 Wilshire Blvd., two blocks E of Fairfax Ave. ☎ (213) 937-2590 for recorded calendar, (213) 857-6111. Map 5D5 🖼️ *(but* 🔢 *second Tues of each month noon-9pm)* 𝒦 🍽️ ⚇ ⇔ *Open Tues-Fri 10am-4.30pm, Sat-Sun 10am-5.30pm. Closed Mon, Jan 1, Thanksgiving, Dec 25.*
This is one of California's best collections, housed in a series of provocative buildings, including the **Robert O. Anderson** building of glass and limestone and, the most recent addition, the **Pavilion of Japanese Art**. Most of the permanent collections are in the central **Ahmanson Gallery** pavilion. Among these, the Heeramaneck collection of Indian, Tibetan and Nepalese art objects are much prized by critics. The Hammer collection of 5,000 Daumier prints is housed here.

The **Frances and Armand Hammer Wing** to the W is used primarily for traveling and temporary exhibitions, but also contains a wide-ranging permanent collection of contemporary works. The **Leo S. Bing Center** to the E has a 500-seat theater in which educational films and old Hollywood classics are shown. A sculpture garden with many Rodin bronzes connects the three pavilions.

George C. Page Museum of La Brea Discoveries
5801 Wilshire Blvd. ☎ *(213) 936-2230, (213) 857-6306. Map 5D5* 🖼️ 🔗
🔗 *Open Tues-Sun 10am-4.45pm. Closed Mon, Jan 1, Thanksgiving, Dec 25.*

This is set amid the famous Rancho La Brea fossil pits from which paleontologists have recovered tons of fossilized remains of Pleistocene creatures and plants. Imaginative displays show not only the bones, but reconstructions of animals, and techniques of the science of paleontology. An observation deck around the outside of the building gives a good view across the fossil pits, which may also be viewed at close range. Exploration continues on the site.

Around the museums and between the fossil pits, Hancock Park also has picnic tables, street musicians, and a parking lot accessible from Curson Ave., opposite Wilshire Blvd.

Hebrew Union College and Skirball Museum
3077 University Avenue (Harbor Freeway/SR-110, Jefferson Blvd. exit, then N via Hoover Blvd.) ☎ *(213) 749-3424. Map 7E8* 🖼️ ✴️ 🔗 *Open Tues-Thurs 8.15am-5pm, Fri 8.15am-4.30pm, Sun 10am-5pm. Closed Sat.*

Opened in 1954, the museum has archeological and biblical exhibits, and a **Walk Through the Past Gallery**. The library specializes in American Jewish literature.

Herald Examiner Building 🏛️
1111 S Broadway (s of junction with 11th St.) ☎ *(213) 744-8000. Map 7E8.*

An imposing, block-long Mission Revival-style building commissioned in 1912 by newspaper baron William Randolph Hearst. Hearst chose architect Julia Morgan, the first woman graduate of Paris' École des Beaux Arts and someone closely involved in the evolution of his fairytale San Simeon retreat, to design the home of his Los Angeles flagship publication. The results remain impressive, and the building is a classic of the genre, marred only by the more recent closing in of its ground-floor arches.

Heritage Square
3800 N Homes St. (Ave. 43 exit from Pasadena Freeway/ SR-110) ☎ *(818) 796-2829, recorded information (818) 449-0193* 🖼️ 🍴 🔗 *Map 2B3. Open Sat-Sun noon-5pm summer, Sun 11am-4pm winter. Closed Mon-Fri summer, Mon-Sat winter.*

An attempt to save at least a portion of Los Angeles' architectural heritage from the path of developers; a kind of rest home for threatened Victorian buildings. So far just seven threatened buildings, rescued from elsewhere in the city, inhabit the 10-acre site. But what is there is interesting, and doubtless more will follow.

Hollywood Bowl
2301 N Highland Ave., Hollywood (w of Highland Ave. exit from the Hollywood Freeway/US-101) ☎ *(213) 850-2000. Map 6B6* 🖼️ *except during concerts* 🅿️ *before concerts* 🔗 *Grounds open daily July-Sept 9am-dusk.*

Frank Lloyd Wright's magnificent 100-foot-wide shell-shaped bandstand faces a 17,619-seat amphitheater surrounded by trees. The acoustics are less than perfect, but the Los Angeles Philharmonic plays light summer concerts in July-Sept; other performances include pop, jazz and rock groups. Easter sunrise services are held, and the annual 4th of July concert climaxes with a firework display. Before the concerts grand picnics are a great tradition. Seats are hard wooden benches, so it pays to bring cushions. Evenings become cool, requiring a sweater or coat.

Hollywood Memorial Cemetery

6000 Santa Monica Blvd., Hollywood (between Santa Monica Blvd., Melrose Ave. and Gower St., behind Paramount Studios) ☎ (213) 469-1181. Map 6C6. Open Mon-Fri 8am-5pm, Sat-Sun 9am-4pm.

A host of Hollywood legends lies behind the high walls of this 65-acre palm-fringed cemetery, including idol of the silent screen Rudolph Valentino, godfather of the movie epic Cecil B. De Mille, motion pictures' original swashbuckler Douglas Fairbanks, Peter Lorre, Tyrone Power, Peter Finch and many more. The mausoleums, statues and adornments are everything one would expect.

Hollywood Sign ★

Durand Dr., off Beachwood Dr., Hollywood. Map 6A6.

Possibly LA's best known landmark, the Hollywood Sign, near the summit of Mt. Lee overlooking the city of Hollywood, was erected by real-estate developers in 1923, when it spelled out "Hollywoodland" in 50ft-high letters. The site and the sign were donated to the city in 1945 and the last four letters were removed. In 1978 the original dog-eared sign was replaced with a new $250,000 sign paid for by celebrities: *Playboy*'s Hugh Heffner bought the "Y," rock star Alice Cooper sponsored an "O."

Huntington Library, Art Gallery and Botanical Gardens ☆

1151 Oxford Rd., San Marino (from Pasadena Freeway/Arroya Parkway, E on California Blvd. to Allen Ave., then S to grounds) ☎ (818) 405-2100. Map 2B3 🔲 ✗ ⬛ ⬛ 🛥 Open Tues-Sat 1-4.30pm, and Sun 1-4.30pm by reservation only (write for Sunday tickets to above address, or ☎ (818) 405-2273 during preceding week). Closed Mon, Oct, hols.

Once the home of railroad tycoon Henry E. Huntington (1850-1927), the 207-acre estate was developed and the collections begun between 1910-25. Today, as a privately endowed museum and study center, it continues to grow in scope and quality.

The art gallery, in what was previously the Huntington mansion, focuses on 18th and early 19thC European painters, most notably works of Gainsborough (including *Blue Boy*), Turner, Reynolds and Romney. The library contains rare books and manuscripts. Items on public display include a Gutenberg Bible, the Ellesmere manuscript of Geoffrey Chaucer's *Canterbury Tales*, and a first folio of Shakespeare's plays.

The surrounding gardens, dating from 1904, include a 12-acre desert succulent and cacti collection filled with rarities; a rose garden with more than 1,000 varieties; 1,500 varieties of camellia; and a Japanese garden with 16thC teahouse and Zen rock garden.

Koreatown

Mid-Wilshire district between Vermont Ave., Pico Blvd., Western Ave. and 8th St. Map 6D7.

Most of California's 200,000-plus people of Korean origin live in Los Angeles, many of them in Koreatown. Anchored by the lively market at the corner of 8th St. and Normandie Ave., the still-expanding *quartier* is characterized by Korean restaurants, food stores, bakeries, small shops and boutiques. The distinctive phonetic calligraphy is hard to miss.

Little Tokyo

Downtown between 1st St., 3rd St., Los Angeles St. and Alameda St., E of Civic Center ☎ (213) 628-2725 (Japanese American Cultural and Community Center) for information. Map 7D9.

Southern California's Japanese-American population numbers considerably more than 100,000, and its cultural focus is downtown's Little Tokyo, centered around the **Japanese Village Plaza** built in 1979. It feels like Japan — clean, compact, with Japanese-influenced architecture, authentic restaurants complete with window displays of plastic food and largely Japanese clientele, bookstores, and shops selling most things Japanese, from groceries to art works, furniture, clothes and cosmetics.

The **Cultural and Community Center** orchestrates major events and festivals such as Nisei week in Aug (see *Calendar of events* in *LA Planning*). Notable are the **Japan American Theater** (☎ *(213) 680-3700*), which stages Asian theater, including Noh and Kabuki, dance and music; the **Higashi Hongwanji Buddhist Temple**, with traditional blue-tiled roof (☎ *(213) 626-4200*); and **JACC Plaza**, a giant rock sculpture dedicated to the earliest Japanese immigrants.

Los Angeles Children's Museum

310 N Main St. (at street level of Los Angeles Mall in the Civic Center) ☎ (213) 687-8800. Map 7D9 🎫 ⚹ 🚗 (fee). Open Mon-Fri noon-5pm, Sat-Sun 10am-5pm summer; call for winter hrs.

The emphasis is on exploring the senses with sticky stuff, strobes, old clothes, butter churns and other familiar or rare items. Some of these whimsical lessons are scheduled classes; others are for those who just drop in. Birthday party programs are available.

Los Angeles Public Library 🏛

630 West 5th St. (between Flower St. and Grand Ave.). Map 7D9 👁 At time of writing, temporarily closed following fire.

Constructed in 1925, and considered by many to be the finest building in Los Angeles, the Public Library is a blend of borrowings from diverse architectural traditions brought together to produce something quintessentially American. Architects Bertram G. Goodhue and Carleton M. Winslow drew upon the styles of Egypt, Byzantium, Rome and the Islamic world and translated them into the Beaux Arts tradition, using 20thC concrete. Aside from the building itself and its pyramid-topped central tower, of particular note are Lee Laurie's exterior sculptures, 9,000sq.ft of mural inside the central **rotunda**, and outstanding illustrations in the **Children's Room**.

Los Angeles State and County Arboretum

301 N Baldwin Ave., Arcadia (S of Foothill Freeway/I-210, via Baldwin Ave. exit directly across from Santa Anita Park thoroughbred race course) ☎ (818) 446-8251. Map 3B4 🎫 (but 👁 third Tues of each month). Streetcar tours available for extra fee K 🅿 🚗 Open 9am-4.30pm. Closed Dec 25.

This horticultural research center covers 127 acres of the property that once belonged to legendary silver miner and rancher Elias Jackson (Lucky) Baldwin, whose ornate Queen Anne cottage still stands. Among plants from every continent are rarities from Australia and South Africa. Remember the *African Queen?* The lake that Humphrey Bogart hauled the boat through is here. Giant palm trees and the orchid collection are well regarded.

Los Angeles Times Building

202 W 1st St. (downtown, near intersection with Main St.)

☎ *(213) 972-5757. Map 7D9* ✗ *Mon-Fri 3pm* 🖾 *Children must be aged at least 10.*

Los Angeles' premier daily newspaper inhabits this monumental 1935 Moderne beige limestone block, and a less distinguished 1973 glass-box addition. Free tours offer a rare opportunity to see a newspaper produced, from newsroom to printing presses.

Lovell Beach House 🏛

1242 West Ocean Front, Balboa Peninsula, Newport Beach (NE corner of 13th St. and Beach Walk). Map 7F4. Private residence: no public access, but can be viewed from outside.

Regarded as a masterpiece of modern architecture, the 1926, Bauhaus-influenced, Rudolph Schindler beach house is an ingenious Constructivist design raised on five concrete cradles. Its clean geometry and thoughtful details make it well worth a visit.

MacArthur Park

Wilshire Blvd., between Alvarado St. and Park View. Map 7D8.

Laid out in 1890 and originally named Westlake Park, the 32-acre public space was renamed for General Douglas MacArthur in 1942. In addition to some 80 rare plants and trees, a small boating lake, a bandstand, picnic areas and a children's playground, the park has a number of specially commissioned works of art. These include a 500ft water spout, a clock tower and two pyramids. Visitors are not advised to visit the park after dark.

Miracle Mile

Wilshire Blvd. (between Sycamore and Fairfax Aves.). Map 5D5.

Among the first Los Angeles strips developed with drivers in mind, Miracle Mile was so named because, at first, most people thought A.W. Ross was crazy when in 1920 he began the development of a commercial center along a dirt road surrounded by farmland and several miles from anywhere. But the visionary Mr Ross foresaw the commuter age, turned his piece of Wilshire into a six-lane boulevard with off-street parking, and ensured that the buildings were attractive, interesting and literally arresting. Those who had doubted the scheme pronounced its success a miracle. Many of the mile's Art Deco buildings have survived, making it one of the more engaging drives/walks in the city.

Mission San Fernando Rey de España †

15151 San Fernando Mission Blvd., Mission Hills (in San Fernando Valley between San Diego Freeway/I-405 and Golden State Freeway/I-5 via San Fernando Mission Blvd. exit) ☎ *(818) 361-0186. Map 2A1* 🖾 ➡ *Open Mon-Sat 9am-5pm, Sun 10am-5pm.*

Founded in 1797, 17th of the missions, San Fernando Rey was one of the most successful. Restoration of the adobe church, *convento* and several outbuildings, along with tableaux of everyday 19thC life, make it instructive to visit. Its gardens enhance the setting.

Mission San Gabriel Arcángel †

537 W Mission Dr., San Gabriel (E from Los Angeles via San Bernardino Freeway/I-10 to New Ramona Ave. exit, then N) ☎ *(818) 282-5191. Map 3B4* 🖾 ➡ *Open 9.30am-4pm.*

Founded in 1771, fourth of the missions, San Gabriel moved to its present site in 1775. The church is styled after the cathedral of Córdoba in Spain. The mission has a museum of religious and Indian artifacts, and its primitive winery, California's oldest, has been restored to give an idea of the original.

Museum of Contemporary Art 🏛 ★
250 S Grand Ave. (downtown at California Plaza, one block s of Music Center) ☎ *(213) 62-MOCA-2, (213) 626-6828. Map 7D9* ▨ *(but* ▣ *Thurs 5pm-8pm)* ♿ *≡* ➡ *Open Tues, Wed, Sat, Sun 11am-6pm, Thurs-Fri 11am-8pm. Closed Mon, Thanksgiving, Dec 25, Jan 1.*

When MOCA opened in 1986, Japanese architect Arata Isozaki's dazzling red sandstone-clad geometric building attracted as much attention as the exhibits. It still does, and the museum is arguably the most important addition to downtown architecture in decades. The permanent and the changing exhibitions of both paintings and sculpture, all displayed in generous well-lit spaces, tend to be equally modern and avant garde.

The museum is especially strong on Pop Art and Minimalism. Notable are works by Roy Lichtenstein, Robert Rauschenberg, Claes Oldenburg and Mark Rothko. In its 200-seat auditorium MOCA also gives regular Art Talks (☎ *(213) 621-1751*), slide presentations giving an overview of exhibitions (☎ *(213) 621-1751*), and occasional symposiums.

Music Center of Los Angeles 🏛
135 N Grand Ave. (downtown adjoining Civic Center at 1st St., one block s of Hollywood Freeway) ☎ *(213) 972-7211. Map 7D9* ▣ *𝕏 compulsory* ➡ *Open for tours May-Oct Mon 10am-2pm, Tues, Fri 10am-5pm; Nov-Apr Mon-Thurs 10am-2pm; Sat 10am-noon year round.*

Guided tours focus on the architecture of the center's **Dorothy Chandler Pavilion** (a 3,197-seat concert hall), **Ahmanson Theater** (a 2,100-seat theater and concert hall) and **Mark Taper Forum** (a 750-seat theater), and the art adorning it. Some love the late-1960s marble-clad rectangles and central cylinder; others hate them. What it lacks in accessibility and warmth it compensates for with extensive basement parking and some impressive sculptures in an otherwise unwelcoming plaza. However, the interior is luxuriously appointed, and the center is home to the Los Angeles Philharmonic and the Center Theater Group (see *LA Performing arts*). It is also the site of special music and theater performances all year round.

National Broadcasting Company Television Studio
3000 W Almeda Ave., Burbank (via Hollywood Way exit from Ventura Freeway/SR-134) ☎ *(818) 840-3537. Map 2B2* ▨ *𝕏 compulsory* ➡ *Open Mon-Fri 9am-4pm, Sat 10am-4pm, Sun 10am-2pm. Closed Jan 1, Thanksgiving, Dec 25.*

The long-running *Tonight Show* comes from here. Guides take visitors on a 75min tour through set construction, special effects, wardrobe departments, prop warehouses and sound stages — including **Studio 1**, where they can stand on Johnny Carson's mark: a star. Tours do not include tickets to taping sessions: for tickets see *Television shows*.

Pacific Asia Museum 🏛
46 N Los Robles Ave., Pasadena (via Ventura Freeway/SR-134, Colorado Blvd. exit, then w) ☎ *(818) 449-2742. Map 2B3* ▨ *Open Wed-Sun noon-5pm. Closed Mon-Tues.*

Housed in a delightfully ornate replica of a traditional Northern Chinese building (1924), originally home and shop for Oriental art dealer Grace Nicholson, the museum stages changing exhibitions of Asian art, both ancient and contemporary. It also has a peaceful courtyard garden, and a gift store selling kitchenware and household objects.

Pacific Design Center 🏛

8687 Melrose Ave., West Hollywood (NE corner of San Vicente Blvd.) ☎ *(213) 657-0800. Map 5C4.*

Conceived as a headquarters for Melrose's fashionable interior design trade, the aircraft-hanger-sized, blue-glass design center was likened by its critics to a beached blue whale. However, the stark elegance of the 1975 Cesar Pelli building and its landmark massiveness have won over most of the critics. Already it has been joined by a Green Whale, and a Red Whale is expected soon.

Paramount Studios

5555 Melrose Ave. (Marathon St. and Bronson Ave., between Gower St. and Van Ness Ave.) ☎ *(213) 468-5575. Map 6C6. Not open to the public.*

Paramount's famous **iron gates**, immortalized in *Sunset Boulevard*, are actually to be found on Bronson Ave. Those on Melrose Ave. are new. Dating from the silent movie era, and featuring stars such as Rudolph Valentino, Marlene Dietrich, Bob Hope and Dorothy Lamour, Paramount is the only great movie studio to have stayed on in Hollywood. Worth the visit just to see those gates.

El Pueblo de Los Angeles State Historic Park 🏛

622 N Main St. (N of downtown between Temple St. and Sunset Blvd.) ☎ *(213) 628-0605. Map 7D9* 🖭 ✗ *Open 10am-10pm summer, 10am-8.30pm winter.*

The park preserves Los Angeles' Spanish-American beginnings in the form of restored buildings, especially the Mexican rustic-style **Plaza Church** (1818), the city's oldest religious building, **Avila Adobe** (1818), the oldest house in Los Angeles, and **Pico House** (1869), in its prime the city's finest hotel. Other early buildings include the **Victorian Fire House No. 1** (1886), the Italianate **Masonic Lodge** (1858), and LA's first theater, the **Merced Theater** (1870); under it ran labyrinthine tunnels, hide-outs for oppressed 19thC Chinese.

However, the park's most visited part is **Olvera Street**, built in the 1920s as a tourist-oriented, block-long marketplace for Mexican restaurants, trinket shops and stalls selling candies. Many consider it to be California's first theme park. This miniature forerunner of Disneyland has a bandstand that serves as the site of *mariachi* concerts throughout the summer. The whole street erupts in fiesta at Cinco de Mayo (May 5).

A map of the four-block park is available at park headquarters next to the Fire House on the plaza E of Main St.

Virginia Robinson Gardens

1008 Elden Way, Beverly Hills. Map 4C2 ☎ *(213) 276-5367* 🖭 ✗ *by reservation only* 🚗 *for cars and vans only, no buses. Open Tues-Fri 10am-1pm. Closed Sat-Mon, major hols.*

Built in 1911, the Robinsons' Beaux Arts house is said to be Beverly Hills' oldest, and it provides a glimpse of the early years of the Los Angeles good life. The 6-acre landscaped estate features terraced hillsides and groves of king palms, azaleas and camellias, the whole crisscrossed by interlocking footpaths.

Rodeo Drive

Beverly Hills, between Wilshire Blvd. and Santa Monica Blvd. Map 4C3.

Rodeo Drive is the apotheosis of Los Angeles' consumer culture. Designer fashions, designer jewelry, designer perfumes, designer adult toys, designer salads, designer people; the place to see and be seen. (See *LA Shopping*.)

Rodia's Watts Towers ★

Willowbrook Ave. and 107th St., midway between Long Beach and Harbor Freeways in Watts district. Map 2D3. Limited public access ☎ *(213) 271-9711, but towers visible from all sides.*

Sabbatino (Simon) Rodia, a tile-setter by trade, spent three decades (1921-54) building this giant, magical, found-object sculpture. The towers — the tallest central tower is 107ft — are made of salvaged steel rods and scrap metal coated with plaster, and decorated with ceramic and glass fragments and 70,000 sea-shells. Once threatened by vandals and demolition plans, the towers are now administered by the Los Angeles Department of Cultural Affairs. Restoration work is well under way.

St Vincent's de Paul Roman Catholic Church

621 W Adams Blvd. (intersection of Adams Blvd. and S Figueroa St.). Map 7E8.

One of southern California's most beautiful churches, St. Vincent's is a splendid example of the ornate Spanish-Mexican Churrigueresque style. Built between 1923-25 with money donated by wealthy oilman Edward Doheny, its most notable features are an entrance screen of Indiana limestone and a brilliantly tiled 45ft-diameter dome.

Santa Monica Pier

At the foot of Colorado St., one block from the end of Santa Monica Freeway/I-10, Santa Monica. Map 2C1.

Of several piers built at the turn of the century, Santa Monica's (1909-21) is the only survivor: a pleasingly raffish collection of restaurants, snack bars, curio stores and bait shops. Fishermen throng the pier, but the high point is the **merry-go-round**, featured in the movie *The Sting* (*open daily in summer, weekends in winter*).

Norton Simon Museum of Art ☆

411 W Colorado Blvd., Pasadena (s side of Ventura Freeway/ SR-134 at Orange Grove Blvd.). ☎ *(818) 449-3730. Map 2B3* 🔲 ✗ ← *Open Thurs-Sun noon-6pm. Closed Mon-Wed, major hols.*

Many critics consider this to be the finest collection in the western United States both for its quality and for the personal vision of the man who assembled it at the cost of an estimated $100 million.

Rodin's *Burghers of Calais* adorn the forecourt. There are fine collections of Indian and Southeast Asian sculpture, both inside and outside the gallery; Old Master paintings and drawings including Rembrandt's *Titus, Bearded Man in Wide-Brimmed Hat* and *Self Portrait*; works by Rubens, Raphael, Goya and Breughel; Francisco Zurbarán's stunning *Still Life — Lemons, Oranges and a Rose*, a superb range of Impressionist and Cubist works including Cézanne's *Tulips in a Vase*, Renoir's *Pont des Arts* and Van Gogh's *Portrait of a Peasant*; a roomful of Degas paintings and sculptures; Picassos; works of the German Expressionists; and an excellent museum shop selling one of Los Angeles' broadest selections of art books, prints and cards.

Six Flags Magic Mountain

26101 Magic Mountain Parkway, Valencia, w of I-5 at Magic Mountain Parkway exit ☎ *(805) 255-4100, from Los Angeles (213) 367-5965. Map 15/6* 🔲 ▣ ♦ ♫ ← AE ● VISA *Open mid-May to mid-Sept Sun-Thurs 10am-10pm, Fri-Sat 10am-midnight; weekends and hols (except Christmas) all year.*

Set in 260 landscaped acres, the newest of the big amusement parks in southern California is something of an anthology of all the rest.

Key among its permanent attractions are its rides, 100 of them, and especially the thrill rides. No other place in California has as much equipment for shaking the boredom out of travel-weary, school-age children. The premier white-knuckle trip is on *Colossus*, a twin-track giant roller coaster 9,200ft long and boasting speeds up to 65mph, but it is only the centerpiece in a collection of heart-stoppers. The park also has a loop roller coaster, a pirate ship that makes vertical swings at speeds useful for training astronauts to live through rocket launches, and the highest double-arm Ferris wheel in the world. Carousels and other more sedate devices suit small children. Still other variations on roller coasters and spinning rides fit between the extremes.

In addition to rides, the spacious park has a dolphin show, a diving exhibition modeled after the famous cliff dives at Acapulco, a petting zoo, and a tots' playground called Children's World that features rides for little people, Warner Bros. cartoon characters and a participatory circus. A section called Spillikin's Handicrafters Junction has artisans in residence demonstrating turn-of-the-century techniques of candy-making, basket-weaving, wood-carving and glass-blowing. Last but not least, the park has regular live music, mime and magic performances plus occasional major shows by big name entertainers. The latter are scheduled for summer evenings.

Like other theme parks, Six Flags Magic Mountain has a number of restaurants with menus ranging from fast-food to fairly elaborate, and from all-American through several national cuisines.

For those who prefer not to make the fairly long drive from Los Angeles, **Grayline** runs tour buses from both LA and Orange County, and **Greyhound** provides a regular bus service.

Southwest Museum ⌂

234 Museum Dr., Highland Park, N of Pasadena Freeway/SR-11, via Pasadena Ave. exit, then Marmion Way, about 2 miles E of Dodger Stadium and Elysian Park ☎ (213) 221-2163. Map 2B3 ▧ ⇔ Open Tues-Sat 11am-5pm, Sun 1-5pm. Closed Mon, major hols.

Greatly transcending its name, the Mission-style museum, begun in 1912, houses a wealth of material on Native Americans from Mexico to northernmost Alaska. Major displays cover the cliff-dwellers of the southwest, the Plains Indians, the North Coast Indians of British Columbia and Alaska, and the Eskimos.

At an institution highly regarded for its anthropological and archeological research, several excellent dioramas depict the rich variety of Indian ways of life. A reminder of the European intrusions that destroyed those ways of life is provided by a depiction of Custer's Last Stand by an Indian participant. Perhaps the strongest collection of artifacts is basketry from every part of the continent W of the Mississippi River. Materials in this and other collections date from 10,000yrs ago to near-contemporary.

The museum hosts a festival of Native American Arts every Oct.

Sunset Strip

Sunset Blvd., West Hollywood, between Crescent Heights Blvd. and Doheny Dr. Map 4C3.

Running for almost 2 miles between Hollywood and Beverly Hills, Sunset Strip was once Hollywood's glossy playground. In the 1930s and '40s stars and starlets flocked by limousine to chic nightclubs such as Ciro's, the Mocambo and the Trocadero. The Strip has undergone several metamorphoses since then, hitting rock-bottom in the 1970s when it was characterized by porno theaters, prostitutes and drug addicts. Nowadays it is peopled by record companies, agents and managers, and movie producers. Fashionable hotels, trendy stores and restaurants, and nightclubs serving up rock-'n'-roll and comedy make for a nightlife almost as lively as the halcyon days.

Château Marmont (*8221 Sunset Blvd.* ☎ *(213) 656-1010*) was built in 1929 along the lines of a Norman castle and is as popular as ever with movie and music stars; Humphrey Bogart and Greta Garbo stayed here. (See *LA Hotels*.) **St James's Club** (*8358 Sunset Blvd.* ☎ *(213) 654-8964*) is a beautifully restored 1931 Art Deco classic. Even harder to miss are the Strip's "vanity boards," enormous elevated billboards advertising who and what's hot in entertainment. Each is hand-painted and merits attention as great popular art.

Tail O' the Pup 🏛
329 N San Vicente Blvd., NW of Beverly Center. Map 5C4.
Displaced from its original site by the new Ma Maison Sofitel hotel, the hot dog and hamburger stand constructed in 1946 in the shape of a hot dog, complete with yellow mustard, is regarded as a Pop Art classic. The hot dogs are so so, but most people are pleased that it has found a new home.

Television shows
The major networks tape a number of shows before live audiences. Tickets are free.

Networks make some tickets available at their offices on the day of taping. The **Los Angeles Visitors and Convention Bureau Visitor Center** (*Arco Plaza, Level B, 6th and S Flower St.*) has daily rations of tickets to many popular shows, also available on the day of taping. Each show or studio has its own minimum age limit for audience guests — the range is 12-18yrs — so families should check in advance. Few shows are taped during Mar-June.

ABC-TV Ticket Office
4151 Prospect Ave., Hollywood, an eastward extension of Hollywood Blvd. ☎ *(213) 557-4103. Map 7B8. Open Mon-Fri 9am-1pm, 2-5pm. Closed Sat-Sun. Tickets also available at ABC Entertainment Center, Plaza level, 2040 Ave. of the Stars, Century City. Map 4D2. Open Mon-Sat 10am-10pm. Closed Sun.*

CBS-TV Ticket Office
7800 Beverly Blvd., Hollywood, at Fairfax Ave. ☎ *(213) 852-4002. Map 5C5. Open Mon-Fri 9am-5pm, Sat-Sun 10am-5pm.*

Fox Television Ticket Office
5746 W Sunset Blvd., Hollywood ☎ *(213) 856-1520; for recorded information (818) 506-0067. Map 6B6. Open Mon-Fri 8.30am-5.30pm. Closed Sat-Sun.*

NBC-TV Ticket Office
3000 W Alameda Ave., Burbank, via Hollywood Way exit from Ventura Freeway/SR-134 ☎ *(818) 840-3537. Map 2B2. Open Mon-Fri 8.30am-5.30pm, Sat-Sun 9am-4pm.*

Paramount Television Audience Shows
780 N Gower St. ☎ *(213) 468-5575 for information. Map 6C6.*

Hollywood on Location
8644 Wilshire Blvd., Beverly Hills ☎ *(213) 659-9165. Map 5D4. Open Mon-Fri 9.30am-5pm. Closed Sat-Sun.*
This provides daily location lists of which TV shows, movies and rock videos are shooting around the city, along with maps and likely stars. However, the service is expensive.

The Temporary Contemporary 🏛
152 N Central Ave. (downtown, near junction with 1st St.) ☎ *(213) 626-6222. Map 7D9* 🔲 *(but* 🔲 *Thurs 5pm-8pm)* ♿ 🚗 *Open Tues-Wed, Sat-Sun 11am-6pm, Thurs-Fri 11am-8pm. Closed Mon, Thanksgiving, Dec 25, Jan 1.*

Architect Frank Gehry renovated two warehouses to create a lofty space of 70,000sq.ft. Initially the Temporary Contemporary was envisaged as just that, a temporary home for MOCA before its California Plaza home was built. But its imaginative exhibitions have given the Temporary a life of its own.

Union Passenger Station 🏛

800 N Alameda St. ☎ (213) 683-6873. Map 7D9 ⊡

The last (1939) grand-scale railroad station to be built out West, it was once the opulent end of the line for passengers chasing the setting sun. Architects John and Donald Parkinson overlaid basic Spanish Colonial Revival with touches of streamlined Moderne and Moorish design, achieving a handsomely proportioned structure where inside and out are interwoven. With its ceramic-tiled floors, wood-beamed ceilings and the many original furnishings still in place, the station is a stylish evocation of southern California's prewar era. The surrounding courtyards provide travelers with an accurate and imaginative reflection of the vivid variety of flora that awaits them.

Universal Studios ☆

100 Universal City Plaza, Universal City (at Lankershim/Universal City exit from Hollywood Freeway/US-101) ☎ (818) 777-3794. Map 2B2 ⊡ ✗ compulsory ▣ ✚ ⇌ Open daily for tours late May-late June 9am-4pm; late June-early Sept 8am-6pm; early Sept-late May Mon-Fri 10am-3.30pm, Sat-Sun 9.30am-4pm. Closed Thanksgiving, Dec 25.

Carl Laemmie moved his studio here from Hollywood in 1915, and soon recognized that the public would pay for a behind-the-screen look at movies; the first visitors paid 25¢. Nowadays it is pricier, but wittily commentated streetcar tours take in tantalizingly familiar sets for Westerns, monster thrillers, sci-fi and every other movie genre. Visitors see through the illusion of some amazing action sequences — for example, a collapsing bridge, the parting of the Red Sea and an alpine avalanche — and visit back-lot departments that reveal more of the tricks used in movie-making. Expect close encounters with King Kong, Jaws and the Bates mansion from Hitchcock's *Psycho*, and to be caught in the crossfire of a space-age laser gunfight.

After the tour the **Entertainment Center** offers a variety of spectacles, including the taping of an episode from *Star Trek*, with members of the audience invited to play starring roles and the results played back on video; the $5 million *Adventures of Conan* sorcery show; an action-packed scene from *Miami Vice*, Cowboy Stuntmen in action; and Animal Actors doing their things. Frankenstein's Monster, Charlie Chaplin and other movie star lookalikes tour the grounds and will pose for pictures. Allow at least 5hrs.

University of California, Los Angeles *(UCLA)*

405 Hilgard Ave., Westwood (between Sunset Blvd., Hilgard Ave., Le Conte Ave., Gayley Ave. and Veteran Ave.). Visitor Center ☎ (213) 206-8147. Map 4C2 ⊡ ✗ ▣ ⇌

The first buildings went up in 1929. Since then UCLA has expanded across more than 400 acres to comprise 13 colleges and 69 departments. The campus grounds are beautifully landscaped and include a traditional **Japanese rock garden**, a delightful **botanical garden** thick with tropical and subtropical plants, and a 5-acre **sculpture garden** peppered with some 50 works by artists such as Rodin, Moore and Matisse.

The buildings are, on the whole, less distinguished. The exceptions include the four original buildings: **Powell Library**, **Kinsey Hall**, **Haines Hall** and **Royce Hall**. All are a combination of red brick and beige stone in Italian Romanesque style. Also on campus are the **Museum of Cultural History** (☎ *(213) 206-1459*), the **Wight Art Gallery** (☎ *(213) 825-9345*) and, best of all, the **Film and Television Archive** (☎ *(213) 206-8013*), an impressive collection of material dating back to the earliest days of cinema, although requests to view must be made well in advance.

Venice
s of Santa Monica via Pacific Ave., or at the w end of Venice Blvd. Map 2C1.
This is the place for a taste of legendary West Coast wackiness. Ocean Front Walk acts as a magnet for all sorts of exhibitionists eager to strut, or more usually roller-skate, their stuff. The vivid boardwalk parade is further enlivened by street performers, musclemen, hawkers and food stalls.

Walk of Fame
Hollywood Blvd. between Gower St. and Sycamore Ave., and Vine Street between Yucca St. and Sunset Blvd. Map 6A6.
Since 1958 almost 2,000 brass-edged stars, inlaid with the names of entertainment industry celebrities, have been embedded in the sidewalk. Volunteer fans polish the stars; Marilyn Monroe has a waiting list.

Wayfarers' Chapel 血 †
5755 Palos Verdes Dr. S, Rancho Palos Verdes ☎ (213) 377-1650. Map 2E2☜ ➡ Open 11am-4pm.
Lloyd Wright, son of Frank Lloyd Wright, designed this famous glass and redwood church erected in 1949 in tribute to theologian and mystic Emanuel Swedenborg. The church, which overlooks the ocean, is open to all.

Will Rogers State Historic Park
14325 Sunset Blvd. ☎ (213) 454-8212. Map 8C1☒ ➡ Park open 8am-7pm summer, 8am-5pm remainder of the year; house open 10am-5pm. Closed Jan 1, Thanksgiving, Dec 25.
The estate of the cowboy philosopher and humorist is one of the finest remaining opportunities to see how movie stars of the grand era lived. Will Rogers' 187-acre property has its own polo field, still in use. There is a collection of memorabilia inside the house.

Where to stay

In hotels, as in everything else, Los Angeles is a great shopper's bazaar for anyone willing to spend. Beyond its vast number of comfortable, conventional modern towers, it has a remarkable supply of unusual places; some are merely distinctive, but others — including a cluster of high-rise glass-walled cylinders, a Norman castle, and a tropical garden hideaway — are unique.

For all the variety, some types of accommodations are lacking. Although **Santa Monica** has a range of hotels and motels near its beach, beach resorts are extremely scarce. **Downtown** has few relatively small, moderately priced old hotels, and most districts have none. In an area where budget-conscious travellers do not find easy pickings, good rooms can be difficult to find in many districts of prime interest to visitors. Alternatives are to shop for weekend or off-season special rates in business-oriented hotels or to seek out the better chain motels. For longer stays of a month or more, investigate very competitively priced efficiency apartments: the **Oakwood Apartments** listed below are a good representative example.

There are tight clusters of hotels **downtown**, in **mid-Wilshire** and especially at the entrance to **Los Angeles International Airport**. But only visitors doing business or in a hurry or both are likely to be attracted to downtown or airport areas; neither is especially lively or interesting, especially after dark.

Otherwise, in keeping with the general nature of Los Angeles, hostelries are usually scattered throughout districts as well as across the length and breadth of the basin. The districts already named, along with **Westside** (Beverly Hills-Westwood-Bel Air-Brentwood), **Hollywood**, Coastal centers such as **Marina del Rey** and **Santa Monica**, as well as Valley towns such as **Pasadena** and **Burbank**, are the most likely headquarters for visitors. When shopping around for bargain rates in less central districts, consider easy access to a freeway as an important advantage.

A hotel tax will be added to quoted rates. The percentage varies by municipality. Los Angeles charges 7.5 percent, Beverly Hills 8.2 percent, Redondo Beach 5 percent. Others fall within that range.

Many hotels are of course members of a chain. In the following pages, pressure of space prevents description of more than one outstanding member of these great chains. Following this will be found a short list of other hotels in the chain, with their locations, telephone numbers and price categories.

Readers wondering about the omission of The Ambassador, home of the legendary Coconut Grove nightclub and site of Robert Kennedy's assassination in 1968, will be saddened to learn that it has finally closed.

Hotels classified by area

Central
Los Angeles Airport Marriott ||||||
Salisbury House |||□

Coastal
Barnaby's |||□ to |||||
Breakers Motel |||□
Carmel |||□
Hotel Queen Mary |||□ to |||||
Huntley |||□ to |||||
Jamaica Bay Inn |||||| to |||||
Marina del Rey |||||| to |||||
Oakwood Apartments Marina del Rey |□ to |||□
Shangri-La |||□ to |||||

Downtown
Best Western Hotel Tokyo |||□
Biltmore |||||
Clark |□
Figueroa |||□
Hyatt Regency-Los Angeles |||||
Mayfair |||||| to |||||
New Otani Hotel & Garden |||||
Sheraton-Grande |||||
Westin Bonaventure |||||

Hollywood
Le Bel Age |||||
Château Marmont |||||| to |||||
Le Dufy |||□ to |||||
Hollywood Roosevelt |||□ to |||||
Ma Maison Sofitel |||||
St James's Club |||||
Sunset Marquis Hotel & Villas |||||

Valleys
Oakwood Apartments Toluca Hills |□ to |||□

Oakwood Apartments Woodland Hills |□ to |||□
Registry |||||
Safari Inn |||□ to |||||
Sportsmen's Lodge |||□

Westside
Bel-Air |||||
Bel-Air Sands |||||
Beverly Hills |||||
Beverly Hilton |||||
Beverly Terrace |□ to |||□
Beverly Wilshire |||||
Century Plaza |||||
L'Ermitage |||||
Four Seasons |||||
Oakwood Apartments Mid Wilshire |□ to |||□
Westwood Marquis |||||
Westwood Plaza (Holiday Inn) |||||

Barnaby's
*3501 N Sepulveda Blvd.,
Manhattan Beach 90266 ☎ (213)
545-8488, (800) 732-1540
℠ 545-8621. Map 2D2 |||□ to |||||. 128
units* ▦ ➡ ⇌ AE CB ◆ ◉ VISA
*Location: 2 miles s of LAX, half a
block s of Rosencrans Ave.* A
family-run hotel of European charm
and elegance set incongruously in
surfuria. Barnaby's decor is hard to
pin down, lying somewhere
between Victorian England and
turn-of-the-century Vienna.
Nevertheless the result is engaging,

and the rooms, both private and public, are a successful blend of antique decor and modern amenity. Service is friendly, the enclosed gardens are especially pleasant, and the restaurant serves good traditional Viennese cuisine. Complimentary London black cabs are available for guests.

⬛ ▢ 🖂 🦶 ⚓ ≋ 🍷 𝄞 ⚲

Le Bel Age 🏨
1020 N San Vicente Blvd., West Hollywood 90069 ☎ *(213) 854-1111. Map 5C4* ▥ *198 units* ▤ 🚗 ≋ *AE CB 🌐 ⓞ VISA*
Location: Half a block s of Sunset Strip. From the outside just another undistinguished Los Angeles building. Inside is a different story: pure luxury. No rooms here, only suites, all of them lavishly done out with original art and fine furniture, three telephones, extra-large TV, and private balcony. Public rooms are equally tasteful, and the atmosphere is one of discretion and exclusivity. Le Bel Age also offers secretarial and limousine services and boasts a fine Franco-Russian restaurant.

⚲ ▢ 🖂 🦶 ≋ 🍷 𝄞

Bel-Air 🏨
701 Stone Canyon Rd., Los Angeles 90024 ☎ *(213) 472-1211. Map 4C1* ▥ *92 units* ▤ 🚗 ≋ *AE CB 🌐 ⓞ VISA*
Location: Directly N of UCLA campus, accessible from Sunset Blvd. All the clichés of the well-heeled southern California life-style are summed up by home-away-from-home Spanish haciendas snuggled into 10 acres of fairytale semitropical gardens in a remote-feeling part of residential Bel-Air. Many of the legendary names of Hollywood hide away here. Suites are luxuriously furnished with antiques; rooms are simpler. The staff cossets guests with skill but without stuffy formality. No conventions or tour groups allowed. Advance deposit required.

⬛ ▢ 🖂 🦶 ⚓ ≋ 🍷 𝄞

Bel Air Summit
11461 Sunset Blvd., Los Angeles 90049 ☎ *(213) 476-6571, (800) 352-6680. Map 2C1* ▥ *181 units* ▤ 🚗 ≋ *AE CB 🌐 ⓞ VISA*
Location: One block w of San Diego Freeway/I-405, Sunset Blvd. exit. Two modern 2-story buildings in a steep hillside garden setting. Lanais (balconies) help bring the outdoors into the large rooms or suites, boldly

decorated in sunny colors. Many units have separate dining nooks. The bar and pool area are popular with locals. Free limousine service to Westwood and Beverly Hills is only one of the extra touches provided by this hotel.

⬛ ⚲ ▢ 🖂 🦶 ⚓ ≋ 🍷 ⚲ 🏆 𝄞

Best Western Hotel Tokyo
328 E First St., Los Angeles 90012 ☎ *(213) 228-8888, (800) 528-1234. Map 7D9* ▥ *174 units* ▤ 🖂 ≋ *AE CB 🌐 ⓞ VISA*
Location: Little Tokyo area, just w of Alameda St. Above-average example of the reliable chain, with the clean and neat Japanese air, and Japanese-speaking staff, to be expected in the heart of Little Tokyo. Convenient for downtown and major freeways.

⚐ ⚲ ▢ 🖂 🦶 🍷 𝄞

☙ Other Best Westerns: **Best Western Farmer's Daughter Motel** (☎ *(213) 937-3930* ▥), in the pleasant Fairfax district of Hollywood; **Best Western Sunset Plaza** (☎ *(213) 654-0750* ▥), close to Sunset Strip. For information on other Best Westerns and reservations in the LA area ☎ (800) 528-1234.

Beverly Hills 🏨
9641 Sunset Blvd., Beverly Hills 90210 ☎ *(213) 276-2251, (800) 792-7637. Map 4C3* ▥ *263 units* ▤ 🚗 ≋ *AE CB 🌐 ⓞ VISA*
Location: In a residential area, less than a mile N of Wilshire Blvd. via Canon Dr. or Rodeo Dr. All of the mythical big deals by Hollywood tycoons and some of the real ones have been fixed over breakfast in the **Polo Lounge** (see *LA Nightlife*) of this grand garden hotel, first opened in 1912. The Polo Lounge feels rather tired these days, but the hotel still provides a perfect atmosphere for a Hollywood deal or for a dip into the milieu. On 12 acres, it has fine gardens with royal palms, banana and jacaranda trees, a huge pool, and floodlit tennis courts. Rooms in the rosy pink, Spanish Colonial-style main building are immense and furnished with quiet luxury. Many have fireplaces and most have bars. Rooms in 20 bungalows dotted around the property are more variable in size, but no less richly furnished. Conventions are not accepted. The hotel is now owned by the Sultan of Brunei. Reservation deposit required.

⬛ ⚲ ▢ 🖂 🦶 ⚓ ≋ 🦶 🏆 🍷 𝄞

Beverly Hilton
9876 Wilshire Blvd., Beverly Hills 90210 ☎ (213) 274-7777. Map **4D3** |||| 592 units ▦ ━ ═ AE CB ⊙ ⊚ VISA

Location: Near the intersection of Wilshire Blvd. and Santa Monica Blvd. The traditional home of the Academy Awards ball is not exactly a typical Hilton. Both public and guest rooms are decorated less functionally than the norm for this far-ranging chain. The lobby is nondescript, but the **International Ballroom** has a glittering opulence that attracts conventions and gala events. All guest rooms are bright, informal and remarkably varied in decor. However, many are small, so visitors wanting a larger room need to ask for one. Rooms facing away from Wilshire Blvd. have private balconies; quite a few overlook a spacious pool and lounge area. Among the restaurants is a well-regarded branch of **Trader Vic's**.
✱ ⚅ ☐ 🖂 ≋ ♈ ♒ ⚑ ⊙ ♉

≋ Other Hiltons: **Los Angeles Hilton** (☎ (213) 629-4321 ||||), downtown; **Pasadena Hilton** (☎ (818) 577-1000 ||||).

Beverly Terrace
469 N Doheny Dr., Beverly Hills 90210 ☎ (213) 274-8141, (800) 421-7223. Map **4C3** ❚❚ to ❚❚ 39 units ▦ ═ AE CB ⊙ ⊚ VISA

A small, intimate hotel unremarkable save for its moderate rates and upscale location. Popular with the design set, supremely convenient for Westside shopping, theaters and restaurants, and so sought after that it's necessary to reserve well in advance.
≋ ☐ 🖂

Beverly Wilshire 🏨
9500 Wilshire Blvd., Beverly Hills 90212 ☎ (213) 275-4282, (800) 282-4804. Map **4D3** |||| 380 units ▦ ━ ═ AE CB ⊙ ⊚ VISA

Location: At the intersection of Wilshire Blvd. and Rodeo Dr. Of all the grand hotels in Los Angeles, the Beverly Wilshire clings faithfully to the starchy era of grand manners. In both the original hotel (the **Wilshire Wing**) and in a modern tower (the **Beverly Wing**) opulence is the watchword. Rooms in the tower are decorated floor by floor, tracing California history from its Spanish beginnings to trendy modern, with plenty of luxury and marble bathrooms. The older wing is more spacious and traditional, suited to the tastes of the hotel's

established guest list, which includes kings, presidents and legendary movie stars. Among the restaurants and bars, **El Padrino** is famous as a meeting place of movie moguls and leading businessmen.
✱ ☐ 🖂 ⚅ ≋ ⚑ ♒ ♈ ⊙ ♉ ♉

Biltmore 🏨 ♣ 🏛
506 S Grand Ave., Los Angeles 90071 ☎ (213) 624-1011, (800) 421-8000, (800) 252-0175. Map **7D9** |||| 700 units ▦ AE CB ⊙ ⊚ VISA

Location: Downtown at 5th St., across from Pershing Sq. A grand old downtown landmark restored to its 1920s glories. Externally the style is Beaux Arts; internally it draws upon a host of traditions, most notably Italian-Spanish Renaissance. The old lobby and **Main Galeria** are magnificent, with acres of marble and lofty hand-painted and gilded ceilings. Some of the suites are as rich in material and detail as the Galeria, although not quite as large. Guest rooms maintain the level of quality but in more modern style. The restaurant **Bernard's** isn't as good as it used to be, but the **Grand Avenue Bar** still has style.
✱ ⚅ ☐ 🖂 ⚑ ≋ ♈ ♒ ⚑ ♉ ⊙ ♉ ♉

The Breakers Motel
1501 Ocean Ave., Santa Monica 90401 ☎ (213) 451-4811, (800) 634-7333. Map **2C1** ❚❚ 34 units ━ AE CB ⊙ ⊚ VISA

Location: In the first block N of the Santa Monica Freeway on Santa Monica's beachfront. The Breakers is a comfortable, old 2-story building with the treble virtues of a useful location, free parking and moderate prices.
☐ 🖂 ⚑ ≋ ♈

Carmel
210 Broadway, Santa Monica 90403 ☎ (213) 451-2469. Map **2C1** ❚❚ 110 units ═ AE ⊙ VISA

Location: Two blocks from Santa Monica Pier. An aged but well-maintained hotel, it has small to medium-sized rooms with just enough Spanish-Mexican touches in the decor to avoid being plain.
✱ ☐ 🖂 ⚑ ♈ ♉

Century Plaza 🏨
2025 Ave. of the Stars, Los Angeles 90067 ☎ (213) 277-2000, (800) 228-3000. Map **4D2** |||| 1,072 units ▦ ━ ═ AE CB ⊙ ⊚ VISA

Location: Century City, opposite ABC Entertainment Center. A member of the uniformly excellent

Westin chain, and once popular with President Ronald Reagan and his entourage, the Century Plaza collects awards annually for its comfort and service. Spacious guest rooms are expensively furnished and have private balconies, some with marvelous views. However, the great curving mass of concrete and glass was designed as an efficiently elegant convention hotel — its primary function — and it lacks warmth and character as a result.

≢ ₺ □ ☐ ⬷ ⇌ ♬ ☺ ♈ Ⴤ ♫

Château Marmont 🏨

8221 Sunset Blvd., Hollywood 90046 ☎ *(213) 656-1010, (800) 242-8328. Map 5B4 //// to //// 63 units* ☷

Location: In Hollywood Hills, w of Fairfax Ave at the E end of Sunset Strip. Even in Hollywood a gray-walled Norman castle with a Mediterranean lobby looks a shade curious, but Château Marmont is prized all the same, or perhaps all the more. The 1920s building has been a favorite haunt of actors of widely separated generations. Carol Lombard and Jean Harlow favored it when it was new, Greta Garbo and Humphrey Bogart stayed here before it declined, and since its 1976 renovation Al Pacino and other New York actors have renewed the glamor. Actor John Belushi died here of a drugs overdose, but the reputation for privacy and discretion survived. The pool-side bungalows are popular, and there are good views from the main balconies.

⌂ ⌁ ≢ □ ☐ ⬷ ⇌

Clark

426 S Hill St., Los Angeles 90013 ☎ *(213) 624-4121, (800) 223-9868. Map 7D9 □ to //☐520 units* ☷ ☷ ☷

Location: Central downtown. The Clark was renovated to a high standard in 1986 and, although less than luxurious, is clean, comfortable and a conveniently located bargain for visitors on a budget who want to stay in the downtown area.

≢ ☐ Ⴤ

Le Dufy

1000 Westmount Dr., West Hollywood 90069 ☎ *(213) 657-7400. Map 5C4 //☐ to //// 121 units* ⌁ ☷ ☷ ☷ ☷ ☷

Location: Three blocks s of Sunset Blvd, one block s of Holloway Dr. A more affordable cousin of **Le Bel Age** (q.v.), Le Dufy is a modern hotel with the feel of an apartment building on a quiet residential street

within striking distance of Beverly Hills. Most suites have a living room with living gas fire and a balcony; some have small kitchens. As well as the pool, there's a rooftop Jacuzzi, self-service laundry and baby-sitting service.

⌂ ⬷ ⇌ ≢ □ ☐ ♬

L'Ermitage 🏨

9291 Burton Way, Beverly Hills 90210 ☎ *(213) 278-3344, (800) 282-4818. Map 4C3 //// 112 units* ☷ ☷ ☷ ☷ ☷ ☷

Location: On a residential boulevard five blocks E of Rodeo Dr., between Santa Monica Blvd. and Wilshire Blvd. L'Ermitage has been called the finest hotel in the USA, and given the prices and the staff-to-guest ratios it ought to be. The frontage has something of the air of an embassy about it and, although the Braques, Dufys and Renoirs on the walls are not originals, the decor is immaculate. Privacy is guaranteed, and service is impeccable, and a French chef presides over a private dining room for residents and their guests. A limousine is at one's disposal at no extra charge. Reservation deposit required.

≢ □ ☐ ♬ ♈ ⬷ ⇌ Ⴤ ♫

Figueroa

939 S Figueroa St., Los Angeles 90015 ☎ *(213) 627-8971, (800) 331-5151. Map 7E8 //☐280 units* ☷ ☷ ☷ ☷ ☷

Location: Downtown, one block from Convention Center. Charming Spanish-style hotel dating from 1927, with a beautiful lobby, huge swimming pool and palm-fringed courtyard. Rooms are of a generous size. The hotel is popular with touring performing arts companies.

♈ ⇌ ≢ □ ☐ ♬ Ⴤ

Four Seasons 🏨

300 S Doheny Dr., Beverly Hills 90048 ☎ *(213) 273-2222, (800) 332-3442. Map 4C3 //// 285 units* ☷ ☷ ☷ ☷ ☷ ☷

Location: Corner of Burton Way. An attractive recent addition to LA's range of hotels, the Four Seasons is a relatively small European-style establishment. Rooms and suites are large and elegantly furnished, and each has a balcony. Public areas are tastefully decorated with marble, original art and fresh flowers. There are all the refinements and amenities one would expect, including 24hr concierge, baby sitting and complimentary limousines to Rodeo Dr.

⌂ ≢ □ ☐ ⇌ ♈ Ⴤ ♫

Hiltons See after **Beverly Hilton**.

Holiday Inns See after **Westwood Plaza**.

Hollywood Roosevelt
7000 Hollywood Blvd., Hollywood 90028 ☎ (213) 466-7000, (800) 858-2244. Map 6B5 ▥▤ to ▥▥▥ 400 units ▤▤ ← ≕ AE CB ◑ ◐ VISA
Location: Across from Mann's Chinese Theater. Recently reopened after a $35 million face-lift, the Roosevelt is back to something like its former self. Site of the first Academy Awards, it was once a favorite with celebrities such as Errol Flynn, Clark Gable, Carol Lombard, Ernest Hemingway and Salvador Dalí. Nowadays movie, TV and music industry types enjoy the echoes. The high-ceilinged Spanish Colonial-style lobby, the Olympic-sized swimming pool and the stylish **Cinegrill Supper Club** are all trendy places to see and be seen.
❤ ➳ ✳ ☐ ▱ ⋒ ⵏ ▶ ⴖ

Hotel Queen Mary
Pier J, PO Box 8, Long Beach 90801 ☎ (213) 435-3511. Map 2E3 ▥▤ to ▥▥▥ 365 units ▤▤ ← ≕ AE CB ◑ ◐ VISA
Location: Harborside, at the s end of Long Beach Freeway/I-710. 1930s-style Art Deco luxury aboard one of the greatest ever ocean liners and a chance to experience how the wealthy traveled before the jet plane. Although restored and kitted out with modern necessities such as telephones and TVs, many of the rooms and suites retain their original furnishings and decoration. The outside rooms, with portholes, are pricier but preferable.
Ġ ✳ ☐ ▱ ⋒ ⵏ ⴖ ▶

Huntley
1111 Second St., Santa Monica 90403 ☎ (213) 394-5454. Map 2C1 ▥▤ to ▥▥▥ 210 units ▤▤ ▱ ≕ AE CB ◑ ◐ VISA
Location: Two blocks from the beach near Wilshire Blvd. In a new tower with fine views across the bay, tastefully decorated and furnished.
▱ ✳ ☐ ▱ ⋒ ⵏ ⴖ ▶

Hyatt Regency-Los Angeles
711 S Hope St., Los Angeles 90017 ☎ (213) 683-1234, (800) 228-9000. Map 7D9 ▥▥▥ 480 units ▤▤ ▱ ≕ AE CB ◑ ◐ VISA
Location: Downtown at 7th St. A great deal of thoughtful, old-fashioned hotel-keeping has been built into this conventional modern tower. One floor is set aside for

nonsmokers. Another floor is titled the **Regency Club**, which has richly comfortable library lounges, a butler to attend to personal needs and to put out afternoon hors d'oeuvres and cocktails, and a concierge to arrange such things as transportation. Throughout the hotel, spacious rooms are furnished in expensive good taste.
✳ ☐ ▱ ⋒ ⵏ ⴖ ▶

✎ Other Hyatts: **Hyatt at Los Angeles Airport** (☎ (213) 670-9000 ▥▥▥), at front entrance to LAX; **Hyatt on Sunset** (☎ (213) 656-4101 ▥▤ to ▥▥▥), in Hollywood; **Hyatt Wilshire** (☎ (213) 381-7411 ▥▥▥), in Mid-Wilshire. For central Hyatt information ☎ (800) 228-9000.

Jamaica Bay Inn
4175 Admiralty Way, Marina del Rey 90291 ☎ (213) 823-5333. Map 2C1 ▥▤ to ▥▥▥ 42 units ▤▤ ← ≕ AE CB ◑ ◐ VISA
Location: On the Marina del Rey Yacht harbor, one block from Washington St. A member of the Best Western chain, the comfortable 2-story motel adjoins a white-sand beach by the sheltered waters of the yacht harbor. Many rooms have patios overlooking the beach and harbor. Advance deposit required.
✳ ☐ ▱ ⋒ ⵏ ➳ ⴖ ▶

Los Angeles Airport Marriott
5855 W Century Blvd., Los Angeles 90045 ☎ (213) 641-5700. Map 2D2 ▥▥▥ 1,019 units ▤▤ ← ▱ ≕ AE CB ◑ ◐ VISA
Location: Near the front entrance to LAX. Spanish overtones in the lobby and subtle earth tones in spacious rooms give real warmth to a modern tower hotel aimed primarily at executive travelers. Suites are luxurious. A 4-story wing surrounds a large swimming pool with gardens and ample terraces around it, suitable for gentle strolls.
✳ Ġ ☐ ▱ ❤ ➳ ⵏ ⴖ ▶

Ma Maison Sofitel ▥▤ ▥
8555 Beverly Blvd., Los Angeles 90048 ☎ (213) 278-5444, (800) 221-4542 ® (213) 657-2816. Map 5C4 ▥▥▥ 311 units ▤▤ ← ≕ AE CB ◑ ◐ VISA
Location: At the intersection of Beverly and La Cienega Blvds., opposite the Beverly Center. Opened in Dec 1988, Ma Maison Sofitel promises to be among Los Angeles' best hotels. The imaginative Post Modern architecture of the building, with hints of French Château and Spanish Colonial Revival, is matched

by the understated pastel elegance of the interiors and a European intimacy. The location is hard to beat for shopping, dining and nightlife. The hotel's name points to what could be its major attraction: the justly famous **Ma Maison** restaurant (see *LA Restaurants*) is relocated here, along with its French/California cuisine. There is also a promising brasserie patterned after La Coupole in Paris.

⇌ ⟵ ⚲ ⇌ 🐾 🏋 □ 🖼 Ⴘ

Marina del Rey
3534 Bali Way, Marina del Rey 90292 ☎ *(213) 301-1000, (800) 862-7462. Map 2C1* ▮▮▮▮ *to* ▮▮▮▮ *160 units* ▤ ⇌ ⇌ AE CB ⊙ ⊙ VISA

Location: 5 miles N of LAX, ¼ mile W of Lincoln Blvd. Surrounded on three sides by water and with its own boat slip, the hotel is perfect for visitors who enjoy boating. Rooms, and the **Crystal Seahorse** restaurant, have excellent views across the marina.

⟵ ⇌ 🐾 ⇌ □ 🖼 Ⴘ

Mayfair
1256 W 7th St., Los Angeles 90017 ☎ *(213) 484-9789. Map 7D8* ▮▮▮▮ *to* ▮▮▮▮ *300 units* ▤ ⇌ AE CB ⊙ ⊙ VISA

Location: Four blocks W of Figueroa St. Among the few LA hotels of a type now common in San Francisco, this is a well-remodeled, middle-sized older building with every comfort in its guest rooms, but not all the public rooms and personal services expected of a grand hotel. Some guest rooms are reserved for nonsmokers. The hotel is sited well nigh perfectly for downtown visitors. Its restaurant, the **Orchid Court**, is useful.

⇌ □ 🖼 ⇌ Ⴘ

New Otani Hotel & Garden 🏨
120 S Los Angeles St., Los Angeles 90012 ☎ *(213) 629-1200, (800) 252-0917. Map 7D9* ▮▮▮▮ *448 units* ▤ ⇌ ⇌ AE CB ⊙ ⊙ VISA

Location: N of downtown in Little Tokyo at 1st St. The 21-story, ultramodern tower hotel is full of surprises. A rooftop terrace has a half-acre impression of the original Otani garden. On one side of it there is an exquisite, glass-walled Japanese restaurant (see **A Thousand Cranes** in *LA Restaurants*). On the other side is a bar decorated in modern Japanese style but dedicated to jazz. In the 3-story lobby/lounge, classical soloists or duettists play beneath imposing paintings by Nong. Large

rooms are expensively furnished with only faint nods to Japan. Suites have Japanese bathrooms and bedrooms, but Western living rooms.

⇌ ⚲ □ 🖼 ⟵ 🏋 Ⴘ 🐾

Oakwood Apartments Mid Wilshire ✿
209 S Westmoreland Ave., Los Angeles 90004 ☎ *(213) 380-4221, (800) 421-6654. Map 6D7.*

Location: Handy for Olympic Blvd. and Santa Monica Freeway.

Oakwood Apartments Toluca Hills ✿
3600 Barham Blvd., Los Angeles 90068 ☎ *(213) 851-3450, (800) 421-6654. Map 2B2.*

Location: S of Universal City, E off US-101, Barham Blvd. exit.

Oakwood Apartments Marina del Rey ✿
4111 S Via Marina, Marina del Rey 90292 ☎ *(213) 823-5443, (800) 421-6654. Map 2C1.*

Location: Just S of Washington Blvd.

Oakwood Apartments Woodland Hills ✿
22122-22222 Victory Blvd., Woodland Hills 91367 ☎ *(818) 340-5161, (800) 421-6654. Map 2B1.*

Location: Near intersection with Topanga Canyon Blvd.

Common to all Oakwood Apartments: ⇌ ▮▮ *to* ▮▮ ▤ 🐾 ⇌ Ⴘ ⇌ ⇌ ⚲ ⇌ AE CB ⊙ ⊙ VISA ⊙

Visitors staying in LA for 30 days or more could do far worse than investigate these short/long-stay apartments. Oakwood have several thousand units in total, and the choice ranges from studios with Murphy bed, kitchenette and bathroom, to family-sized units with living room, two bedrooms, kitchen and bathroom. All come fully equipped with linen and kitchenware, most have a balcony, and communal facilities include pools, clubhouse, gymnasiums, barbecues and coin-laundry. Electricity and cleaning are extra, but the deal is still hard to beat, and what the Oakwoods lack in architectural distinction they make up for with their friendliness. The only drawback is that guests must make their own arrangements with the telephone companies to have telephones connected and pay your bill. Unless a friend on the spot can arrange it for you beforehand, this can take a few days.

Registry
555 Universal Terrace Pkwy., Universal City 91608 ☎ *(818)*

506-2500. Map 2B2 **IIII** 450 units
▦ ▦ ▭ AE CB ▢ ▢ VISA

Location: At Lankershim Blvd. exit from US-101. The Registry is the younger and more luxurious next-door neighbor of the Sheraton Universal, a fact reflected in prices that begin where the Universal's leave off. Both are so entertainment-oriented that some guests have a hard time getting away for the studio tours.

‡ □ ▭ ▨ & ◁ ≈ ≛ ♈ ♫ ≱

Safari Inn

1911 W Olive Ave., Burbank 91356 ☎ *(818) 845-8586, (800) 845-5544. Map 2B2* **III** to **IIII** 110 units **▦ ▭ ▭ AE CB ▢ ▢ VISA**

Location: sw of I-5, Olive Ave. exit. A popular 1950s motel with character, pleasant rooms and a perfect location for Burbank's entertainment industry. Universal Studios, NBC, Disney and Warner Bros are all near.

≈ ‡ □ ▭ ▨ ♈

St James's Club ▥

8358 Sunset Blvd., Los Angeles 90069 ☎ *(213) 654-7100, (800) 225-2637. Map 5B4* **IIII** 74 units **▦ ▭ ▭ AE CB ▢ ▢ VISA**

Location: On Sunset Strip. Just a few years ago this landmark 1931 Art Deco delight was dilapidated and inhabited only by squatters. The new British owners spent $40 million restoring it, and the result is an exclusive, lavishly furnished club/hotel.

≈ ♈ □ ▭ ♈

Salisbury House ▤

2273 W 20th St., Los Angeles 90018 ☎ *(213) 737-7817. Map 7E8* **III** 5 units **AE ▢ VISA**

Location: Two blocks n of I-10, two blocks w of Western Ave. Small bed-and-breakfast establishments are commonplace in San Francisco but rare in Los Angeles. Salisbury House is one of only a handful, and has the added attraction of being an historic Craftsman-style bungalow built in 1909. Weekly rates available.

▨

Shangri-La

1301 Ocean Ave., Santa Monica 90401 ☎ *(213) 394-2791. Map 2C1* **III** to **IIII** 55 units **▦ ▭ AE CB ▢ ▢ VISA**

Location: One block s of Wilshire Blvd., across from Palisades Park. Refurbished 1939 Art Deco hotel, with splendid ocean views and sea breezes. Rooms are decorated in period style and most have fully equipped kitchenettes. The hotel is

well placed for Santa Monica's many attractions, not least the beach.

‡ □ ▭ ▨ ⚘ ⚑

Sheraton-Grande ▥

333 S Figueroa St., Los Angeles 90071 ☎ *(213) 617-1133, (800) 325-3535. Map 7D9* **IIII** 470 units **▦ ▭ ▭ AE CB ▢ ▢ VISA**

Location: Adjoining the Harbor Freeway near 3rd St. Among the newest (1982) of downtown LA's grand hotels may also be the grandest of them. The amazing mass of glass that is its front elevation hides not only a soaring atrium lobby and luxury rooms, but a splendid movie theater (the first new one in downtown in four decades) and several fine restaurants (particularly **Ravel**). The emphasis throughout is on personal service, with a butler for each story and multilingual concierges. Subtly decorated guest rooms are tranquil retreats; 65 of them are suites.

‡ □ ▭ ▨ ⚘ ◁ ≈ ≛ ♈ ♫ ≱

⚘ Other Sheratons:
Miramar-Sheraton (☎ *(213) 394-3731* **IIII**), facing beach at foot of Wilshire Blvd.; **Sheraton Plaza-La Reina** (☎ *(213) 642-1111* **IIII** to **IIII**), a dramatic 1981 tower near LAX; **Sheraton-Town House** (☎ *(213) 382-7171* **IIII**), a stately, comfortably old-fashioned 1929 tower in Mid-Wilshire; **Sheraton-Universal** (☎ *(818) 980-1212* **IIII**), at Universal Studios, Universal City. For central information ☎ (800) 325-3535.

Sportsmen's Lodge

12825 Ventura Blvd., North Hollywood 91604 ☎ *(818) 769-4700. Map 2B2* **III** 196 units **▦ ▭ ▭ AE CB ▢ ▢ VISA**

Location: One mile s of US-101 Coldwater Canyon exit. Almost the countryside in the city; greenery, waterfall and ponds around a charming, moderately priced hotel. About 20mins n of downtown, and supremely convenient for the Valley, Universal City, Beverly Hills and Burbank Airport. A good restaurant and a coffee shop are attached.

≛ ≈ ♈ ‡ □ ▭ ▨ ♈ ♫

Sunset Marquis Hotel & Villas

1200 N Alta Loma Rd., West Hollywood 90069 ☎ *(213) 657-1333. Map 5B4* **IIII** 120 units **▦ ▭ ▭ AE CB ▢ ▢ VISA**

Location: Half a block s of Sunset Blvd. An intimate and fashionable hotel popular with visiting entertainers; Mick Jagger has been known to stay here. All you would expect of an upscale hotel conveniently placed for Hollywood nightclubs, theaters, restaurants and shops. Most suites have equipped kitchens.

🏠 🚗 ♨ ♥ ☎ □ 🖻 ⚡ 🍴 ♪

Westin Bonaventure 🏨 🏛

404 S Figueroa St., Los Angeles 90071 ☎ (213) 624-1000, (800) 228-3000. Map 7D8 ▦▦ 1,474 units

🖩 🖻 🚗 AE CB ⚡ ⊡ VISA

Location: Downtown at 5th St. Five clustered cylinders sheathed in glass look like a 35-story, multi-stage rocket waiting for its nose cone. Dating from 1976, John Portman's building symbolizes Los Angeles perfectly as a city of the future. The medium-sized rooms, aside from having nonparallel side-walls and slightly curved window walls, are conventional in design and decor. The 6-story lobby is striking: Portman used cast concrete to achieve such astonishing effects as miniature cocktail lounges cantilevered into space and called, appropriately, cocktail pods. Six levels of shops and several interesting restaurants rim the walls (see *LA Shopping*).

♨ ♿ □ 🖻 ﴾ 🚗 🏊 ♨ ☎ ♪ ♥ 🈂

Westwood Marquis 🏨

930 Hilgard Ave., Los Angeles 90024 ☎ (213) 208-8765, (800) 352-7454. Map 4D2 ▦▦ 258 units

🖩 🖻 🚗 AE CB ⚡ ⊡ VISA

Location: In Westwood village, adjoining UCLA campus to the e. This is an excellent example of something Los Angeles seems to do particularly well: a modern tower filled with rooms evoking the past. All suites, the

Westwood is in every sense a luxury hotel. Furnishings are antique, eclectic as to period and style, but reliably comfortable and tasteful. Public rooms are sunny and cheerful. The pool and surrounding garden are pleasantly private. High tea and Sunday brunch are popular.

🏠 ♨ ♿ □ 🖻 ﴾ 🚗 🏊 ♨

Westwood Plaza (Holiday Inn)

10740 Wilshire Blvd., Los Angeles 90024 ☎ (213) 475-8711, (800) 238-8000. Map 4D2 ▦▦ 300 units

🖩 🖻 🚗 AE CB ⚡ ⊡ VISA

Location: e of Westwood Blvd. A modern 19-story tower, the hotel is set apart from standard Holiday Inns by a number of grace notes. Guest rooms are fairly spacious, with well-appointed, modern bathrooms. The largely European staff offers concierge and other extra services.

♨ ♿ □ 🖻 🛇 ﴾ 🚗 🏊 ☎ ♪

✑ **Holiday Inns**

All the hotels in this reliable chain can be expected to have comfortable, conventionally modern rooms of very similar decor. Those listed below are in useful locations for tourists. ☎ (213) 688-7313 for central reservations for these and eight other Holiday Inns in the greater LA area, plus eight in Orange County.

Holiday Inn-Convention Center (Los Angeles) (☎ (213) 748-1291 ▦▦ *to* ▦▦), downtown; **Holiday Inn-Convention Center (Pasadena)** (☎ (213) 449-4000 ▦▦), in downtown Pasadena; **Holiday Inn-Downtown** (☎ (213) 628-5242 ▦▦), downtown; **Holiday Inn-Los Angeles International Airport** (☎ (213) 649-5151 ▦▦), near LAX entrance.

Where to eat

The amazing range of cuisines, along with top-quality ingredients and boundless enthusiasm for experiment, make Los Angeles a strong contender for the title Culinary Capital of the United States and, some would argue, the World. And if it isn't the best, it is certainly the most interesting. This is scarcely surprising, given a population that hails from the four corners of the globe, loves food and the dining experience, and has the wherewithal to pay for it. None of which is to say that the food is universally good. For every restaurant of note there are dozens that can disappoint. Quality is not always determined by the size of the check, just most of the time, and it is remarkably easy for two people to spend $100 and more for dinner with wine. Still, the better chain restaurants and fast-food joints succeed in satisfying most people for under $20 for two. If Los Angeles is short of anything it is distinctive, small, moderately priced restaurants.

One heady complication in choosing among famous places is stargazing. If the probable presence of movie celebrities and other glitterati is a factor, remember that movie stardom does not necessarily confer a great palate. Put another way, not all of the stars' favorite haunts serve great food, and not all great restaurants are haunted by stars. Furthermore, today's hottest spot could be stone cold tomorrow. On average, scores of restaurants open or change hands each year, and two-thirds of new restaurants fail within the second year. Angelenos are frequently seduced by novelty, sometimes with spectacular consequences. But for the visitor, the tried, tested and consistent may be a better bet than the latest gimmicky fashion.

With or without famous fashionable faces, the range is dazzling. Perhaps the most novel experience awaiting visitors is home-grown California cuisine. The underlying characteristic is the use of fresh, in-season ingredients lightly cooked. If this sounds suspiciously like *nouvelle cuisine*, it is no mistake. Many of the techniques find their antecedents in French cooking. But the ingredients — and especially the combinations of ingredients — are peculiarly Californian. And such is the eclecticism of Los Angeles chefs that they feel free to draw upon any influences that take their fancy, be they Japanese, Chinese, Mexican, Italian, Thai or whatever. There are many unprecedented results; from *la nueva cocina mexicana*, with Mexican ingredients and French techniques, to *nouvelle* Chinese, mixing ingredients and techniques from East and West. The most recently consummated marriage is between French and Japanese foods. If Los Angeles hasn't got it they ship it in.

In addition to the innovators, there are many who adhere to ethnic and national culinary traditions. There are excellent French, Italian and Mexican restaurants; good Chinese, Thai, Korean, Vietnamese and Jewish restaurants; and greater Los Angeles has more Japanese *sushi* bars than McDonald's outlets.

Serious restaurants often announce their choice of dishes not on a printed menu but posted on a blackboard or recited by the waiter. Waiters (and diners) in really serious restaurants often have to be able to memorize the equivalent of a three-act play. One likely explanation is that restaurants base menus on the best produce available on a given day. Another is the seemingly tireless quest for novelty.

Connoisseurs of that other major southern California genre, fast food, will not be disappointed. Born out of the hamburger drive-in and multiplied to include fried chicken, fish and chips, *tacos*, pizza and barbecue, they are legion. Franchised fast-food joints are amusingly easy to spot. They have vast expanses of window glass, eye-catching signs, and roof-lines somewhere between mansard and Mayan.

The geography of outstanding food is more predictable. The Wilshire axis serves well, along with West Hollywood-Beverly Hills, where there is a dense concentration of famous places (the gastronomic heart of Los Angeles beats near the intersection of La Cienega Blvd. and Melrose Ave.). But other hallowed names are downtown and in Santa Monica, Wilshire itself has some very good restaurants, and most districts can claim more than one establishment worth the drive.

Parking is a consistent, expensive problem. Most of the better restaurants have a valet parking system. Many of the cheaper places have no parking at all except on the street. Reservations are mandatory, unless noted otherwise. Visitors should also note that Angelenos eat early by European or New York standards; it can be difficult to order food after 10pm.

Restaurants classified by area

Downtown to Mid-Wilshire
Bernard's ⅢⅢ
Bicycle Shop Café Ⅲ to Ⅲ
Cassis Ⅲ to ⅢⅢ
Chan Dara Ⅲ to Ⅲ
City Restaurant ⅢⅢ to Ⅲ
Lawry's California Center Ⅲ
The Original Pantry Café Ⅲ to Ⅲ
Pacific Dining Car Ⅲ to Ⅲ
Rex, Il Ristorante ⅢⅢ
Downtown/Chinatown
Mon Kee Live Fish Sea Food Ⅲ to Ⅲ
Downtown/Little Tokyo
Horikawa ⅢⅢ
Oomasa Ⅲ to Ⅲ
A Thousand Cranes ⅢⅢ
Yagura Ichiban Ⅲ to ⅢⅢ
Hollywood/West
Hollywood/Beverly Hills
Antonio's Ⅲ
Benihana of Tokyo Ⅲ to ⅢⅢ
The Bistro ⅢⅢ
The Border Grill ⅢⅢ
Chan Dara Ⅲ to Ⅲ
Chez Hélène Ⅲ
Chianti Cucina ⅢⅢ to ⅢⅢ
Citrus ⅢⅢ
Le Dôme ⅢⅢ
L'Ermitage ⅢⅢ
Ginger Man Ⅲ to ⅢⅢ
Gitanjali Ⅲ to ⅢⅢ
Hampton's Ⅲ
Lawry's The Prime Rib Ⅲ
Ma Maison ⅢⅢ
The Mandarin Ⅲ to Ⅲ
Matsuhisa Ⅲ to ⅢⅢ
Moustache Café Ⅲ to ⅢⅢ
Musso & Frank Grill Ⅲ to ⅢⅢ
L'Orangerie ⅢⅢ

Le St Germain ⅢⅢ
La Scala ⅢⅢ to ⅢⅢ
Spago ⅢⅢ
La Toque ⅢⅢ
Trumps ⅢⅢ
West LA/Westwood/Brentwood
Harry's Bar and American Grill Ⅲ to ⅢⅢ
Homer & Edy's Bistro Ⅲ
Lew Mitchell's Orient Express ⅢⅢ to ⅢⅢ
Peppone ⅢⅢ
Studio Grill ⅢⅢ
Toledo Restaurant ⅢⅢ
Coastal
Belle-Vue Ⅲ
Chinois on Main ⅢⅢ
Famous Enterprise Fish Co. Ⅲ to Ⅲ
Michael's ⅢⅢ
Pioneer Boulangerie Ⅲ
Sabroso Ⅲ
St Estephe ⅢⅢ to ⅢⅢ
72 Market Street ⅢⅢ
Valentino ⅢⅢ
West Beach Café ⅢⅢ
Valleys
Benihana of Tokyo Ⅲ to ⅢⅢ
Café Jacoulet ⅢⅢ
The Chronicle ⅢⅢ to ⅢⅢ
Dragon Regency Ⅲ
L'Express (1) Ⅲ to ⅢⅢ
L'Express (2) Ⅲ to Ⅲ
Fragrant Vegetable Ⅲ to Ⅲ
Hampton's Ⅲ
Holly Street Bar and Grill Ⅲ to Ⅲ
Jerry's Famous Deli Ⅲ to Ⅲ
Jitlada Ⅲ
Katsu Ⅲ to ⅢⅢ
Wonder Seafood Ⅲ to Ⅲ

Antonio's
7472 Melrose Ave., LA ☎ (213) 655-0480. Map 5C5 Ⅲ ☐ ♈
⇔ by valet Ⅲ ⅢⅢ Ⅲ Open Tues-Fri noon-2.30pm, 5-11pm, Sat-Sun 5-11pm. Closed major hols.
Innovations at newer places have made the once radical Antonio's look positively traditional. But among regular dishes at this renowned restaurant, the *tamales* are worth a drive, and special goodies are offered in the list of daily specials, all drawn from the area around Mexico City. The bar serves excellent margaritas.
Specialties: *Mole negro Oaxaqueno, pollo en pipian, ropa vieja, albondigon rebozado.*

Belle-Vue
101 Santa Monica Blvd., Santa Monica ☎ (213) 393-2843. Map 2C1 Ⅲ ☐ ▩ Ⅲ Ⅲ Ⅲ Ⅲ Open 11.30am-2pm, 6-10pm.
A cozy neighborhood restaurant in a refurbished landmark building stuffed

with antiques chosen to produce a country French atmosphere. Its long menu blends local dishes and pure French classics with intelligence. The Fri-only *bouillabaisse* is something of a legend. **Specialties:** *Squid, stuffed crab, sea bass Grenobloise, calves' brains.*

Benihana of Tokyo
38 N La Cienega Blvd. ☎ (213) 655-7311, map 5E4, and 16226 Ventura Blvd., Encino ☎ (818) 788-7121, map 2B1 Ⅲ to ⅢⅢ ☐
▩ ♈ ⇔ by valet Ⅲ ⅢⅢ Ⅲ Ⅲ
Ⅲ Open Mon-Thurs 11.30am-2pm, 5.30-10pm, Fri 11.30am-2pm, 5.30-11pm, Sat 5.30-11pm, Sun 4.30-10pm.
The decor at this popular chain "Japanese" restaurant is very Japanese; the food isn't. However, the Westernized hybrids on offer are good, and the *teppan* chefs provide one-man floor shows as they work with lightning speed and skill at the individual grills set inside

horseshoe-shaped tables. With a few Japanese beers or jars of warm sake, it's lots of fun. *Specialties: Hitachi steak, lobster and chicken.*

Bernard's
515 S Olive St., LA ☎ *(213) 624-0183. Map 7D9* 📞 ▭ 🔜
➡ *by valet* 🅰 🆑 💿 🔘 🆅 *Open Mon-Thurs 11.30am-1.45pm, 6-10pm, Fri 11.30am-1.45pm, 6-11pm, Sat 6-11pm.*

This grand old institution in the **Biltmore Hotel** (see *LA Hotels*) has kept its reputation as a fine French restaurant. Dim lights, plush furnishings and a harpist make the room as romantic as one could hope. The staff is impeccably attentive. The emphasis is on fish and inventive seasonings. *Specialties: Sole in lobster sauce, sea bass with ginger and lime.*

Bicycle Shop Café ♣
12217 Wilshire Blvd., LA ☎ *(213) 826-7831. Map 4D1* 📞 *to* 📞 ▭
🔘 🆅 *Open Mon-Fri 7am-midnight, Sat-Sun 7am-1am. Closed Jan 1, Thanksgiving, Dec 25.*

A cloud of bicycles hangs from the ceiling to justify the name of a restaurant that is a happy, noisy hangout for neighborhood regulars. Omelets, sandwiches and crepes are mainstays, but the menu ranges into conventional entrées. *Specialties: Terrine of sweetbreads, Pacific red snapper in lemon sauce, El Steak Bravo.*

The Bistro
246 N Canon Dr., Beverly Hills ☎ *(213) 273-5633. Map 4C3* 📞 ▭
🔜 ⬟ ➡ *by valet* 🅰 🆑 💿 🔘 🆅 *Open Mon-Fri noon-3pm, 6-11pm, Sat 6-11pm.*

One of the summits of Beverly Hills chic is usually crowded with movie people. Although star-watching counts for much here, the French and continental menu has more ups than downs. Daily blackboard specials are of particular interest. The mirrored downstairs room is quite small but still one of the most handsome around. *Specialties: Brains beurre noir, chicken grandmère.*

The Border Grill
7407½ Melrose Ave., LA ☎ *(213) 938-2155. Map 5C5* 📞 ▭ 🅰 💿
🆅 *Open Mon-Sat 11.45am-11.45pm, Sun noon-11.45pm.*

The kitchen is one of the ablest interpreters of *la nueva cocina mexicana*, but the dining room is a particular LA type: small and bare, full of local heavyweights who come in their grubbies to spend considerable money on unusual food. *Specialties: Grilled turkey, sabana (very thin steak marinated in lime juice, served with scallions and jalapeno peppers).*

Café Jacoulet
91 N Raymond Ave., Pasadena ☎ *(818) 796-2233. Map 2B3* 📞 ▭
🔜 💿 🔘 🆅 *Open for lunch Mon-Fri 11.30am-2.30pm, Sat noon-3pm; for dinner Mon-Thurs 6-9.30pm, Fri-Sat 6pm-midnight, Sun 5.30-9.30pm.*

A light, airy atmosphere matches a light, airy menu compounded from diverse sources. Jacoulet was a French painter much influenced by Japan; the food reflects both of those cuisines plus California and Italy. *Specialties: Duck with raspberry sauce, lobster ravioli with spinach pasta, fresh salmon poêle with fresh spinach sauce.*

Cassis
8450 3rd St., LA ☎ *(213) 653-1079. Map 5C4* 📞 *to* 📞 ▭ 🔜 🔜 ➡ *by valet* 🅰 🆑 💿 🔘 🆅 *Open Mon-Fri 10.30am-3pm, 6-11pm, Sat 6-11pm.*

This is a charming, romantic French restaurant. The structural interior is Art Deco; the decoration is an extension of the garden in the form of potted plants and cut flowers. A luncheon clientele anchored by neighborhood television and recording studio employees has the best of the atmosphere, but dinner patrons get the best of the menu. *Specialties: Duck in peppercorn sauce, rack of lamb in honey-vinegar sauce.*

Chan Dara
1511 N Cahuenga Blvd., Hollywood ☎ *(213) 464-8585, map 2B2, and 310 N Larchmont Blvd., Hancock Park* ☎ *(213) 467-1052, map 6C6* 📞 *to* 📞 ▭ ⬟ ➡ 🅰 💿
🆅 *Open Mon-Fri 11am-11pm, Sat-Sun 5-11pm.*

Long-established (by Los Angeles standards) and popular, Chan Dara's Thai cuisine is extremely good and consistently so. Both locations can be crowded, so expect a wait. *Specialties: Barbecued chicken, sausage with lime and ginger, satay.*

Chez Hélène ♣
267 S Beverly Dr., Beverly Hills ☎ *(213) 276-1558. Map 4D3* 📞 ▭
🔜 🍴 ➡ 🅰 💿 🔘 🆅 *Open Tues-Sat noon-3pm, 6.30-10pm, Sun 6.30-10pm.*

Chez Hélène has long since been discovered as a place that offers

75

excellent value. In fact the discovery is so complete that reservations are virtually mandatory at this unpretentious but solid French restaurant. **Specialties:** *Chicken Chez Hélène, lamb with provençale herbs, bouillabaisse.*

Chianti Cucina

7383 Melrose Ave., LA ☎ *(213) 653-8333. Map 5C5* ▥▥ *to* ▥▥ ▭ ⬛ ⬛ *Chianti open nightly 5-11pm; Cucina open Mon-Sat 11.30am-midnight, Sun 5pm-midnight.*

Chianti and Cucina are two rooms on either side of one Tuscan kitchen. Chianti is the quieter, darker and more expensive side. The food in both is the same, and at the head of the city's list of Italian restaurants. The menu changes every day or two to reflect what is freshest in the market.

Chinois on Main

2709 Main St., Santa Monica ☎ *(213) 392-9025. Map 2C1* ▥▥ ⬛ ⬛ ⬛ ⬛ *Open Mon-Sat 6-11pm, Sun 5.30-10.30pm.*

Wolfgang Puck — the youthful wonder who invented and still runs **Spago** (q.v.) — has reinvented Chinese cooking by mixing Asian and French techniques and California ingredients and built a startlingly original room in which to serve the results. Amid riveting expanses of copper, marble, and what the proprietors call "screaming art," diners confront such as *chèvre*-stuffed bao, *sashimi*-like Spanish mackerel, and mandarin orange-flavored *crème brulée*. **Specialties:** *Sizzling catfish, Mongolian lamb.*

The Chronicle

897 Granite Dr., Pasadena ☎ *(818) 792-1179. Map 2B3* ▥▥ *to* ▥▥ ▭ ⬛ ⬛ ⬛ ⬛ ⬛ ⬛ *Open Mon-Thurs 11.30am-2.30pm, 5.30-10.30pm, Fri-Sat 11.30am-2.30pm, 5.30-11.30pm, Sun 5-10pm.*

The Chronicle is located in an old wood-frame house refurbished with frilly, flowery but unfussy turn-of-the-century decor. It offers continental menus with a certain soberness of style and a blackboard with long lists of daily specials led by such unusual fish as John Dory, grouper and pompano. Outstanding California wines. **Specialties:** *Fresh fish in orange sauce with hazelnuts, roast duckling au porto, chicken or veal Oscar.*

Citrus

6703 Melrose Ave., Hollywood ☎ *(213) 857-0034. Map 6C5* ▥▥ *to* ▥▥ ⬛ ▭ ▭ ☕ ⬛ *by valet* ⬛ ⬛ ⬛ *Open Mon-Sat noon-3pm, 6.30-11pm.*

Many hold Citrus, owned and run by Michel Richard, LA's premier *pâtissier*, among the city's top California/French restaurants. Its clean chic lines are enlivened by a fashionable clientele, a kitchen visible through a glass wall, and exceptionally good *nouvelle* bistro food. The leafy patio is generally less crowded than the main dining room. **Specialties:** *Scallops with maui onions, lamb with ravioli, pear sorbet.*

City Restaurant

180 S La Brea Ave., LA ☎ *(213) 938-2155. Map 5C5* ▥▥ *to* ▥▥ ▭ ⬛ ⬛ ⬛ *Open Mon-Sat 11.45am-2pm, 5.45-11.45pm, Sun 5-11pm.*

By Susan Feniger and Mary Sue Milliken (also the owner-chefs of **The Border Grill**, q.v.), City's menu is what one dazzled admirer calls "off-the-wall eclectic." Not everyone is dazzled, but, if not exactly like anything else, the food is earthy and vital. Northwest razor clams come with Mexican sauces; flank steaks are tandoori baked; etc. Preparations are impeccable, and the puddings are exceptional. The atmosphere, meanwhile, is stark high tech, or very close to it. The clientele is as off-the-wall as the food. **Specialties:** *Poona pancake, vegetable vermicelli.*

Le Dôme △

8720 Sunset Blvd., LA ☎ *(213) 659-6919. Map 5B4* ▥▥ ▭ ⬛ ⬛ *by valet* ⬛ ⬛ ⬛ *Open Mon-Fri noon-1am, Sat 6pm-1am.*

Le Dôme has begun to cast off its reputation as a trendy hangout for recording stars in favor of status as a serious restaurant. The original clientele still comes around. The original decor, a mishmash of Art Deco, chrome, velvet, and Chinese pottery, also survives. As the clientele has enlarged without being revolutionized, so has the menu. **Specialties:** *Grilled shark with anchovy butter, boudin noir.*

Dragon Regency

120 S Atlantic Blvd., Monterey Park ☎ *(818) 282-1089. Map 2C3* ▥▥ ▭ ⬛ ⬛

Yet more evidence of Monterey Park's emergence as a center of Chinese culinary excellence. Neither the shopping mall location nor the decor are anything special. But the food, especially the seafood, is as good as any Chinese fare available in LA. **Specialties:** *Double pleasure sole, pan-fried crab, salt fried shrimp.*

L'Ermitage
730 N La Cienega Blvd., LA
☎ (213) 652-5840. Map 5C4 ⫿⫿⫿⫿ ▭
🍴 🚗 by valet AE CB 🔘 🔘 VISA
Open Mon-Sat 6.30-10.30pm.
The late proprietor, Jean Bertranou, is widely credited with starting gastronomy on its dizzying climb to excellence in Los Angeles. Always formal to formidable in atmosphere and decor, L'Ermitage has lost some of the experimental edge Bertranou maintained in its menu, but there is still an insistence on quality ingredients and masterful preparation. Reservations are required well in advance. *Specialties: Pigeon pâté with green peppercorns, squab with spinach and blackcurrant sauce.*

L'Express
14910 Ventura Blvd., Sherman Oaks ☎ (818) 990-8683, map 2B1 and 3575 Cahuenga Blvd., Studio City ☎ (213) 876-3778, map 2B2 ⫿⫿⫿ to ⫿⫿⫿⫿ ▭ 🍷 🚗 by valet AE 🔘 VISA Open 7am-2am.
Fairly standard brasserie food in exceptional settings designed by Johannes van Tilburg. The clientele is a mix of local, young professional, and entertainment industry, who enjoy the chic ambience and the piped rock music. *Specialties: Duck salad, croque monsieur, pizza.*

Famous Enterprise Fish Co.
174 Kinney St., Santa Monica
☎ (213) 392-8366. Map 2C1 ⫿▭ to ⫿⫿▭ 🍴 🍷 AE 🔘 VISA Open Sun-Thurs 11.30am-10pm, Fri-Sat 11.30am-11pm.
Grilled fresh fish is the basic dish in a big, comfortable converted warehouse where formality is forbidden. The cooking is no fancier than the decor, but anything listed on the blackboard is indeed fresh. Not only is it not overcooked, it will be brought undercooked on request. *Specialties: Snapper, shark and other freshly caught fish, Alaskan king crab.*

Fragrant Vegetable
108 N Garfield Ave., Monterey Park ☎ (818) 280-4215. Map 2C3 ⫿▭ to ⫿⫿▭ ▭ 🍴 AE 🔘 VISA Open Mon-Thurs 11am-9.30pm, Fri-Sun 11am-10pm.
The Fragrant Vegetable is sited in an otherwise undistinguished shopping mall in what's fast becoming known as Little Taiwan. It offers vegetarian food with a difference, drawing on centuries of Chinese magic with vegetables, fungi and bean curds to produce flavor-full dishes, many of them artfully resembling meat or fish.

The decor is tasteful and restrained and the service friendly, with patient waiters happy to explain dishes to the uninitiated. *Specialties: Eight precious assorted appetizer, Buddha's cushions, mixed mushrooms and water chestnuts.*

Ginger Man
369 N Bedford Dr., Beverly Hills ☎ (213) 273-7585. Map 4C3 ⫿⫿▭ to ⫿⫿⫿⫿ ▭ 🚗 by valet AE 🔘 VISA Open Mon-Sat 11.30am-3pm, 5.30pm-2am (supper only after 10.30pm), Sun 11am-3pm, 4-11pm.
Ginger Man offers its trendy clientele an unaffected Californian menu of fresh salads and hamburgers, plus some pleasant surprises. Dinner reservations are always required, lunch reservations advised. Sun afternoons are devoted to Dixieland by the Beverly Hills Unlisted Jazz Band, with George Segal and other celebrities in the chairs.

Gitanjali ✿
414 N La Cienega Blvd., LA
☎ (213) 657-2117. Map 5C4 ⫿⫿▭ to ⫿⫿⫿⫿ ▭ 🚗 AE 🔘 🔘 VISA Open Mon-Thurs 6-10.30pm, Fri-Sat 6-11pm, Sun 5.30-10.30pm. Closed Thanksgiving, Dec 24-25, 31.
The decor sketches a mood of northern India in a handsome room. The cooking is meticulous and the menu includes vegetarian dishes. Spicy fires range from faint glow to conflagration. *Specialties: Lamb Kathmandu, tandoori chicken, tikka grills.*

Hampton's
4301 Riverside Dr., Toluca Lake
☎ (818) 845-3009, map 2B2, and 1342 N Highland Ave., Hollywood ☎ (213) 469-1090, map 5B5 ⫿▭ ▭ 🍷 🚗 by valet 🔘 VISA Open Sun-Thurs 11am-10pm, Fri-Sat 11am-11pm.
Hampton's is said by many to serve the finest burgers in LA. Certainly they're fresh, cooked precisely to order, and come with all imaginable, and some unimaginable, toppings. There's also a help-yourself fresh salad bar. *Specialty: Hamburgers.*

Harry's Bar and American Grill ✿
2020 Ave. of the Stars (lower level, ABC Entertainment Center), LA ☎ (213) 277-2333. Map 4D2 ⫿▭ to ⫿⫿⫿⫿ ▭ 🍷 AE 🔘 VISA Open Mon-Sat 11.30am-11.30pm, Sun 4.45-10.30pm. Closed Jan 1, Labor Day, Dec 25.
The staff says this Harry's is a precise copy of the one in Florence. A connoisseur swears it feels more like

the one in Venice. Either way, unornamented dark wood, creamy white plaster and good paintings make an elegant setting for some proper Florentine cookery.

Specialties: *Paglia e fieno, vermicelli all'Amatriciana, veal tonnato.*

Holly Street Bar and Grill
175 East Holly St., Pasadena
☎ *(818) 440-1421. Map 2B3 ▯ to*
▯▯▯ ▭ ⅄ ▰ AE CB ▢ ▢ VISA
Open Mon-Sat 11am-12.20am.
Relaxing pastel decorations, a pleasant airy space adjoining a courtyard, attentive service and well-prepared food all bode well for this recently opened restaurant. Ideally located for lunch or dinner before or after a visit to the Norton Simon Museum. **Specialty:** *Fettucine alfredo with mushrooms, spicy angel hair with shrimp, chorizo, diced tomato, black beans and white wine.*

Homer & Edy's Bistro
2839 S Robertson Blvd., LA
☎ *(213) 559-5102. Map 5E4 ▯▯▯ ⦿*
▰ AE CB ▢ ▢ VISA *Open Tues-Fri 11.30am-3pm, 6-11pm, Sat 6-11pm, Sun 5-11pm.*
Homer & Edy's is so far off the beaten track that it has one of the rarest gifts in Los Angeles: free parking. It is even farther away from New Orleans, but hear the piano player and smell the food, and there is no room for doubt that this restaurant in a converted one-time residence is the real thing.
Specialties: *Gumbo, oysters Bienville, southern fried frogs' legs.*

Horikawa
111 S San Pedro St., LA ☎ *(213) 680-9355. Map 7E8 ▯▯▯ ▭ ▰*
▰ *by valet* AE CB ▢ ▢ ▢ *Open Mon-Thurs 11.30am-2pm, 5.30-11.30pm, Fri 11.30am-2pm, 5.30-11pm, Sat 5-11pm, Sun 5-10pm.*
This all-purpose Japanese restaurant has one of the largest *sushi* bars in the city, a comparable *teppan* section, and a regular dining room. All three are well regarded. **Specialties:** *In the teppan section, where chefs give amazing tableside displays of cutting and chopping as part of the entertainment: lobster and filet mignon. In the dining room: iso-yaki, shabu-shabu.*

Jerry's Famous Deli
12655 Ventura Blvd., Studio City
☎ *(818) 980-4245. Map 2B2 ▯▯▯ to*
▯▯▯ ▭ ⅄ ▰ AE CB ▢ *Open 24hrs.*
Like all LA delis, Jerry's staples, from pastrami on rye to cheesecake, seem to fall short of the same dishes served

up in New York; this in spite of the fact that many of the ingredients here are imported from there. Maybe they lose something on the journey. Nevertheless, quality at Jerry's is high, service is brisk and helpful, and both the Valley clientele and the artworks covering the walls are stimulating.
Specialties: *Over-stuffed sandwiches, salads.*

Jitlada
11622 Ventura Blvd., Studio City
☎ *(818) 506-9355. Map 2B2 ▯▯▯ ▭*
⅄ ▢ ▢ *Open Tues-Thurs 11am-10pm, Fri-Sat 11am-11pm, Sun 4-11pm.*
Anyone who claims that the Thai food at this unpretentious restaurant in the Valley is superb hasn't been to Bangkok. Probably they're just reflecting the fact that Thai is the hottest (figuratively and literally) new fad in Los Angeles. Still, it is pretty good, and ranks highly among the rapidly increasing number of Thai restaurants on the West Coast. Most of the authentic ingredients appear to be on hand, although a few are obviously missing, service is friendly, prices reasonable, and there's excellent imported Thai beer.
Specialties: *Stuffed chicken wings, mee krob, yam yai.*

Katsu
1972 N Hillhurst Ave., Los Feliz
☎ *(213) 665-1891. Map 6B7 ▯▯▯ to*
▯▯▯ ▭ ▰ ⅄ ▰ *by valet* AE CB ▢
▢ VISA *Open Mon-Fri noon-2pm, 6-10pm, Sat 6-10pm.*
Minimalist black and white decor, avant garde tableware plus what may be the best *sushi* in Los Angeles. The dishes, employing only the freshest seafood, are a visual as much as a culinary delight. Arrive early or expect to wait. Reservations a must for tables. No reservations accepted for sushi bar. **Specialty:** *Sushi.*

Lawry's California Center
570 W Ave. 26, LA ☎ *(213) 224-6850, (213) 224-5783. Map 7C10 ▯▯▯ ▭ ▰▰ ⬛ ⬛ ⅄ ⑂ ▰ AE*
▢ *Open daily 11am-3pm all year, May-Oct Mon-Fri 5-10pm, Sat-Sun 4-9pm. Call for holiday schedules. Also ✗ of food plant Mon-Fri 11.30am, 1.30pm, 2.30pm.*
Shops and a multi-faceted restaurant that is mostly garden and patio adjoin Lawry's food-processing and packaging plant out among the warehouses E of Dodger Stadium. The restaurant menu is mostly California-Mexican and the food is consistently good.

Lawry's The Prime Rib
55 N La Cienega Blvd., Beverly Hills ☎ *(213) 652-2827. Map 5C4* ⅢⅢ ▭ ▯ ⬚ *AE* ⬚ *VISA Open Mon-Thurs 5-11pm, Fri-Sat 5pm-midnight, Sun 3-11pm.*
The menu pretty much repeats the name of the place. The side dishes are Yorkshire pudding and salad. Otherwise, prime rib it is, and in such quantities that the staff takes it in its stride each year when the opposing Rose Bowl football teams come in and try to eat everything but the walls. No reservations are accepted.

Lew Mitchell's Orient Express
5400 Wilshire Blvd., LA ☎ *(213) 935-6000. Map 5D5* ⅢⅢto ⅢⅢ ▭ ▯ 🔥 ⬚ ⬚ *VISA Open Mon-Fri 11.30am-3pm, daily 6-11pm or later.*
The dark rose and charcoal gray interior of this great example of Los Angeles eclectic has severe lines and rich textures that make it look as if a contemporary Italian had designed it. The huge, happily uncrowded room makes a perfect backdrop for a collection of fine Chinese art. The menu, created by Mitchell's Chinese wife, reverses the East-West proportions. It is nearly all traditional Hunanese and Szechuan with a small but thoughtful selection of Western dishes. ***Specialties:*** *Crab cake, whole rock cod, beef hunan.*

Ma Maison
8555 Beverly Blvd. (Ma Maison Sofitel Hotel), Mid-Wilshire ☎ *(213) 655-1991. Map 5C4* ⅢⅢ ▭ ▯ 🔥 *by valet AE CB ⬚ ⬚ VISA*
Many credit Patrick Terrail and his original Ma Maison on Melrose Ave. (1973-85) with a central match-making role in LA's love affair with chic restaurants. The new setting is Hollywood French, with a garden feel and sliding glass roof. It's probably too early to rate the food, although initial reaction has been guarded. ***Specialties:*** *Smoked salmon, warm lobster salad, sautéed bass.*

The Mandarin
430 N Camden Dr., Beverly Hills ☎ *(213) 272-0267. Map 4D3* ⅢⅢ to ⅢⅢ ▭ 🔥 🔥 *AE CB ⬚ ⬚ VISA Open Mon-Fri noon-11pm, Sat 5-11pm, Sun 5-10.30pm.*
A clone of Cecelia Chiang's excellent San Francisco temple of imperial Chinese gastronomy. It is the equal of its forerunner in opulence of decor and breadth of menu. The Peking duck must be ordered in advance. ***Specialties:*** *Prawns Szechuan, Peking duck, noodles.*

Matsuhisa
129 N La Cienega Blvd., West Hollywood ☎ *(213) 659-9639. Map 5C4* ⅢⅢ to ⅢⅢ ▭ 🔥 *AE ⬚ ⬚ VISA Open Mon-Fri 11.45am-2.30pm, 5.45-10.30pm, Sat-Sun 5.45-10.30pm.*
Another contender for the title "best *sushi* bar in town," Matsuhisa is small, nothing special to look at, and the service can be erratic. However, the seafood dishes, both cold and hot, are excellent. Reservations are essential. ***Specialties:*** *Sushi rolls, bonito.*

Michael's
1147 3rd St., Santa Monica ☎ *(213) 451-0843. Map 2C1* ⅢⅢ ▭ 🔥 *AE CB ⬚ ⬚ VISA Open Tues-Fri noon-2pm, 6.30-10pm, Sat-Sun 10.30am-2pm, 6.30-10pm. Closed Jan 2, Dec 24.*
One of the most ambitious and highest-priced restaurants in the Los Angeles basin, Michael's is generally French but particularly Californian. One of the motivations is a quest by owner Michael McCarty for perfect ingredients arrayed in striking new combinations. The spectacular wine list is revised twice weekly. As usual among perfectionists, the failures are almost as dramatic as the successes. Most of the tables are outdoors in a delightful garden. ***Specialties:*** *Poulet grillé — cresson nature et beurre d'estragon, pigeon grillé sur foie gras de canard au vinaigre de framboise, faux-filet de veau — citron caramelisé.*

Mon Kee Live Fish Sea Food 🍴 ♠
679 N Spring St., LA ☎ *(213) 628-6717, (213) 628-1090. Map 7D9* ⅢⅢ to ⅢⅢ ▭ 🔥 ⬚ ⬚ *VISA Open 11.30am-10pm.*
The place is as bare and plain as only inexpensive Cantonese restaurants can be, but the claim of live fish is true. Tanks full of fish await the cooks, who work in the Hong Kong style. A few chicken, pork and beef dishes supplement five pages of fish on the menu. ***Specialties:*** *Bird's nest of grated potato with conch, squid, shrimp, scallops or rock cod, lobster or crab in gingery hoisin-style sauce.*

Moustache Café
8155 Melrose Ave., LA ☎ *(213) 651-2111. Map 5C4* ⅢⅢ to ⅢⅢ ▭ 🔥 ⬚ ⬚ *VISA Open Sun-Thurs 11.30am-midnight, Fri-Sat 11.30am-1am. Closed Jan 1, Thanksgiving, Dec 24-25.*
The place looks like a bistro: it has a café-style interior and a patio shielded

from the street by tenting. The food includes undistinguished bistro fare anchored by sandwiches and crepes, and ranges into fuller meals more typical of a brasserie. But the heart of Moustache is the clientele, which is pure Hollywood bent on a relaxed good time. *Specialties: Canard au Muscadet, daily meat and fish entrée, chocolate soufflé.*

Musso & Frank Grill
6667 Hollywood Blvd., Hollywood
☎ *(213) 467-7788, (213) 467-5123.*
Map 6B5 ▥ to ▥▥ ▢ ⟶ nearby
▣ ▣ ▣ ▣ *Open Mon-Fri 11am-10.45pm. Closed major hols.*

While actors and directors parade through ultra-chic spots in Beverly Hills, writers hang out in the worn, warm confines of an old-fashioned Hollywood joint that resembles a stage set of a New York bar and grill, where the guy in the next booth looks like Philip Marlowe, private eye, and the waiters look just slightly cynical. Atmosphere is the main event. (A second room with tables has slightly less of it, but is easier to get into.) The kitchen produces satisfying but not stylish food from a long, New York-style menu. *Specialties (one each day): Corned beef and cabbage, sauerbraten, chicken pot pie, braised short ribs of beef.*

Oomasa
350 E 1st St., LA ☎ *(213) 623-9048. Map 7D9 ▥ to ▥▥ ▢*
▤ ▣ ▣ *Open Tues-Sun 11.30am-10pm.*

Scores of *sushi* bars contend for top honors. Oomasa is one of the best and has an appropriate location on Japanese Village Plaza. The restaurant also serves dinners in booths at one side of the *sushi* bar. *Specialties: Sushi, sashimi, unikirage (sea urchin and jellyfish), unagi kabayaki (grilled freshwater eel with sweet sauce).*

L'Orangerie ⌂
903 N La Cienega Blvd., West Hollywood ☎ *(213) 652-9770. Map 5C4 ▥▥ ▢ ☞ ⓨ ⟶ by valet* ▣
▣ ▣ ▣ *Open 6-10pm.*

Hiding behind a stony facade, this temple of *nouvelle cuisine* manages to be at once beautiful, formal and welcoming. Service is splendid, and the French food can be among the best in Los Angeles, appreciably more distinctive and intense in flavor than typical *nouvelle. Specialties: Eggs in shells with caviar, grilled sea bass with fennel, veal medallions in cream and mustard, apple tart.*

The Original Pantry Café
877 S Figueroa St., LA ☎ *(213) 972-9279. Map 7D8 ▢ to ▢ ▢*
▰ *Open 24hrs.*

This big, plain barn of a place is worth knowing about for hearty breakfasts and nourishing if unimaginative main meals. No beer or wine, or other grace notes, and fast service is counted as good service. *Specialties: Steak with hash browns, selection of daily specials.*

Pacific Dining Car ♺
1310 W 6th St., LA ☎ *(213) 483-6000. Map 7D8 ▥▥ to ▥▥▥*
☞ ⓨ ⟶ *by valet* ▣ ▣ *Open daily 24hrs.*

Every city claiming greatness should have a round-the-clock restaurant serving properly grilled meats and fish in an atmosphere that permits conspiracy without encouraging it. LA has this one dating back to 1921. Breakfast (*1-11am*), lunch (*11am-4pm*) and dinner (*4pm-1am*) menus all have a selection of steaks and other grills. Reservations advised at mealtimes. Incidentally, a small part of the premises is indeed a railroad dining car. The bar, in Stygian darkness, offers four whiskeys (The Glenlivet, Chivas Regal, Jack Daniels and Jim Beam) plus white liquor for the timid, and good California wines by the glass. *Specialties: Grilled beef, plus daily specials such as broiled rabbit, grilled sole.*

Peppone ⌂
11628 Barrington Ct., LA ☎ *(213) 476-7379. Map 2C1 ▥▥ ▢*
⟶ ▣ ▣ ▣ ▣ *Open Tues-Fri 11.30am-2.30pm, 5.30-11.30pm, Sat-Sun 5.30-11.30pm. Closed Sept 1-15, Thanksgiving, Dec 25.*

Frequently chosen as LA's best Italian restaurant, although critics believe it's been passed in recent years. Its owner-chef hopes guests will ignore the menu and give him instructions to extemporize, perhaps using one or two dishes from an encyclopedia-length list of daily specials. The style is southern, with subtle but unwavering enthusiasm for tomatoes and garlic. The room is dark, but not quite dark enough to hide the paintings of miserably weeping children, the only drawback. *Specialties: Fusili carbonara, green fettucine with anchovy and garlic sauce, sweetbreads Pompeii, calamari.*

Pioneer Boulangerie ♺
2012 Main St., Santa Monica
☎ *(213) 399-7771. Map 2C1 ▥▢ ▰*
▰ ⟶ ▣ ▣ *Open for breakfast*

8-11am, lunch and dinner 11am-9pm. Closed Jan 1, Dec 25.
First and foremost, this enterprise is a splendid bakery. Secondly, because baked-on-the-spot croissants, breads, cinnamon and other sweet rolls dominate and the espresso is rich, it is excellent for cafeteria breakfasts. The sunny patio is only an extra blessing. Thirdly, it is an inexpensive and hearty Basque dinner house with one seating nightly, Wed-Sun by reservation only.

Rex, Il Ristorante ⌂

617 S Olive St., LA ☎ (213) 627-2300. Map 7E8 ▥▥ ▭ ▪▬ ☒ Y
▬ by valet at dinner only ▣▣ ▣▣
▣ ▣▣ ▥▥ Open Mon-Fri noon-2pm, 7-10pm, Sat 7-10pm. Closed Sept 1-15.
The style is *nuova cucina*, the regional touches mostly Roman. Rex's decor announces that it is for serious eaters. Walls have paneling, chairs are plush, upholstered for long sitting. The center of an uncrowded room is given over to a display of food artful enough to go in a museum. The effect of all this is magnified by a gilded exterior. Reservations are required, often difficult for a single nightly seating. Up on the mezzanine there is an Art Deco bar and a tiny floor meant for cheek-to-cheek dancers. *Specialties: Terrine of duck with pistachios and small salad of cucumbers and duck hearts, fettucine with porcini (wild boletus mushrooms), baby red snapper in tomato sauce, grilled entrecôte and eggplant.*

Sabroso

1029 W Washington Blvd., Venice ☎ (213) 399-3832. Map 6E7 ▥▥ ▭
▬ Open Tues-Fri noon-2pm, 6-10pm, Sat-Sun 6-10pm.
There's a jukebox playing Mexican hits, cacti on the patio and an anarchic air. The fare is *nouvelle* Mexican and the menu, which changes often, is written up on a large blackboard. The food seldom disappoints. *Specialties: Cazuela ranchera, cactus salad, chocolate flan.*

St Estephe

2640 Sepulveda Blvd., Manhattan Beach ☎ (213) 545-1334. Map 2D2 ▥▥ to ▥▥ ▭ ▬ ▣▣ ▣▣ Open for lunch Mon-Fri 11am-2pm, for dinner Tues-Sat 6-10pm.
The name comes from an old bottle of Cos d'Estournel that dazzled the owners, but that is the most of the French inspiration. The cookery of the American southwest is the greater half

in a signal variation on *la nueva cocina mexicana*. The presentation is stunning. *Specialty: Salmon painted dessert.*

Le St Germain ⌂

5955 Melrose Ave., LA ☎ (213) 467-1108. Map 6C2 ▥▥ ▭ ▬ Y
▬ by valet ▣▣ ▣▣ ▣ ▣▣ ▥▥ Open Mon-Fri noon-2pm, 6-10.30pm, Sat 6-10.30pm.
A pleasant old building painted yellow, a terrace full of flowers and rosy-hued walls hung with pastoral paintings create a perfect illusion of a French country restaurant right next to one of LA's busiest streets. Several small dining rooms, plus tables on the terrace, sustain a mood of intimacy. This triumph of imagination is equaled by one of the earliest, most intelligent weddings of French culinary technique with fresh California ingredients on a menu that has been around so long it no longer smacks of the experimental. *Specialties: John Dory, rabbit in wine, cream and mustard sauce, veal sautéed with mushrooms and crayfish, California salad.*

La Scala ⌂

410 N Canon Dr., Beverly Hills ☎ (213) 275-0579. Map 4C3 ▥▥ to ▥▥ ▭ ▬ ▣▣ ▣ ▣▣ ▥▥ Open Mon-Fri 11.30am-2.30pm, 5.30pm-midnight, Sat 5.30pm-midnight.
The funny, half-fancy, half-Chianti-bottle decor of this durable restaurant could probably double as a stage set for some light-hearted opera, but it is apt where it is. Since its beginnings, La Scala has been both a showplace for celebrities (the bar is a good place for stargazing) and a good northern Italian restaurant with, maybe, a few Spanish touches. The menu has kept pace with rising culinary standards without losing its earthy vitality. A meal of pasta at an off-peak hour is a bargain. The wine list, Italian, French and Californian, is excellent. Proprietor Jean Leon has a less formal place, **La Scala Malibu**, in a shopping center called Malibu Country Mart (*3835 Cross Creek Rd.*). Same clientele in less fancy dress; similar menu, but simpler and fresher. *Specialties: Mussels, Melanzane nostra, mignonettes Rossini, veal scallopine piccata.*

72 Market Street

72 Market St., Venice ☎ (213) 392-8720. Map 2C1 ▥▥ ▭ Y
▬ by valet ▣▣ ▣ ▥▥ Open Tues-Thurs 8-10.30am, 11.30am-2.30pm, 6-10.30pm, Fri

8-10.30am, 11.30am-2.30pm, 6-11.30pm, Sat 6-11.30pm.
Dudley Moore and Liza Minelli are among the owners of this chic restaurant, where the architecture is as noteworthy as the cuisine. The airy, high-ceilinged space was once used as a studio by architect Frank Gehry, and the high-tech conversion suits the arty showbiz crowd who go for the all-American food and the prospect of hearing Moore tinkling the ivories, something he does more often than you'd expect. Good, long list of daily specials. *Specialties: Meatloaf, chili, grilled fish.*

Spago
8795 Sunset Blvd., LA ☎ (213) 652-4025. Map 5C4 ▥ ☐ ▽ ☛ by valet AE ◎ VISA Open 6pm-2am.
Wolfgang Puck was a legend before he left the then ultra chic Ma Maison to open .... a pizzeria! He has become a bigger legend since, as Spago has turned out to be to pizzerias what Maseratis are to Fiats. Dough is rolled to order, fresh tomatoes replace tomato sauce; the galaxy of toppings includes artichokes, eggplants and goat cheeses. Not only that: this is where the hot names of Hollywood come to see, to be seen, and — not incidentally — to eat Puck's spectacular reinventions of old Italian standbys. If they're able to get a table, mere passers-through eat pretty well toward the back of the room, where the views are modest but the fare is every bit as good as it is out front where the social lions lounge, and where Puck still treats familiars pretty much as if they were in his dining room at home. When he is not at Spago, he is at his other place (**Chinois on Main**, q.v.) shattering other culinary icons. The name Spago is, incidentally, an irreverent shorthand for spaghetti, which also finds new levels here. *Specialties: Pizza, pasta, Sonoma baby lamb.*

Studio Grill
7321 Santa Monica Blvd., LA ☎ (213) 874-9202. Map 5C5 ▥ ☐ ■ ☛ ☚ AE ◎ VISA Open Mon-Fri noon-2.15pm, Sun-Thurs 6-10.15pm, Fri-Sat 6-11.15pm.
This is almost beyond doubt the ultimate example of Los Angeles reverse chic. The dusty white facade is in the middle of a particularly dull-looking stretch of Santa Monica Blvd., but the room within is elegant and the eclectic menu one of the finest in the city. The style is light without being *nouvelle.* Reservations required. The list has many well-aged wines at fair prices. *Specialties:*

Carpaccio, shrimp with ginger and lime, roasted peppers with anchovies.

A Thousand Cranes △
120 S Los Angeles St. (New Otani Hotel), LA ☎ (213) 629-1200. Map 7D9 ▥ ☐ ■ ☚ ☛ AE CB ◎ VISA Open 6-10.30pm.
Because the menu is aimed largely at Japanese guests in an elegant hotel, A Thousand Cranes has a luxurious breadth of dishes both in its *à la carte* and set dinner lists. The room could hardly be lovelier. One side has Japanese tables (with welcome foot wells for the less than limber), the other conventional Western furnishings. A glass wall looks onto a garden with pools and waterfalls. *Specialties: Salt roasted clams, shabu shabu.*

Toledo Restaurant
11613 Santa Monica Blvd., LA ☎ (213) 477-2400. Map 2C1 ▥ ☐ ■ ☚ AE ◎ VISA Open Tues-Thurs 11.30am-2.30pm, 5.30-10.30pm, Fri 11.30am-2.30pm, 5.30-11pm, Sat 5.30-11pm, Sun 4-10pm.
The decor is worthy of an urbane restaurant in Spain, and so is the menu, which has some hints of Castile and many of Andalucía. Preparation and service live up to appearances. Toledo's long wine list also waves the Spanish flag. *Specialties: Paella, pato Sevilla.*

La Toque
8191 Sunset Blvd., West Hollywood ☎ (213) 656-7515. Map 5B4 ▥ ☎ ☐ ■ ▽ ☛ by valet AE CB ◎ VISA Open Mon-Thurs noon-2pm, 6.30-10.30pm, Fri noon-2pm, 6-10.30pm, Sat 6-10.30pm.
La Toque is a small restaurant with a big reputation that is well deserved. The restaurant avoids novelty for novelty's sake, serving just the freshest ingredients prepared in both classical and restrained *nouvelle* French fashion. The menu changes with the seasons, the fish dishes and puddings are especially good, and the ambience is quiet and charming. *Specialties: Sea bass rolled with crayfish, rabbit in mustard sauce, fresh fruit tarts.*

Trumps △
8764 Melrose Ave., LA ☎ (213) 855-1480. Map 5C4 ▥ ☐ ▽ ☛ by valet AE ◎ VISA Open Mon-Thurs noon-3pm, 6.30pm-midnight, Fri-Sat noon-3pm, 6.30pm-12.30am.
Among all the experimental kitchens in this open-minded city, trendy

Trumps is alone on a new frontier. Almost no combination is too outlandish to consider. The architecture echoes the menu. Late-night suppers are less bizarre and a better value. *Specialties: Potato pancakes with goat cheese, cold lobster pesto, scallops with pine nuts.*

Valentino △
3115 Pico Blvd., Santa Monica ☎ *(213) 829-4313. Map 2C1* ▥ ▰ ▢ ▰ ♆ ⇝ *by valet* ⒶⒺ ⒸⒷ ⊙ ⒸⒹ ▨ *Open Mon-Sat 5.30-11.30pm; lunch Fri only 11.30am-2.30pm.*
Recently revamped, Valentino's stylish decor is now worthy of its splendid Italian food and exceptional wine list. Ignore the *à la carte* and choose from a long list of daily specials, which include well-executed traditional dishes and more innovative creations. *Specialties: Daily specials, antipasto, pasta.*

West Beach Café
60 N Venice Blvd., Venice ☎ *(213) 832-5396. Map 2C1* ▥ ▢ ▰ ⒶⒺ ⊙ Ⓒ ▨ *Open 10am-1am, except Mon lunch.*
One of the more versatile demonstrations of modern California changes the contemporary paintings on its walls each month, and changes its "*nouvelle* California" and/or "minimalist" menu weekly. Snow white, rectilinear and skylit, this is

every bit as good a restaurant as it is a gallery. Specialties change seasonally and weekly, but typical are Hawaiian tuna with sea urchin sauce, and breast of turkey in vinegar and honey.

Wonder Seafood
2505 W Valley Blvd., Alhambra ☎ *(818) 308-0259. Map 2C3* ▥▢ *to* ▥ ▢ ⊙ ▨ *Open 11.30am-10pm.*
Cantonese chefs have little if anything to learn about getting the best out of fresh seafood, and it doesn't come much fresher than at Wonder Seafood, where many of the live ingredients-in-waiting can be seen swimming about in large water tanks. The traditional Cantonese food is so authentic you could be in Hong Kong. *Specialties: Snake soup, crab with black beans, prawns baked in salt.*

Yagura Ichiban
101 Japanese Village Plaza, LA ☎ *(213) 623-4141. Map 7D9* ▥▢ *to* ▥ ▢ ♆ ⒶⒺ ⊙ ▨ *Open Mon-Fri 11am-2.30pm, 5-10.30pm, Sat 11am-10.30pm, Sun noon-10.30pm. Closed first week of Jan.*
The dining rooms evoke Japanese country inns to the satisfaction of visiting Japanese. The most praised of several restaurants within a restaurant is the *robata yaki* bar, a sort of country barbecue style of cooking done in front of the diners.

Moderate and inexpensive restaurants

American lunch or dinner
O'Shaughnessy's Downtown (*505 S Flower St., ARCO Plaza* ☎ *(213) 629-2568*); **Stepps on the Court** (*330 S Hope St., Crocker Center* ☎ *(213) 626-0900*).

BBQ
Dr. Hogly-Wogly's Tyler Texas BBQ (*8136 N Sepulveda Blvd., Van Nuys* ☎ *(818) 780-6701*).

Breakfast places
Croissants USA (*9536 Brighton Way, Beverly Hills* ☎ *(213) 271-2535*); **Old World Restaurant** (*1019 Westwood Blvd., LA* ☎ *(213) 208-4033*), a UCLA favorite, with health foods and burgers too.

Delicatessens
Art's Deli (*12224 Ventura Blvd., Studio City* ☎ *(818) 769-9808*); **Langer's Deli** (*704 S Alvarado St., downtown* ☎ *(213) 483-8050*); **Stage Deli** (*Century City Marketplace, 10250 Santa Monica Blvd.* ☎ *(213) 553-DELI*).

Fish & chips
H. Salt (*4795 Vineland Ave., North Hollywood* ☎ *(818) 761-1750*).

Hamburgers and hot dogs
Cassell's (*3300 W 6th St., Mid-Wilshire* ☎ *(213) 480-8668*); **Hard Rock Café** (*Beverly Center at 8600 Beverly Blvd., Mid-Wilshire* ☎ *(213)*

276-7605); **Pink's** (*711 N La Brea Ave., Hollywood* ☎ *(213) 931-4223*); **Russell's** (*5656 E 2nd St., Naples* ☎ *(213) 434-0226*); **Tail O'the Pup** (*329 N San Vicente Blvd., West Hollywood* ☎ *(213) 652-4517*); **The Wiener Factory** (*14917 Ventura Blvd., Sherman Oaks* ☎ *(818) 789-2676*).

Inexpensive Chinatown

Grandview Gardens (*944 N Hill St., LA* ☎ *(213) 624-6084*) for *dim sum*; **Hunan** (*980 N Broadway, LA* ☎ *(213) 626-5050*) for truly spicy foods; **Mandarette** (*8386 Beverly Blvd., Beverly Hills* ☎ *(213) 655-6115*).

Korean

Dong Il Jang (*3455 W 8th St., Mid-Wilshire* ☎ *(213) 383-5757*); **Hanil** (*989 Dewey Ave., Mid-Wilshire* ☎ *(213) 480-8141*); **Korea Gardens** (*950 S Vermont Ave., Mid-Wilshire* ☎ *(213) 388-3042*).

Omelets, sandwiches, salads

Alice's Restaurant (*1043 Westwood Blvd., Westwood* ☎ *(213) 478-0941*); **Café Rodeo** (*360 N Rodeo Dr., Beverly Hills* ☎ *(213) 273-0300*); **The Egg and the Eye** (*5814 Wilshire Blvd., LA, in the Craft and Folk Art Museum* ☎ *(213) 933-5596*); **TGI Friday** (*13470 Maxella St., Marina del Rey* ☎ *(213) 822-9052*).

Pizza

California Pizza Kitchen (*Beverly Center, LA* ☎ *(213) 854-6555; also 207 S Beverly Dr., Beverly Hills*); **Little Toni's** (*4745 Lankershim Blvd., North Hollywood* ☎ *(818) 763-0131*); **Mario's** (*1001 Broxton St., Westwood* ☎ *(213) 208-7077*); **Palermo** (*1858 N Vermont Ave., Los Feliz* ☎ *(213) 663-1430*); **La Strega** (*400 S Western Ave.* ☎ *(213) 385-1546*); **Wildflour Boston Pizza** (*2807 Main St., Santa Monica* ☎ *(213) 399-9990*).

Nightlife

Los Angeles has an overwhelmingly rich nightlife that tends, like everything in the greater city, to be spread out across a wide area and subject to a deeply fickle clientele. As for stargazing, the conventional wisdom is that "when the rich party they like to dive." So you are more likely to see Eddie Murphy or Jack Nicholson at nondescript **On the Rocks** on Sunset Blvd. than in the **Polo Lounge**, although it is probably easier to *get* into the Polo Lounge. However, at most places the door policy is pretty relaxed, and you don't have to be famous, beautiful or both to win admittance, although, of course, it helps.

Most of the comedy clubs are in Hollywood. The after-dark street scene on Sunset and Hollywood Blvds. cannot be called uplifting, but the clubs sometimes are, and the lack of polish is compensated for by the vividness. Much of the sleaze was cleaned up prior to the 1984 Olympics and has not returned. Slightly trendier hangouts are to be found on La Cienega Blvd. and Melrose Ave.

Jazz may be the richest vein of all; Los Angeles always has a number of well-known players in residence. Their numbers are augmented by film and studio players who sometimes put stars in the shade. In contrast, the rock scene can look somewhat dated. Many of the bands are caught in a pre-1980s time-warp, although Angelenos seem not to have noticed.

The following list notes only a handful of the best-known clubs. In addition to checking magazines and daily newspapers for information on what, where and who's hot, look for copies of the free tabloid *LA Weekly,* distributed in a variety of public places and at some hotels. It offers exhaustive surveys and listings of available entertainment.

The bigger the name on the marquee, the more advisable it is to reserve in advance. Most clubs sell advance tickets at the door. Check with **Ticketron** (☎ *(213) 670-2311*) and **Mutual** (☎ *(213) 627-1248*).

Bars

Barney's Beanery
8447 Santa Monica Blvd., West Hollywood ☎ *(213) 654-2287. Map 5C4* ⬛️🚻 *to* ⬛️🚻 ⚞ *Open 6am-2am.*
A small neighborhood bar immortalized by sculptor Ed Kienholz and boasting more than 200 different beers. Friendly no-nonsense atmosphere.

Carlos 'N Charlie's
8240 Sunset Blvd., West Hollywood ☎ *(213) 656-8830. Map 5B4* ⬛️🚻 ⚞ ● 🎵 ♪ 👤 *by valet* AE 🔘 VISA *Open 11.30am-2am.*
Carlos 'N Charlie's is much more than a bar. It has a goodish Mexican restaurant attached, and the upstairs space functions as disco, cabaret and comedy workshop. The regular singles crowd is smart but more relaxed than the preening fashion victims that inhabit some LA nightspots.

Carlos & Pepe's
2020 Wilshire Blvd., Santa Monica ☎ *(213) 828-8903* ⬛️🚻 *to* ⬛️🚻 ⚞ 🚗 AE 🔘 VISA *Open 11am-2am.*
Stylish Mexican-style decor, central bar and a young Westside clientele who crowd the place around happy hour. Good bar snacks.

Grand Avenue Bar
506 S Grand Ave., LA (Biltmore Hotel) ☎ *(213) 624-1001* ⬛️🚻 ⚞ AE CB 🔘 🔘 VISA *Open Mon-Fri 11.30am-1.30am, Sat 6.30pm-1.30am.*
This is an interior-designed bar with Italian marble tables, Mies van der Rohe chairs, artworks changed seasonally, and live jazz in the evening. The bar attracts an upscale business crowd, but most of the action is around the lunchtime buffet and early evening.

Nicky Blair's
8730 Sunset Blvd., West Hollywood ☎ *(213) 659-0929. Map 5B4* ⬛️🚻 ⚞ 🚗 *by valet* AE CB 🔘 VISA *Open 6pm-2am.*
A glossy high-energy designer-clad clientele makes this a popular watering hole with entertainment industry high fliers and hangers-on. It can all be a bit intimidating, but ideal for beautiful people or beautiful people-watching.

Polo Lounge
9641 Sunset Blvd., Beverly Hills (Beverly Hills Hotel) ☎ *(213) 276-2251. Map 4C3* ⬛️🚻 ⚞ 🚗 *by valet* AE 🔘 🔘 VISA *Open 7.30am-1.30am.*
Once *the* place to see, be seen, do deals and generally feel good about the good life in Los Angeles, this is nowadays essentially an exercise in nostalgia.

Rainbow
9015 Sunset Blvd., West Hollywood ☎ *(213) 278-4232. Map 4C3* ⬛️🚻 🎵 ⚞ ● 🎵 ✕ AE 🔘 VISA *Open nightly 6pm-2am.*
Marilyn Monroe and Joe Di Maggio were engaged here (before its current incarnation, of course), and the restaurant still claims to serve the best chicken soup in California. Less than elegant, but it has evolved into something of a local institution since it converted to the Rainbow in 1972. The dark and atmospheric bar, restaurant and new wave music disco are popular with young ultra-hip singles on the prowl.

Rangoon Racket Club
9474 Santa Monica Blvd., Beverly Hills ☎ *(213) 274-8926. Map 4C3* ⬛️🚻 ⚞ 🚗 *by valet* AE CB 🔘 🔘 VISA
Hollywood colonial, with ceiling fans, rattan and waiters dressed for the Raj. Sleek Beverly Hills clientele.

Rebecca's
2025 Pacific Ave., Venice ☎ *(213) 306-6266. Map 2C1* ⬛️🚻 ⚞ 🚗 *by valet* AE CB 🔘 🔘 VISA *Open Sun-Thurs 6pm-midnight, Fri-Sat 6pm-2am.*
Desperately fashionable bar/restaurant designed by architect Frank Gehry and frequented by over-achieving singles who tend to drive European cars and wear expensive European clothes. The atmosphere, however, is pure conspicuous-consumption LA. Inexplicably, alligator- and octopus-shaped objects hang from the ceiling; the tables are of black marble. Not for those lacking in self-esteem. The Mexican food is good but expensive.

Ye Olde King's Head
116 Santa Monica Blvd., Santa Monica ☎ *(213) 451-1402. Map 2C1* ⬛️🚻 ⚞ *Open 11am-2am.*
The name says it all. A "British" pub complete with darts, fish & chips and warm draft beer. Popular with homesick expatriates and young anglophile locals alike.

LA Nightlife

Cabaret and comedy

Chippendales
3739 Overland Ave., West LA
☎ *(213) 202-8850. Map 4F3* 🚭 ⊠
🆎 🅾 🖩 *Open Sun-Thurs*
6.30pm-2am, Fri-Sat 6.30pm-4am.
Shows continuous. Variable cover
charge.

Good-natured cabaret with male
exotic dancers strutting their
well-muscled stuff for an all-female
audience. Male customers are
admitted after 10pm.

Comedy Store
8433 W Sunset Blvd., West
Hollywood ☎ *(213) 656-6225. Map*
5B4 🚭 ⊠ *Shows nightly from*
about 8.30pm. Variable cover
charge plus two-drink minimum.

The fare is comedy and occasional
magic acts. The store has three rooms:
The Main Room (the best local
comedians mixed with big names
trying out new acts for Las Vegas); the
Original Comedy Store (a smaller
room given over mostly to rising
young acts); and **The Belly Room**
(intimate, for female performers only).
Weekends draw the sharpest talent;
Mon is the night when anyone can get
up on stage.

A branch, **Comedy Store West**
(*1621 Westwood Blvd., Westwood*
☎ *(213) 477-4751*), books some of
the same acts, but has only a beer and
wine license, and admits minors.

Groundlings Theater
7307 Melrose Ave., West
Hollywood ☎ *(213) 934-9700. Map*
5C4 🚭 *Shows nightly from about*
8pm. Variable cover charge.

Among the best laughs in town.
Resident talented cast with polished
sketches, routines and improvisation.
Alumni include Pee-wee Herman.

Improvisation
8162 Melrose Ave., West
Hollywood ☎ *(213) 651-2583.*
Map 5C4 🚭 *Shows nightly from*
about 8.30pm. Variable cover
charge plus two-drink
minimum.

There is a weekly cycle, which
includes Off the Wall improvisational
theater (Mon), new comic faces and
singers (Tues-Wed), stand-up comics
(Thurs), and booked acts plus
drop-ins, the latter sometimes
including big names (Fri-Sat). Sun is
for auditions.

La Cage aux Folles
643 N La Cienega Blvd., West
Hollywood ☎ *(213) 657-1091. Map*
5C4 🚭 ☷ *Open Tues-Sat*
7pm-2am ☎ *for show times.*
Variable cover charge.

Long-running female impersonator
show spun off from the movie. Plenty
of outrageousness and glitter. Not for
the prudish.

Rose Tatoo
655 N Robertson Blvd., West
Hollywood ☎ *(213)* 🚭 ☷ 🍸 ⊠
Open nightly 5.30pm-2am. Shows
9pm-1am. Variable cover charge.

Fashionable club with a clientele that
is predominantly gay but welcomes
women. Entertainments include '50s
and '60s groups, singers, exotic
revues and talent contests.

Verdi Ristorante di Musica
1519 Wilshire Blvd., Santa Monica
☎ *(213) 393-0706* 🚭 ☷ *Open*
Tues-Sun 6pm-2am.

Theater/restaurant with a refined
atmosphere and resident repertory
group performing opera and
Broadway hits.

Jazz

At My Place
1026 Wilshire Blvd., Santa Monica
☎ *(213) 451-8596. Map 2C1* 🚭
🍸 *Open Mon-Sat 7pm-2am, Sun*
3pm-1am. Shows nightly ☎ *for*
times. Variable cover charge.

The hangout for many of LA's best
studio musicians leans towards jazz,
but also offers rock, R&B, comedy.

Baked Potatoe
3787 Cahuenga Blvd.,
N Hollywood ☎ *(818) 980-1615.*
Map 2B2 🚭 🍸 *Open 7pm-2am.*
Show times vary ☎ *for times.*
Variable cover charge.

Contemporary jazz in intimate
surroundings is the main point. But as
the name suggests, baked potatoes
are a specialty for those who arrive
hungry.

Concerts by the Sea
100 Fisherman's Wharf, Redondo
Beach ☎ *(213) 379-4998. Map 2D2*
🚭 ☷ ⊠ *Open Thurs-Sun*
8.30-2am. Show times and cover
charge variable.

Not exactly luxurious surroundings,
but there are big name mainstream
performers and a musically
sophisticated clientele.

Donte's
*4269 Lankershim Blvd., N
Hollywood* ☎ *(818) 769-1566* 🔳
═ ☥ *Variable cover charge. Open
7.30pm-2am.*
Established jazz supper club serving
Italian food to the sound of fusion,
mainstream and big band sounds.
Chuck Mangione debuted here.

Linda's
6715 Melrose Ave., Hollywood
☎ *(213) 934-6199. Map 5C5* 🔳 ═
☥ *No cover. Open 6pm-midnight.*

Very hip Hollywood club/restaurant
with off-the-wall decor and nightly
cabaret from owner Linda Keegan
and guests.

Nucleus Nuance
7267 Melrose Ave., Hollywood
☎ *(213) 939-8666. Map 5C5* 🔳 ═
☥ ☙ *Open nightly 6pm-2am.
Two-drink minimum, shows from
9.30pm.*
Top name artists play jazz and blues
in a chic, relaxed setting favored by
young professionals.

Rock

Club Lingerie
6507 W Sunset Blvd., Hollywood
☎ *(213) 466-8557. Map 6B6* 🔳 ☥
🔀 *Open Mon-Sat 9pm-2am.*
Well-established venue for new wave,
rock and reggae, that is known to
regulars as Club Underwear. The
fashion show staged by the chic
clientele is sometimes better than the
music.

Lighthouse
30 Pier Ave., Hermosa Beach
☎ *(213) 376-9833. Map 2D2* 🔳 ☥
*Open Mon-Fri 4pm-1.30am,
Sat-Sun 10am-1.30am. Show
times and cover charges vary, so
check first.*
For years Lighthouse was advertised
as a jazz club and waterfront dive.
Now, after a face-lift, the musical fare
has changed to reggae, R&B and
rock.

Lhasa Club
1110 N Hudson Ave., Hollywood
☎ *(213) 461-7284. Map 6B6* 🔳
*Open Wed-Sat. Times and cover
charge vary.*
As one would wish of somewhere as
avant garde as Lhasa, it isn't very
predictable. Events, happenings and
acts change by the night, ranging
from local bands to new wave cabaret
to poetry readings and performance

art. The young street-stylish clientele
is as engaging as the artwork on the
walls.

The Palace
1735 N Vine St., Hollywood
☎ *(213) 462-3000. Map 6B6* 🔳 ═
☥ *Open Sun-Thurs 9pm-2am,
Fri-Sat 9pm-4am. Cover charge
varies.*
Beautifully converted 1927 theater
with three bars, major rock names,
jazz, R&B and dancing all under the
same roof.

The Palomino
*6907 Lankershim Blvd., North
Hollywood* ☎ *(818) 764-4010. Map
2B2* ═ ☥ *Open Mon-Sat 10am-
2am, Sun 4pm-2am. Cover varies.*
LA's major country music showcase
looks rather shabby these days, but
some would say it always did, and it
still attracts major names and the
crowds. Also rock, R&B, blues.

Roxy
*9009 Sunset Blvd., West
Hollywood* ☎ *(213) 276-2222. Map
5C4* 🔳 🎵 ☥ *Show times vary.
Two-drink minimum.*
Not the premier rock venue that it
once was, but still a comfortable Art
Deco spot featuring up-and-coming
local bands.

Performing arts

Unsurprisingly, motion pictures in LA are fresh from the cutting rooms.
Less expected, and contrary to belief outside the city, theater here is alive
and flourishing. There are a staggering 150 legitimate theaters. Classical
music and dance are less well represented, but they are here.

The following list notes only a selection of the major venues for the
performing arts. The "Sunday Calendar" section of the *Los Angeles Times*
runs complete listings of current theater, music and dance, and
California Magazine can also be useful.

Buy tickets in advance from agencies such as **Ticketron** (☎ *(213) 670-2311)* and **Mutual** (☎ *(213) 627-1248)*.

Ballet and classical music

The **Ambassador Auditorium** (*300 W Green St., Pasadena* ☎ *(818) 304-6161)* is part of a religious college campus. The luxuriously appointed, architecturally splendid auditorium annually books as many as 100 concerts. Nearly all of the performers and performing groups are of international stature.

The **Dorothy Chandler Pavilion** (*Los Angeles Music Center, 135 N Grand Ave.* ☎ *(213) 972-7211)* is a splendid 3,197-seat downtown concert hall, home of the Los Angeles Philharmonic and the Joffrey Ballet. Other orchestras and recitalists also guest here.

A huge, recently renovated hall in downtown, the **Shrine Auditorium** (*665 Jefferson Blvd.* ☎ *(213)(213) 748-5116)* is used primarily for touring dance troupes, and the American Ballet Company regularly performs here. And in the Mid-Wilshire district, the **Wilshire Ebell Theater** (*4401 W 8th St.* ☎ *(213) 939-1128)* is a wonderful old period theater used by the Los Angeles ballet.

Outdoor theaters used for classical music and ballet include the **Greek Theater** (*2700 N Vermont Ave.* ☎ *(213) 410-1062)* in Griffith Park, an outdoor amphitheater that books a broad range of entertainment from classical ballet to light opera and rock concerts. The **Hollywood Bowl** (*2301 N Highland Ave.* ☎ *(213) 850-2000)*, a natural amphitheater in the hills N of Hollywood, hosts scores of concerts as well as the summer season by the Philharmonic. It also presents pop concerts.

Cinema

Predictably, Los Angeles has movie theaters by the hundred. **Hollywood** and **Universal City** have some state-of-the-art movie theaters with the most technically advanced projection and sound systems. **Downtown** has the greatest architectural wonders, though most of the movies are in Spanish. But **Westwood Village** is the focal point for first-run movies.

Theater

The major theaters are downtown, in Hollywood and in Beverly Hills.

The **Ahmanson Theater** (*Los Angeles Music Center, 135 N Grand Ave.* ☎ *(213) 410-1062)* is a major downtown theater with 2,100 seats, used for major dramas and by the Center Theater Group, and occasionally by the Los Angeles Civic Light Orchestra. It presents touring troupes mostly doing musicals and musical comedy.

The **Mark Taper Forum** (*Los Angeles Music Center, 135 Grand Ave.* ☎ *(213) 410-1062)*, a 750-seat house, is used primarily by the local Center Theater Group and Mark Taper Forum/Laboratory, who offer a consistent diet of new, often experimental works. A festival of new plays is held every spring.

The **Pantages Theater** (*6233 Hollywood Blvd.* ☎ *(800) 852-9772)*, LA's largest theater, with 2,288 seats, is used for touring Broadway and other companies.

The **Pasadena Playhouse** (*37 S El Molino Ave.* ☎ *(818) 356-75290)* was founded in 1917 and restored and relaunched in 1986. The 700-seat auditorium stages major drama with some of the best actors in town.

The **Shubert Theater** (*2020 Ave. of the Stars, ABC Entertainment Center* ☎ *(800) 233-3123)* is a 1,828-seat palace for Broadway-produced, long-running plays and musicals.

Many small theaters put on contemporary or experimental plays. A bonus is modest ticket prices. See newspaper listings.

Shopping

Want to shop till you drop? Los Angeles is the place. Its wealth and huge population, for whom consumerism is not a dirty word, and cheerful shop assistants, for whom service is more a pleasure than a chore, ensure great shopping. Choice and quality are outstanding. However, districts with tight clusters of attractive stores are rare, so for the full range visitors will need to drive.

Apart from well-known streets such as **Rodeo Dr.** and **Melrose Ave.**, some of the best shopping is in the huge shopping malls, which are generally well designed, user-friendly and anchored by one or more major department stores. Major malls include **Arco Plaza**, **The Beverly Center**, **Century City**, **Glendale Galleria**, **Santa Monica Place**, **Sherman Oaks Galleria**, **Westside Pavilion** and **Woodland Hills Promenade**. Well-stocked chain stores include **The Broadway**, **Bullock's**, **I. Magnin**, **May Company**, **Neiman-Marcus**, **Nordstrom**, **Robinson's** and **Saks Fifth Avenue**. Parking beneath the malls is easier than on fashionable streets, and many stores will validate parking. Sales are frequent and well publicized in the local press. Specialty stores will probably require a longer haul; it's prudent to telephone before setting out.

On the following pages the main shopping areas of Greater Los Angeles are described, with details of special-interest shops beginning on page 93.

Coastal

Santa Monica has the best shopping of the coastal cities, in its range of stores, their easy accessibility and civilized atmosphere. Cooling sea breezes add to the pleasures of strolling and browsing.

Main St. (*s of the end of Santa Monica Freeway*) was horribly run-down until ten years ago; now it rivals Melrose Ave. for trendiness. The mix is familiar enough: fashion, antiques, art galleries, gifts, home accessories, sportswear and goods, including surfer's heaven at **Horizons West** (*2011 Main St.*). But in all there are about 100 stores along nine manageable blocks, and peppered between them are pleasant restaurants, cafés and pubs, making for a very relaxed morning's or afternoon's meander.

Montana Ave. (*10 blocks N of Santa Monica Freeway*) rivals Main St. in its range of stores. The best of them are on the ten blocks between 7th St. and 16th St. and include good clothing stores, especially for children, as well as a variety of stores selling gifts, jewelry, stationery, rugs etc.

Santa Monica Place (*Broadway, between 2nd St. and 4th St.*), designed by the ubiquitous Frank Gehry, is a bright, skylit 3-story mall with ocean views and about 160 small shops plus branches of **The Broadway** and **Robinson's** department stores. The fast-food outlets are well placed for people-watching, the *sushi* bar being especially recommended. Nearby is **Santa Monica Mall** (*3rd St., between Broadway and Wilshire Blvd.*), a pedestrian mall with a range of shops that are cheaper, on the whole, than those in the other main shopping areas.

Venice (*just s of Santa Monica*) is best known for the nonstop carnival that enlivens its **Boardwalk**. Also on the Boardwalk is an open-air market selling sportswear, posters, sunglasses etc. The quality isn't Rodeo Dr., but neither are the prices. Elsewhere, notably on **Market St.**, are some interesting galleries.

Downtown

Nowadays downtown is best known for several diverse, indoor plazas in business and hotel towers. It also has fine stores on the street, notably around Chinatown, Olvera St. and Little Tokyo. The only drawback is that downtown parking can be expensive, so be sure to ask stores for validation.

ARCO Plaza (*Flower St., between 5th St. and 6th St.*) has two large underground levels of 60 restaurants and stores (excellent needlepoint, jewelry, wine, clothes, shoes, books). The **Visitor and Convention Bureau Visitors Center** is also here.

Bonaventure Shopping Gallery (*Figueroa St., between 4th St. and 5th St.*) has six circular levels of restaurants, services and shops.

Broadway Plaza (*W 7th St. and Figueroa St.*) has a multilevel 30-shop gallery anchored by the department store **The Broadway**, where good clothes, cosmetics and kitchenware are moderately priced.

Seventh Market Place (*Figueroa St. and 7th St.*) is the newest and most attractive of the downtown malls, with 60 shops and specialty stores in an airy, open environment.

Also downtown: **Chinatown** (*within Ord St., Alameda Ave., Barnard St. and Yale St.*) has scores of small shops selling foodstuffs, imported silks, *objets d'art*, traditional medicines and household goods; the **New China Emporium** (*727 N Broadway*) is a small department store selling inexpensive goods from the PRC; **Little Tokyo** (*within 3rd St., Alameda Ave., 1st St. and 3rd St.*) has two major shopping areas — **Japanese Village Plaza** (*327 E 2nd St.*) and **Little Tokyo Sq.** (*333 S Alameda Ave.*) — with boutiques and small shops selling Japanese goods, books and magazines; go to **Olvera St.** for Mexican handicrafts; **The Garment District** (*Los Angeles St., from 7th St. to Washington Blvd.*) has excellent clothing bargains, both from shops along the street and at outlets in the **Cooper Building** (*near 9th St.*) and **The California Mart** (*Olympic Blvd.*) — many are designer label seconds, so check carefully.

Other downtown services and shops: Brooks Bros. (*530 W 7th St.*), traditional clothing for men and women; **Henry's Camera Hi-Fi and Video** (*516 W 8th St.*), a wide selection, discounts and a multilingual staff; **Western World Apparel** (*615 W 7th St.*) for leatherwear, Levis, Stetsons; **Thomas Bros. Maps and Books** (*603 W 7th St.*), with absolutely the best maps to Los Angeles and California, plus travel books and accoutrements.

Hollywood

Stylish West Hollywood is altogether more interesting to shoppers than Hollywood proper. The latter is best for bookstores, cameras and a few novelty stores, including the fantasy lingerie of Frederick's of Hollywood. The former has The Beverly Center, one of LA's best shopping malls, varied and fashionable shops including some of the best galleries and antique stores on and around Melrose Ave., plus the rather touristy delights of Farmers' Market.

The **Beverly Center** (*at Beverly Blvd. and La Cienega Blvd.*), with its dour concrete facade, is not much to look at from the outside. However, inside it is an attractive, spotlessly clean, galleried mall of 900,000sq.ft with some 200 quality shops and restaurants, 14 movie theaters and, at ground level, **Irvine Ranch Market**, probably the best-stocked supermarket in Los Angeles. At one end of the mall is **The Broadway** department store; at the other is the slightly more upscale store **Bullocks**. Beneath are four levels of parking.

Farmers' Market (*W 3rd St. and Fairfax Ave.*) is best known for its produce and food stalls. In all, the open-air complex has 150 shops selling fresh fruits, vegetables, meats, seafood, breads and pastries, souvenirs and gifts. Pricier than the neighborhood supermarket, but more fun.

La Cienega Blvd. (*N from the Beverly Center to Melrose Ave.*) ought to be renamed "Carpet Canyon"; stores selling Eastern and native American rugs and carpets occupy almost every inch. Farther up La Cienega (*between Melrose Ave. and Willoughby Ave.*) are more than a score of art galleries. The other major attraction is the frankly-named **Trashy Lingerie** (*402 La Cienega Blvd.*). A small membership fee dissuades passing voyeurs from ogling the corseted saleswomen, but the erotic merchandise is displayed in the windows.

Hollywood Blvd. (*w of intersection with Vine St.*) is not nearly as sleazy as it used to be, at least not in daytime. However, there is not much to interest shoppers, save a few discount clothing stores, vendors of over-priced Hollywood memorabilia, some decent bookstores clustered near the intersection with Cherokee Ave., including the movie buffs' favorite **Larry Edmunds** (*6658 Hollywood Blvd.*), and the original **Frederick's of Hollywood** (*6608 Hollywood Blvd.*) for extravagantly styled, moderately priced lingerie. Newspapers and magazines from across the world are available at **World Book and News** (*1652 N Cahuenga Blvd.*).

Melrose Ave. (*between Doheny Dr. and Highland Ave.*) is not quite as exclusive or as expensive as Rodeo Dr., but it is probably the snazziest and most interesting shopping strip in LA. And, with a concentrated 40-blocks-worth before the glamor peters out after Highland Ave., it is also the longest. (Valley enthusiasts might claim this for Ventura Blvd., but that admirable street lacks the density of stores; walking the 3-mile length of Melrose at one go would be a chore, but walking Ventura would be an Olympian task.) The western stretch is the more expensive, featuring scores of antique stores (with the fanciest on **Melrose Pl.**), galleries, and stores selling specialist books, furniture and home accessories (especially Art Deco) and designer fashions. Going E from Fairfax Ave., privilege gives way to punk, the stores are progressively less pricey, the California-style fashions younger, the artwork not originals but numbered prints, the jewelry paste rather than precious stones. The gift stores are full of amusing gadgets and nicknacks, and **Vinyl Fetish** (*7350 Melrose Ave.*) is one of LA's best record stores for imports.

Sunset Blvd. (*going w from intersection with Crescent Heights*) is notable primarily for the high-fashion outlets at **Sunset Plaza** (*on Sunset Strip*) and **Tower Records** (*8801 Sunset Blvd.*), billed as the largest record store in the world, which reputedly has in stock, or is able to find, just about any disc. Across the street is **Tower Video** (visitors from overseas should remember that tapes are in the US "NTSC" system and may not work in their home country).

Valleys

Like everything else in the Valleys, the shopping is very spread out. Each community has its own concentration, some better than others. Traveling from E to W, the more noteworthy are indicated below.

Pasadena's best shopping is on **Lake St.** (*between Colorado Blvd. and California Blvd.*) and at **Pasadena Plaza** (*opposite Pasadena Hilton on Los Robles Ave. and Colorado Blvd.*). In addition to the usual range of clothing and other stores, the former has branches of **I. Magnin** and **Bullock's** and some elegant arcades. The recently opened Plaza has 120 shops. Less predictable is the **Rose Bowl Flea Market** (*Rose Bowl Dr.*), held on the second Sun of each month.

Glendale Galleria (*Central Ave. and Colorado Blvd.*) is vast, with some 250 shops. Although not the swankiest mall in town, it has plenty to offer, including outposts of department stores **Nordstrom** and budget-conscious **J.C. Penny**.

Ventura Blvd. (*from Studio City to Woodland Hills*) runs through half a dozen communities, with clumps of excellent shops along its length. (Specific stores are detailed below.) Of the malls, **Sherman Oaks Galleria** (*Ventura Blvd. and Sepulveda Blvd.*) and the adjacent open-air **Sherman Oaks Fashion Square** are popular with Valley residents; **Woodland Hills Promenade** (*Topanga Canyon Blvd. and Oxnard St.*), anchored by **Robinsons** and **Bullocks Wilshire**, is generally regarded as being among the poshest in town; and **Topanga Plaza** (*Topanga Canyon Blvd. and Vanowen St.*), although less upscale, is bigger and its choices more varied. Unless you have a specific chore on Ventura Blvd., Topanga Plaza is more easily accessed via the Ventura Freeway.

Westside
Beverly Hills
Much of the best, and perhaps inevitably the most expensive, shopping in Los Angeles is to be found within the so-called "Golden Triangle" bordered by **Wilshire Blvd.** on the s, **Little Santa Monica Blvd.** on the N and **Crescent Dr.** on the E. Slicing across the triangle is **N Rodeo Dr.**, 2½ blocks of ritzy stores where consumption is about as conspicuous as it gets, even in LA. Most of the big international names in fashion, jewelry, accessories and cosmetics are represented along the tree-lined, flower-bedecked street. Forget the parking meters, which will eat up your change; there is public parking opposite the Beverly Rodeo Hotel that is free for 2hrs. Other free parking lots are located throughout Beverly Hills.

Among the establishments on Rodeo Dr. are:

Adult toys   **Hammacher Shlemmer** (*no. 309*), gadgets for people who have almost everything.

Beauty parlors   **Elizabeth Arden** (*no. 434*); **Vidal Sassoon** (*no. 405*).

Home accessories   **La Provence of Pierre Deux** (*no. 428*).

Jewelers   **Cartier** (*no. 370*); **Fred Joaillier** (*no. 401*); **Van Cleef & Arpels** (*no. 300*).

Men's and women's fashions   **Fred Hayman**, previously Giorgio (*no. 273*), American and European clothes, with cocktails and coffee from an antique Gaggia. Buyers for the TV soap *Dallas* shop here.

Men's fashion   **Battaglia** (*no. 306*), Italian designer labels; **Bijan** (*no. 420*), by appointment, the most expensive menswear in town; **Jerry Magnin/Polo** (*no. 323*), both conservative and trendy attire.

Women's fashions   **Celine** (*no. 460*), natural fabrics, classic clothes and leather; **Collections A** (*no. 458*), top Japanese designers; **Courrèges** (*no. 447*), French fashions; **Rodeo Collection** (*between Little Santa Monica Blvd. and Brighton Way*), a Post-Modernist 5-level mall hosting 35 big-name retailers including **Fogal**, **Gianni Versace** and **Louis Vuitton**.

Leather and silks   **Gucci** (*no. 347*); **Hermès** (*no. 343*), handmade leather accessories and classic silks.

Adjacent streets too have much to interest the serious shopper. On Wilshire Blvd. near the intersection with Rodeo Dr.: **Abercrombie & Fitch** (*no. 9424*), sporting goods; **Brentano's** (*no. 9528*), for a wide range of books; **I. Magnin** (*no. 9634*), California-based specialist in fine clothes and sportswear; **Neiman-Marcus** (*no. 9700*), Dallas-based, famous for imported accessories and fashions; **Robinson's** (*no. 9900*), department store strong in clothes and gifts; **Saks Fifth Avenue** (*no. 9600*), designer collections and distinctive accessories; **Tiffany & Co.** (*no. 9502*), distinguished New York jewelers and silversmiths.

Other stores worthy of special note are: **Advance Coin & Stamp Co.** (*9857 Little Santa Monica Blvd.*), antique coins, stamps, and paper money; **Banana Republic** (*9669 Little Santa Monica Blvd.*),

LA flagship of the San Francisco-based retailer of safari chic; **Church's English Shoes** (*9633 Brighton Way*), bench-made men's footwear; **Francis-Orr** (*320 N Camden Dr.*), luxury stationery; **Galatee** (*419 N Bedford Dr.*), imported lingerie; **Hunter's Books** (*420 N Beverly Dr.*), excellent bookstore specializing in showbiz and the arts; **Kron Chocolatier** (*9529 Little Santa Monica Blvd.*), hand-made chocolates; **The Scriptorium** (*427 N Canon Dr.*), historical manuscripts, letters; **The Sharper Image** (*Little Santa Monica Blvd. at Camden Dr.*), gadget heaven; **Williams-Sonoma** (*317 N Beverly Dr.*), designer kitchen goods.

Farther down Wilshire Blvd. toward downtown: **Bullock's Wilshire** (*no. 3050*), a superb 1920s Art Deco department store, with a chandeliered tearoom by Herman Sach.

Century City Shopping Center (*Ave. of the Stars and Little Santa Monica Blvd.*), an 80-shop open-air complex diagonally opposite ABC Entertainment Center, is one of LA's earliest malls. It has the usual designer clothing, gift and accessory stores, plus a lively food hall, **Century City Magazines**, with a wide range of newspapers and magazines, **Nickelodian** for records, tapes and video discs, and a number of good restaurants.

Westside Pavilion (*Pico Blvd. and Westwood Blvd.*) is a newer mall in Post Modern style. The overall effect is less elegant than Century City, but there is a wider range of shops and prices.

Westwood Village (*N of Wilshire Blvd. at Westwood Blvd.*), being adjacent to the UCLA campus, is excellent for discount bookstores, stationers, art materials, casual preppie clothing, sportswear and handicrafts.

Specialty shops
Art galleries
In by far the largest art market in the western US, **West Hollywood** (especially **La Cienega Blvd.** and **Melrose Ave.**) has the greatest concentration of galleries. **Downtown** is the new boom area. Artists are named only to indicate a gallery's style, not its whole roster. Hours are mostly Tues-Sat 10am-5pm and by appointment.

Ankaum Gallery (*657 N La Cienega Blvd.*), Bob Kane, David Remfry, Jan Sawka, Morris Boderson, plus other well-known contemporary artists; **Antiquarius LA Antique Market** (*8840 Beverly Blvd.*), some 70 stalls with a wide range of antiques and *objets d'art*; **Antique Amusements** (*14502 Ventura Blvd.*), vintage pinball machines, jukeboxes and vending machines, all lovingly restored; **ARCO Center for Visual Art** (*505 S Flower St., B level*), photographs, graphics, sculpture, and paintings by West Coast contemporary artists; **Fantasies Come True** (*7408 Melrose Ave.*), Disney artwork from Mickey Mouse onward; **Dorothy Goldeen Gallery** (*1547 9th St., Santa Monica*), contemporary paintings and sculpture, with emphasis on new artists; **Harry A. Franklin** (*9601 Wilshire Blvd.*), traditional tribal sculpture from sub-Saharan black Africa plus pre-Columbian artifacts; **Galerie Marumo** (*8424 Melrose Ave.*), Los Angeles branch of Paris firm specializing in Impressionists and 19th and 20thC French masters; **Gallery of Eskimo Art** (*2665C Main St.*), Eskimo art from Alaska and Canada; **Gemini G.E.L.** (*8365 Melrose Ave.*), art publishers with gallery showing works by Sam Francis, David Hockney, Jasper Johns, Robert Rauschenberg, plus sculpture by Noguchi, di Suvero, Serra; **Gideon** (*8748 Melrose Ave.*), 17th-19thC maps and wildlife and botanical prints; **Goldfield** (*8400 Melrose Ave.*), Remington, Russell, Bierstadt, Payne and other 19th-20thC painters of the American West; **Kirk de Gooyer** (*1308 Factory Pl.*), abstract paintings, drawings and sculptures by Tom Lieber, Robert Hernandez, Karla Klarin and others; **G. Ray Hawkins**

(*7224 Melrose Ave.*), art photography by Ansel Adams, Max Yavno and many others; **Margo Leavin** (*812 N Robertson Blvd.*), paintings, drawings and graphics by Johns, Hockney, Rauschenberg, Jim Dine, Charles Gaines, Robert Motherwell, Edward Ruscha and Andy Warhol; **B. Lewin** (*266 N Beverly Dr.*), Mexican masters; **Main St. Gallery** (*2803 Main St.*), Japanese antiques and folk art; **Many Horses Gallery** (*740 La Cienega Blvd.*), American Indian art; **Neil G. Ovsey Gallery** (*705 E 3rd St.*), Woods Davy, Vivian Kerstein, Constance Mallinson, Claes Oldenburg, Ruscha plus other contemporary Californians and New Yorkers; **Peterson Galleries** (*270 N Rodeo Dr.*), Californian western Impressionists and masters; **M. M. Shinno** (*5820 Wilshire Blvd.*), contemporary Japanese prints plus work in many media by local artists of Asian descent; **Tortue Gallery** (*2917 Santa Monica Blvd.*), broad range from young Californians to European masters; **Stephen White** (*752 N La Cienega Blvd.*), 19th and 20thC photographers.

Bookstores

Westwood Blvd.   **David & Schorr Art Books** (no. 1547), out-of-print and rare books; **Bernard H. Hamel** (*no. 2325*), Spanish books; **George Houle Rare Books** (*no. 2277*), autographs, first editions and rare books, particularly concerning California and the West; **Hyman & Sons** (*no. 2315*), new and out-of-print Egyptology and archeology; **Victor Kamkin** (*no. 2320*), Russian books; **Howard Karno** (*no. 2367*), antiquarian specializing in books on Latin America; **Barry R. Levin** (*no. 2253*), rare and out-of-print science fiction and fantasy; **Needham Book Finders** (*no. 2317*), general secondhand books; **Technical Book Co.** (*no. 2056*), large stocks of science, health science and law texts.

Melrose Ave.   **Art & Architecture Books of the Twentieth Century** (*no. 8375*); **Bennett & Marshall** (*no. 8214*), antiquarian specializing in early science, medicine and travel; **Bodhi Tree** (*no. 8585*), occult and religion; **Canterbury** (*no. 8344*), out-of-print history, literature and philosophy; **Cosmopolitan** (*no. 7007*), secondhand and out-of-print titles; **William & Victoria Daily** (*no. 8216½*), art and rare books, fine prints; **Golden Apple** (*no. 7753*), comics, science fiction, fantasy; **Michael R. Thompson** (*no. 8320*), fine printing, rare and scholarly books, manuscripts.

Specialists elsewhere   **Amerasia Bookstore** (*129 Japanese Village Plaza*), specializing in books on Asia from history to cooking; **Book Soup** (*8818 Sunset Blvd.*), general-interest books;) **Cherokee Book Store** (*6607 Hollywood Blvd.*), first editions and rare Americana; **Larry Edmund's Cinema & Theater Books** (*6658 Hollywood Blvd.*), new and secondhand books, current and back-issue magazines on all the performing arts, and studio photos of stars (some autographed).

Chain and general bookstores   **Children's Book & Music Center** (*2500 Santa Monica Blvd.*), books for children of all ages; **Crown Books** (*throughout Los Angeles*), current titles in hardback and paperbacks at attractive discount prices; **Dutton's** (*11975 San Vicente Blvd., 5146 Laurel Canyon Blvd.*), new and used titles; **B. Dalton** (*throughout Los Angeles*), full range of current titles.

Westernwear

King's Western Wear (*6455 Van Nuys Blvd., Van Nuys*); **Nudie's** (*5015 Lankershim Blvd., North Hollywood*); **Western Frontier Establishment** (*Farmer's Market, 3rd St. and Fairfax*).

Wine

Greenblatt's (*8017 Sunset Blvd., Hollywood*); **Vendome** (*327 N Beverly Dr., Beverly Hills*); **Lawry's California Center** (*570 W Ave. 26, Los Angeles*); **Wally's Liquor & Gourmet Foods** (*2107 Westwood Blvd.*); **The Wine Merchant** (*9701 Santa Monica Blvd.*).

Sports and recreation

In Los Angeles, recreation means beaches before anything else. There are hundreds of public tennis courts and scores of public golf courses, but local pressure on these is intense enough to limit their use by visitors, although the situation is easier on weekdays and during school term.

Beaches

With a few short interruptions, the whole sandy arc of Santa Monica Bay is a public beach. Sections of particular interest, from N-S, are:
Santa Monica Beach is one of the best for location, cleanliness and amenities, but draws huge crowds. **Muscle Beach**, close to Santa Monica Pier, is the place for body builders. **Venice Beach**, directly S, has a particular charm, mainly because the walkway behind it is a meeting place for roller-skaters, skateboard fans and practitioners of other arcane styles of locomotion. The beach has good amenities. **Marina del Rey**, adjoining Venice, has excellent ocean beaches and a sheltered sandy beach, suitable for small children, inside the huge yacht harbor. S of LAX, **Manhattan Beach** finds favor with volleyball and Frisbee enthusiasts, **Hermosa Beach** is a toned-down version of Venice popular with surfers, and **Redondo Beach** is similar to Manhattan Beach, only less glossy.

Fishing

Pier fishing is available at **Santa Monica Pier**, **Venice Pier** and **Redondo Beach Municipal Pier**. Party boats for offshore trips berth at Santa Monica Pier, **Marina del Rey**, and **King Harbor** at Redondo Beach. See Yellow Pages under "Fishing Parties" for a complete list of boat operators.

Fitness facilities

Few cities are as devoted to the body beautiful as Los Angeles. Gymnasiums and fitness centers abound. Joggers often head for the beaches. The bigger hotels have responded to the demand among visitors by installing their own facilities, and others often have relationships with nearby clubs. In addition, YMCAs will sell daily memberships at reasonable prices. For information on temporary use of outside fitness centers, gymnasiums, aerobics classes etc., consult the ads in *LA Weekly*, *Los Angeles Magazine* and the Yellow Pages.

Golf

Los Angeles has more public courses than any other city in the United States. Most central of the public courses are **Harding**, 6,945yds, par 72, rated 70, and **Wilson**, 6,945yds, par 72, rated 71.5 (both are in *Griffith Park*). Local registered players may reserve starting times; visitors must wait for openings. For information on LA's seven 18-hole courses ☎ (213) 485-5555, and on LA County's 16 courses (mostly in the San Fernando Valley) ☎ (213) 738-2961.

Horseback riding

Once again, *Griffiths Park* is the place, with 250 miles of trails. Four stables rent out horses (see Yellow Pages under "Stables"). Or contact **Griffith Park Equestrian Center** (☎ *(818) 840-9063*).

Tennis

Visitors who are intent on playing tennis in LA should stay at a hotel with its own courts, or one that has arrangements with a nearby club. City residents may reserve court time at the 12-court **Vermont Canyon Center** (*Griffith Park on Vista del Valle Dr.*); visitors must wait for an opening. Nearby, the 4-court **Peppertree Lane** is first-come first-serve. There is an hourly charge for play at both places. For information on the city's 60 facilities ☎ (213) 485-5566.

Sailing and windsurfing
Marina Beach at Marina del Rey is excellent for both, and boats and boards can be rented by the half-day (see Yellow Pages).

Environs and excursions

As ever with LA and southern California, mobility is the key. All the areas and specific destinations listed below are easily accessible by one or other means of transportation — automobile, bus, plane, boat or train. And some of them are closer in time and effort than crossing Greater LA in rush hour. Angelenos do it, so why not visitors?

Catalina Island
*Map **15**J6. 27 miles offshore from Los Angeles. Served daily by a fleet of tour boats from San Pedro and Long Beach (reservations usually required summer and weekends) i Catalina Chamber of Commerce, PO Box 217, Avalon 90704 ☎ (213) 510-1520; Visitors' Information and Service Center ☎ (213) 510-2500; Catalina Cruises ☎ (213) 775-6111/832-4521.*
Movie stars escape to Catalina on their yachts or in their airplanes, followed by crowds of tourists who make the 2hr crossing on a fleet of comfortable passenger ferries and hydrofoils. Standard day-trip crossings allow passengers 4hrs ashore. Special cruises allow a full day trip. Spring and fall are the best times to visit.

For all the summer crowds, the 28-mile-long island (officially called Santa Catalina Island) remains a fine place for escapists. Its only town, **Avalon**, is a quiet beach resort with the air and architecture of a Mediterranean village. A particular charm is the near absence of cars, which are replaced by a sort of zoo-train, and bicycles that can be rented inexpensively. Avalon has overnight accommodations; the Chamber of Commerce makes reservations. The rest of the island, 86 percent in fact, is untamed natural beauty protected by the Santa Catalina Conservancy: mountains, canyons, cliffs, coves, sandy beaches and free-roaming wildlife.

Sights and places of interest
Catalina Casino
The 12-story building, Art Deco with overlays of Spanish Colonial, houses a movie theater, a museum (🖼 *open Easter-end Oct 1-4pm, 8-10pm; remainder of year Sat 1-4pm, 8-10pm, Sun and hols 1-4pm ; entrance fee includes tour of building*) and, far from least, the **Avalon Ballroom**, which once drew 6,200 to a single dance. Crowds today are not quite that large, but big bands do book here, mostly on weekends.

Recreation
Avalon has two sand beaches lapped by warm ocean waters ideal for swimming. **Crescent Beach** is in front of the town. **Pebble Beach** is E of the arrival pier. **Catalina Island Golf Course** (*PO Box 1564, Avalon 90704 ☎ (213) 510-0530*) has a 9-hole layout. It also has hourly-fee tennis courts.

Excursions
Catalina offers a number of tours. The most unusual are an after-dark flying fish boat trip (spotlights excite the fish to soar alongside and even over the boat), and a glass-bottom boat trip across Avalon's undersea gardens.

Bus tours of the unspoiled interior leave from the Island Plaza at the center of town, or from the nearby pier.

Long Beach

Map 15l6. On San Pedro Bay, 21 miles s of Los Angeles via the Long Beach Freeway/SR-7, or via the San Diego Freeway/I-405. Long Beach Airport served daily by PSA; bus connections from Los Angeles International by Airport Service Inc. ☎ *(714) 776-9210. City served daily by Greyhound Lines and Trailways, Inc.* i *Long Beach Visitors and Convention Bureau, 180 E Ocean Blvd., Long Beach 90802* ☎ *(213) 436-3645.*

Long Beach is one of a number of cities lost, in many ways, in the giant sandwich of Greater Los Angeles. Looking for identity beyond being a center of oil production, a US Navy base and a deepwater freight harbor, the city has made a bid for the tourist trade with the *Queen Mary,* and a large convention center used almost as much for concerts as for business meetings. At the same time, it has managed to make a fair secret of having one of the finest family beaches in all of southern California. Coves with even gentler shores, marinas and a fishing pier add luster.

Event   Long Beach Grand Prix. Conventional auto race through downtown. Mid-Mar.

Sights and places of interest
Long Beach Museum of Art
2300 E Ocean Blvd., Long Beach, adjoining the beach 1.4 miles E of Long Beach Convention Center ☎ *(213) 439-2119* 🖸 *Open Wed-Sun 1-5pm. Closed Mon, Tues, major hols.*
Permanent collection of works by contemporary southern Californians, in 1912 Craftsman-style building.
Port Adventure Harbor Cruise
Pier J Long Beach ☎ *(213) 547-0802* 🔳 *Cruises daily.*
A comfortable boat takes 90min trips through the busy maze of Long Beach and San Pedro Harbors, visiting areas inaccessible by land.
RMS Queen Mary and the Spruce Goose ★
Pier J Long Beach. At end of Long Beach Freeway/SR-7 ☎ *(213) 435-3511 (both sights), (213) 435-4747 (Queen Mary), (800) 421-3732 (Spruce Goose)* 🔳 *Open 10am-6pm, June 22-Labor Day 9am-9pm.*
There are three ways to go aboard this great old ship: as a hotel guest (see **LA Hotels**, as a visitor to the restaurants and shops, or on a self-guided tour.

The 50,000-ton *Queen Mary,* launched in 1934 and bought by Long Beach after its retirement in 1964, is the largest, most luxurious ocean liner still afloat. Elegant furnishings and fittings and painstaking craftsmanship reflect 1930s Art Deco styles. The period menus on display are not to be missed; prewar appetites appear to have been prodigious. There is also a sound-and-light show and a lifeboat demonstration. Children will enjoy **The Living Sea**, a museum devised by Jacques Cousteau.

The astonishing dome — the world's largest clear-span geodesic dome — alongside RMS *Queen Mary* houses Howard Hughes' *Spruce Goose.* Having a 320ft wingspan, it was the largest wooden airplane ever to fly, though it did so just once, and barely, for one mile on Nov 2, 1947.

One ticket buys both giants, plus exciting audiovisual displays.

Orange County

Map 15J6. Straddles both San Diego Freeway/I-405 and Santa Ana Freeway/I-5 and adjoins Los Angeles County to the N. Served daily by AirCal and Western Airlines (John Wayne-Orange County Airport at Costa Mesa); Airport Service Inc. bus from John Wayne-Orange County and Los Angeles International to Disneyland and Grand hotels; Amtrak (stops at Fullerton, Santa Ana, San Juan Capistrano and San Clemente); Greyhound Lines and Trailways, Inc. (no local service within county or from Los Angeles); RTD (☎ *(213) 626-4455) has bus service between Los Angeles downtown and Disneyland and*

LA Environs and excursions/Orange County

Knott's Berry Farm. Local transportation: Orange County Transit District (☎ (714) 636-7533), a countywide public transit system; Fun Bus (☎ (714) 635-1390), a loop run encompassing many hotels, Disneyland and Knott's Berry Farm **i** *Anaheim Area Visitors and Convention Bureau, 800 W Katella Ave., Anaheim 92802 ☎ (714) 999-8999; visitor center at the Anaheim Convention Center across Katella from Disneyland. American Express Travel Service Office: South Coast Plaza, 3333 Bristol St., Costa Mesa 92626 ☎ (714) 540-3611.*

Orange County is known from afar for **Disneyland** and **Newport Beach**, and for returning arch-conservatives to Congress. As the first two parts of its reputation promise, it is one of the most famous playgrounds in a state full of famous playgrounds.

Disneyland and the kindred **Knott's Berry Farm** anchor a series of parks and entertainments in the Anaheim-Buena Park area. Except for these, the industrial-residential towns in flat northern Orange County are of limited interest to visitors. (Between 1955 and 1965 the orange groves that gave the county its name were torn out, and the area became what Los Angeles has often been accused of being: 49 suburbs in search of a city.) The beach towns in the hilly s, on the other hand, uphold the paradisaical view of southern California.

Newport Beach is the home of the most affluent society of boat people on the whole Pacific Coast. Marinas, shops and restaurants, as well as many beach homes, are crowded onto a long, low-lying peninsula. Islands inside the bay have more of the same, and so does the mainland shore. Adjoining Corona del Mar is the tennis and golf suburb. This area is within easy reach of Disneyland and John Wayne-Orange County Airport.

More remote **Laguna Beach** began as an art colony and still has some of that flavor. Its gallery-lined shopping streets have a small-town atmosphere. Without a harbor, it is much more beach-oriented than Newport Beach. Other shoreside towns N and S beg not to be overlooked: **Huntington Beach** for surfing; **Capistrano Beach** for beaches and its mission; nearby **Dana Point** for beaches and boating; **San Clemente** also for its beach.

If Orange County lacks a center, at least its web of freeways makes travel simple. To get around reasonably well, visitors need only know freeways I-405, I-5 and SR-55, plus the Pacific Coast Highway/SR-1, Beach Blvd./SR-39, Harbor Blvd. and MacArthur Blvd.
Events Dana Point Harbor Festival of Whales. First three weekends in Feb. Celebrates the migration of gray whales with offshore tours plus lectures and other programs on sea life (**i** *Dana Point Harbor Association, 25102 Del Prado, Dana Point 92629*).

Festival of the Arts and Pageant of the Masters. Irvine Bowl, Laguna Beach. Early July-late Aug. Most celebrated aspect is locals portraying figures in living tableaux of famous paintings (**i** *Festival of Arts of Laguna Beach ☎ (714) 494-2685*).

Sights and places of interest

Although the county is compact enough to be explored as a whole, sights and places of interest are divided into those inland in the general area of Anaheim/Buena Park and those along the shore.
Anaheim Stadium
2000 State College Blvd., Anaheim, adjacent to Orange Freeway/SR-57 at Katella Ave. exit ☎ (714) 634-1002.
The 70,000-seat stadium is the home of the California Angels baseball team and the Los Angeles Rams football team (☎ (714) 937-6761).
Bowers Memorial Museum
2002 N Main St., Santa Ana, near Main St. exit from Santa Ana Freeway/I-5 ☎ (714) 972-1900 🔄 ➤ *Open Tues-Sat 9am-5pm, Sun noon-5pm. Closed Mon, major hols.*

Orange County does have a past, much of it locked up in this museum.
Displays include some fine Indian and early Californian relics, important
documents of the Mexican and Spanish eras, and early California art.

Disneyland ★

*PO Box 3232, Anaheim 92803, Santa Ana Freeway/I-5 to Harbor Blvd.
exit in Anaheim; entrance on Harbor Blvd. between Ball Rd. and Katella
Ave. ☎ (714) 999-4565 ▩ ✗ ◼ ✦ ℥ ▰ ㉏ Open daily 9am-midnight
May-Sept; remainder of year Wed-Fri 10am-6pm, Sat-Sun 10am-7pm,
but schedule expands for some hols (check with above address).*

Walt Disney's inspired marriage of the amusement park and the Hollywood set
opened on July 17, 1955 to rave reviews. The park has never lost that original
luster in spite of gaining at least a score of imitators. One of its secrets is
constant renewal of the major attractions. As important, the management pays
great attention to such finicky details as putting a little fun into standing in lines,
and getting to and from the parking lots, no small matter when attendance runs
at some 12 million a year. In the same vein, there's a baby care center (facilities,
no sitters), a day kennel, lockers and plentiful rest rooms.

No description of Disneyland will produce willing suspension of disbelief,
but the *place* does with margin to spare. An outline can only give hints.

Disneyland consists of seven "theme" lands. Main Street USA is the gateway,
and the plaza extending from it leads to the gates of other sections, in
clockwise order: Adventureland, Frontierland, New Orleans Square, Bear
Country, Fantasyland and Tomorrowland. All sections have strolling musicians,
street performers and living, breathing hosts dressed as Disney cartoon
characters, including Mickey Mouse, 60 years old in 1988. ("I hope we never
lose sight of one thing," said Walt Disney, "that it all started with a mouse.")

The sections are also populated by remarkably lifelike human and animal
characters animated by a Disney invention called Audio-Animatronics. The
audio part explains itself; the figures are wired for sound. The animatronics that
make them move are an ingenious combination of electronic signals and
pneumatic joints hidden under uncannily flesh-like hides. The technique is also
applied to animals, birds and flower figures.

Adventureland has flat-bottom boats that tour re-creations of Asia, Africa
and the South Pacific. Each stream has an animated adventure to go with it.
Hippos charge, elephants bathe, crocodiles stand sulky guard over temple
ruins, and the Swiss Family Robinson makes an appearance.

Bear Country is a re-creation of America's North West wilderness, the
vehicle a Davy Crockett canoe, the entertainment by animated bears.

Fantasyland features characters from Disney Studio movies, who gather
inside the gates of Sleeping Beauty's castle to conduct dressed-up carnival
rides. An anachronistic flivver re-creates Mr. Toad's Wild Ride through 19thC
England. There is a wilder ride to be had in whirling cups from the Mad
Hatter's Tea Party. But the real white-knuckle trip is the 14-story drop from the
top of the Matterhorn in a bobsled. More sedately, a circus train visits
Cinderella, Pinocchio and the Three Little Pigs, and a carousel has knightly
horses from King Arthur's court.

Frontierland is where the whole of the pioneering Old West is represented
one way or another. On the rivers of America are a Mississippi stem-wheeler,
the *Mark Twain*, and a square-rigger, *Columbia*. Visitors can pole out to Tom
Sawyer's island on the raft and, in a nifty piece of navigation, go for a voyage
on the *Columbia*. Big Thunder Mountain Railroad goes through a mine in
splendid style in spite of rock-slides, floods and bats.

Main Street USA is turn-of-the-century Americana; horse-drawn wagons and
buggies are the only vehicles in a town of nickelodeons, ice cream parlors, and
other shops perfectly scaled for children. Inside the Opera House, in a show
called Great Moments With Mr Lincoln, an animated figure of Abraham Lincoln
gives a lecture on American history.

New Orleans Square has Mardi Gras parades and Dixieland jazz (by real
players, not mechanical animations this time) and some eerie sides of the Old
South, including boat trips through a pirate-infested Caribbean, and a journey
through a house haunted by hologram ghosts.

Tomorrowland changes constantly, trying to keep up with its subjects:
space and science. Among the latest innovations are Star Tours, a stunning
journey through outer space re-created on a 40-passenger flight simulator, and
"Captain Eo," a 3-D space adventure starring Michael Jackson. The rides —
Submarine Voyage, Star Tours and Space Mountain — still thrill.

In addition to these more or less permanent attractions, the park schedules
rock, pop and folk concerts, and big-band concerts with dancing. The fullest
schedules are on summer evenings and at Christmas. A fine fireworks display
goes up at 9pm.

Disneyland "Passports" include admission and unlimited use of all attractions, except arcades; there are seasonal discounts for people aged over 60, and 2- or 3-day "passports." Food and gift stores will run costs higher. Tackling the densely packed park within a single day is nigh on impossible. The Disneyland Railroad provides previews of each section. The train departs on its 1½-mile loop from Main Street USA.

Each section of the park has a share of Disneyland's 25 restaurants ranging in style from fast food to fairly elaborate dinner houses.

Garden Grove Community Churches 🏛 †

12141 Lewis St., Garden Grove, SE of Disneyland near Chapman Ave. exit from Santa Ana Freeway/I-5 ☎ (714) 971-4000.

Southern California has a long history of attempts to fit religion to local climate and society. None has produced a more remarkable set of buildings than the Crystal Cathedral and two earlier structures. The **Crystal Cathedral**, 128ft (39m) high and 410ft (125m) long, towers above the flat landscape, an abstract geometric form of white steel trusses cloaked in silver tempered glass. Designed by architects Philip Johnson and John Burgee and opened in 1980, the church seats 2,862. Pastor Dr Robert Schuller had earlier (1955) commissioned a steel and glass building by International Style architect Richard Neutra with the novel intent of making his church services visible (and audible through speakers) to drive-in worshipers in a 1,400-capacity parking lot. In this most automobile-oriented region of the world, the idea worked well enough to require not only the Crystal Cathedral, but also a 15-story administration building called Tower of Hope, designed by Dion Neutra, Richard's son.

Knott's Berry Farm

8039 Beach Blvd., Buena Park, Beach Blvd. exit from Riverside Freeway/SR-91; main entrance on Beach Blvd. between La Palma Ave. and Crescent Ave.; auxiliary entrances on La Palma Ave. and Western Ave. ☎ (714) 827-1776 🔲 📶 ⬤ 🟰 AE 🔲 🔳 🔲 Open May-Sept, Sun-Thurs 9am-midnight, Fri-Sat 9am-1am; remainder of year Mon-Tues 10am-6pm, Fri-Sun 10am-9pm, but schedule expands for some hols (check first). Closed Dec 25.

This is the other major theme park in Orange County. Knott's Berry Farm is bigger than Disneyland (135 acres) and older (the first restaurant dates back to 1934, the first amusement rides to the 1940s, when the Knott family still had a working berry farm), but the main distinction between it and its near neighbor is that the themes in Knott's focus entirely on nostalgia rather than fantasy. Also, there is greater emphasis on thrill rides in the theme sections called Fiesta Village, Old West Ghost Town and Roaring Twenties. There are age and height restrictions on some rides.

In **Fiesta Village**, a loop roller coaster called Montezooma's Revenge is a white-knuckle trip. The theme of Mexico and early California is carried into shops, demonstrations of crafts and a Mexican restaurant. El Cinema Grande shows movies on a 180' screen and well-known rock bands play live music.

Bandits in the **Old West Ghost Town** hold up every trip of the Butterfield Stage and every run of the Denver Rio Grande narrow-gauge railroad. The thrill ride is in hollowed-out logs on an old-fashioned, Paul Bunyanesque logging flume. Visitors looking for quieter thrills can pan for gold. The saloon serves sarsaparilla or boysenberry punch, and has can can dancers. Fried chicken is the specialty of the restaurant, a much enlarged successor to the original.

The big thrill ride in the **Roaring Twenties** is a corkscrew roller coaster. Amid considerable attention to pioneer flying, there is a 20-story parachute tower (the chutes drop on guy wires with riders securely perched on small platforms). Well-known entertainers and/or ice shows play at the Good Time Theater. A dance hall, Cloud 9, helps keep the Charleston alive and kicking.

Oak Canyon Nature Center

200 S Anaheim Blvd., Anaheim; from Riverside Freeway/SR-91, s on Imperial Highway to Nohl Ranch Rd.; E to Walnut Canyon Rd., then follow it to its end ☎ (714) 998-8380 🔳 but donation welcome. Open 9am-5pm except major hols.

Within 58 compact acres, a hands-on interpretive center, six miles of hiking trails and staff naturalists teach useful lessons about everything from roadrunners to rattlesnakes to anyone wishing to explore regional wilderness safely and intelligently in any season.

Newport Beach and the Coast

Huntington Beach Pier

Pacific Coast Highway/SR-1 at the foot of Main St., Huntington Beach.
If there is one perfect place to watch surfers at peak form, this is it. Wave action

around the pier makes top-drawer riders in this area use its pilings as a sort of
slalom course. Waves just alongside are reliable for long rides. .

Mission San Juan Capistrano †
31882 Camino Capistrano, one block w of SR-74 junction with I-5
☎ *(714) 493-1111* 📷 *Open 7am-5pm.*
Founded by Father Junipero Serra in 1776, San Juan Capistrano, seventh of the
missions, is one of the most moving to visit. Its ornately decorated church is the
only known remaining site at which Serra said mass. Its wider fame is as the
home to which the swallows return every year, in romantic tales, on St Joseph's
Day, Mar 19. The birds migrate s around Oct 23, the date on which the patron
saint of the mission died.

Newport Harbor Art Museum
850 San Clemente Dr. ☎ *(714) 759-1122. Donation requested. Open
Tues-Sun 11am-5pm, Fri 6-9pm. Closed Mon.*
Permanent and rotating exhibitions are devoted almost entirely to
contemporary southern California artists.

Wild Rivers
*8800 Irvine Center Dr., Irvine, adjacent to San Diego Freeway/I-5 at Irvine
Center Dr. exit* ☎ *(714) 768-9453* 📷 ♿ *Open 10am-8pm mid-June to
mid-Sept: 11am-5pm weekends and hols mid-May to mid-June and
mid-Sept to end Sept. Closed remainder of year.*
The theme is water, most of it wild, but some of it tame. Of 40 water rides and
attractions in the 20-acre park, 19 plummet from 5-story-high Wild River
Mountain. On the Bombay Blaster, one plummets the five stories in five
seconds inside a soft foam tube. A more sedate section called Explorers Island
has gentle, drifting rides, and three huge swimming pools.

Recreation
Beaches and recreation are almost synonymous in Orange County,
but fishing, boating, tennis and golf count for almost as much with
locals and visitors alike. For visitors, beaches and fishing are
accessible everywhere. Tennis and golf are associated primarily with
hotels because of heavy local pressure on public courts and courses.

Beaches
From the Los Angeles County line at Seal Beach s to Newport Beach,
the Orange County coast is low-lying, virtually one continuous sandy
beach. From Newport Beach s the coast grows more rugged, and
sandy beaches are more apt to be short, at the back of coves. Much
of the shore is state beach property. Most of the vacation and resort
beaches range s from Huntington Beach.

Beaches of particular interest, N to S: **Santa Ana River County
Beach** is Newport Beach's share of the long sandy strand. Surfing is
good at the mouth of the **Santa Ana River** and at **Newport Pier**;
the latter is also a favored place for pier fishermen. At the tip of the
Balboa peninsula, a spot called **The Wedge** is legendary among
body surfers.

Laguna Beach has a length of white sand for swimmers and
sunbathers extending s from a small developed park area at Laguna
Canyon Rd./Broadway. The park has picnic tables, volleyball nets
and other amusements. Some miles s, **Aliso Beach County Park**
has picnic tables and lawns, and a fishing pier. The beach is good for
swimming, and surfing is reliably excellent here.

Doheny State Beach, adjoining Dana Harbor to the s and forming
the shore of Capistrano Beach, is one of the most popular in the
system. Surfing is good at the mouth of a lagoon. Inside Dana
Harbor, a sheltered beach is excellent for families with small children.

Palm Springs
*On SR-111, 103 miles E of Los Angeles via I-10. Palm Springs
Airport served daily by Alaska Airlines, American Airlines,
TWA, Western Airlines, and commuter lines from Los Angeles
and San Diego. City served daily by Greyhound Lines. Useful
publications: Key, Palm Springs Life's Desert Guide. Local
transportation: most hotels provide van or limousine service to*

and from the airport. Sunline ☎ (619) 323-8157) provides useful intercity service in the Coachella Valley. Downtown Palm Springs has a London double-decker called the Sun Special
i Palm Springs Convention & Visitors Bureau, 255 N El Cielo Rd., Suite 315, Palm Springs 92262 ☎ (619) 327-8411.

Palm Springs is to deserts what *Carmen* is to operas. What other opera has such tunes in such a straightforward story? What other desert has 70 lush golf courses, 600 tennis courts and 7,500 swimming pools?

In strictest truth, Palm Springs has only a fraction of either total. The rest are in the connected communities of **Cathedral City**, **Rancho Mirage**, **Palm Desert** and **La Quinta**, all farther down the Coachella Valley. However, Palm Springs is good shorthand for the lot because it was the first link in the chain and gave rise to the rest.

On alluvium at the foot of the steep, barren San Jacinto Mountains, Palm Springs started as a winter retreat for the stars in the early days of Hollywood. Today, the stars still come to the resort, but it has also become a retirement town for the wealthy. For vacations, rich or not so rich, spring and fall have become popular seasons as well as winter, but only confirmed desert rats spend much time in this town in the heat of summer.

Sights and places of interest

Desert Museum 🏛

At 101 Museum Dr., two blocks W of North Palm Canyon Dr., via Tahquitz-McCallum Way ☎ (619) 325-7186 ▪ 🚗 Open Tues-Sat 10am-5pm, Sun 1-5pm. Closed Mon.

In the fine natural history section, permanent dioramas explain the basics of the local desert ecosystem. There are also changing displays of art relating to the desert. The pure art sections include attractive sculpture gardens and several galleries. A small permanent collection of paintings is continuously augmented by traveling exhibitions.

Living Desert ☆

At 47-900 Portola Ave., 1½ miles S of SR-111 ☎ (619) 346-5694 ▪ ✱ 🚗 Open 9am-5pm Sept-May. Closed (except to Grayline tours) June-Aug.

On 350 acres of ridge and wash there are living specimens of most of the plants and animals native to the area. The plants and some of the animals are easy to see on either of two walks, one a stroll in the 20 acres nearest the parking lot, the other a stiff 5-mile hike covering the whole reserve. The highlight is a building where a special lighting system turns day into night so that the desert's nocturnal creatures can be seen going about their business.

Palm Springs Aerial Tramway

Lower station is 3½ miles off SR-111 on Tramway Rd. at Palm Springs N city limit ☎ (619) 325-1391 ▪ 🚗 Open Mon-Fri 10am-9.15pm, Sat-Sun 8am-9.15pm. Closed Sept.

Two 80-passenger streetcars give riders dramatic views of Palm Springs and the desert between Chino Canyon (2,643ft/806m elevation) and Mountain Station (8,516ft/2,596m). Evening passengers can eat dinner at a steak house at the top. Mountain Station is the gateway to 13,000-acre **Mt San Jacinto State Park**, a well-used hiking area from spring to fall, and a modest snow-sports area in winter.

Nearby sights

Cabot's Old Indian Pueblo Museum 🏛

67624 Desert View Ave., Desert Hot Springs ☎ (619) 329-7610 ▪ 🚗 Open Wed-Mon 9.30am-4.30pm. Closed Tues, major hols.

Cabot Yerxa belonged to the legion of desert eccentrics. His 35-room Pueblo-style house, built mostly with homemade adobe and salvage, is testimony not only in itself, but through its random collections of Indian and Eskimo memorabilia and general souvenirs of Yerxa's life.

Joshua Tree National Monument

From Los Angeles, 124 miles E via I-10 and SR-62 to Twentynine Palms.

In 870sq. miles of rolling to mountainous desert, the national monument preserves the greatest natural stands of the spiky tree after which it is named. Joshuas (*Yucca brevifolia*) grow at relatively cool elevations above 3,000ft

(914m); the stubbier Mojave Yucca (*Yucca schidigera*) grows lower down. The great desert preserve also supports fine herds of desert bighorn sheep, although few visitors catch glimpses of these shy animals. Only lightly touched by man, the park still has as one of its most intriguing aspects the abandoned ranch of William Keys, ghostly subject of daily free tours from park headquarters at Twentynine Palms.

Joshua Tree NM lies within easy reach of Palm Springs. Although the park has campgrounds, most have no water or fuel; campers must bring their own. Also, day trippers from nearby desert communities must bring water for themselves and their car radiators.

Salton Sea
45 miles SE of Palm Springs on SR-111.
This accidental inland desert sea, 38 miles long, 228ft below sea level and stocked with salt-tolerant corvina, is one of southern California's most popular fishing lakes in summer, but is more pleasant to visit in winter. Along the eastern shore the extensive **Salton Sea State Recreation Area** caters to campers, swimmers and boatmen, and has a natural history interpretive center. At the S tip of the lake, a national wildlife refuge is a stopover for 250 species of migrating shore birds. Nearby are several mineral hot springs.

Recreation
Golf and tennis
Greater Palm Springs has numerous courses and courts open to the public, others described as "semi-private" where visitors are sometimes welcome, and still more that are strictly private. For a comprehensive list see the Convention and Visitors Bureau monthly *Palm Springs Life's Desert Guide* (☎ *(619) 325-2333*).

San Diego
On the Pacific Coast 127 miles S of Los Angeles via I-5. Served daily by AirCal, American Airlines, Braniff, Continental Airlines, Delta Airlines, Eastern Airlines, National Airlines, Northwest Airlines, Ozark Airlines, PSA, Pan-American Airways, Southwest Airlines, TWA, United Airlines, Western Airlines and commuter airlines, Amtrak, Greyhound Lines and Trailways, Inc. i San Diego Convention & Visitors Bureau, 1200 Third Ave., Suite 824, San Diego 92101 ☎ (619) 232-3101; recorded calendar of events ☎ (619) 239-9696. Local transportation: San Diego Transit, regional transit system serving city and suburbs (☎ (619) 233-3004); Light Rail Transit, the San Diego trolley (☎ (619) 231-1466). City tours: Grayline Tours (☎ (619) 231-9922); Harbor Excursions (☎ (619) 234-4111); San Diego Mini Tours (☎ (619) 234-9044). Useful publications: San Diego Tribune, San Diego Union, especially Fri and Sun editions; San Diego Magazine is monthly; advertiser-oriented monthlies free in hotel rooms include Where Magazine, Today in San Diego (tabloid). Emergency information: Police ☎ 911; hospital ☎ 911.
California began at San Diego in 1542 when Juan Rodriguez Cabrillo made the first landfall by a European at Point Loma. In 1769, Gaspar de Portola founded a presidio and Padre Junipero Serra planted a cross near the mouth of the San Diego River, establishing the first European settlement within the state.

Traces of Spanish history linger, but are scattered in this strikingly American city, the second largest in California. Perhaps the Middle America impression is exaggerated because the US-Mexican border and the city of Tijuana are just 18 miles S, but San Diego is still surprising after the Mediterranean flavors of other coastal cities all the way N to San Francisco.

Contemporary San Diego is a huge military port, major tuna fishing harbor and commercial center with literally hundreds of square miles of suburbs sprawling across a series of hills and mesas separated from each other by steep-sided arroyos (streams). For most visitors, however, all of these facets are of less interest than San Diego's zoo

103

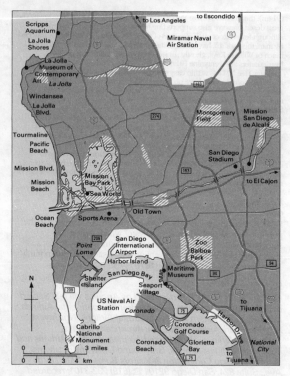

and superb year-round beach resorts.

The **zoo**, in Balboa Park near the city center, is one of the most famous in the world. The beaches at **La Jolla**, **Pacific Beach**, **Mission Bay** and **Coronado** have four entirely different characters. La Jolla smells even more of money than it does of salt water; it has the chic touches. Tom Wolfe found The Pump House Gang of surfers at Windansea at La Jolla in the early 1960s; today surfers still reign from Windansea s through Pacific and Mission Beaches to the San Diego River mouth, although nonsurfers also will be charmed by the affluent resort. The great recreation area of Mission Bay has no permanent population, only hotel guests, while Coronado is a peaceful, quiet, low-key community of people who delight in their isolation on the sandy peninsula that forms the outer side of San Diego Bay.

If San Diego's long history is not a magnet of quite the same power, it does lend some interesting fillips. **Cabrillo National Monument**, **Old Town** and **Balboa Park's museums** hold the highlights.

Events　　Theater festival, Old Globe Theatre in Balboa Park. Early June through summer. Three plays by a repertory company (*i (619) 231-1941*).

San Diego Air Show. Miramar Naval Air Station. Aug. Contemporary military aircraft in flight and on the ground.

Sights and places of interest
Balboa Park
The oldest and one of the largest of the great municipal parks on the Pacific

Coast, Balboa contains not only San Diego's great zoo but most of the city's museums, and still has room to spare for outdoor theaters, a municipal golf course, picnic lawns and playgrounds. Near downtown, the park's main features are on or near El Prado, between the 6th Ave. and Laurel St. entrance and any of several entrances off Park Blvd. Entry to the park is free of charge, but most of the exhibitions have an entrance fee.

The **Aero-Space Museum** (*s of El Prado at 2001 Pan American Plaza* ☎ (619) 234-8291 ▨ *open 10am-4.30pm, closed hols*) contains a replica of Charles Lindbergh's *Spirit of St Louis*, built in San Diego by craftsmen from the Ryan company, as was the original. But the most striking flying machine in the hall is Leonardo da Vinci's uncanny anticipation of the hang-glider. Other original and reproduction small aircraft span the age of flight from the Wright brothers to US Navy carrier jets. Under the same roof, the **International Aero-Space Hall of Fame** honors great fliers with displays of memorabilia.

The **Botanical Building** (*ε half of El Prado* ▢ *open Sat-Thurs 10am-4.30pm, closed Mon-Wed and hols*) is an old railroad depot that now houses collections of tropical and subtropical plants.

The **Reuben H. Fleet Space Theater and Science Center** (*ε end of El Prado* ☎ (619) 238-1233, *open 10am-9pm*) is a single building that houses two attractions. The multimedia **Space Theater** (★ ▨) creates eerie illusions of travel in space via movies shown on a hemispheric screen that is also used for conventional planetarium shows. The adjoining **Science Center** (★ ▨ ✳) teaches a broad range of lessons through displays that visitors operate themselves. Weekend crowds often overwhelm both facilities.

The **Museum of Man** (*w end of El Prado* ☎ (619) 239-2001 ▢ *open 10am-4.30pm, closed Jan 1, Thanksgiving, Dec 25*) has major sections dealing with prehistoric man and North American Indians. But by far the most intriguing permanent displays are Mayan. Lucid translations of religious symbols and the Mayan arithmetic system accompany massive original carved stones. Artisans sometimes demonstrate old crafts in the main foyer.

The **Museum of Natural History** (*ε end of El Prado* ☎ (619) 232-3821 ▨ *open 10am-5pm mid-June to Sept, 10am-4.30pm remainder of year, closed Jan 1, Dec 25*) contains paleontologic and contemporary displays of animals, plants and minerals.

The **Old Globe Theatre**, newly rebuilt after a fire, is a reconstruction of the Bard's original and the site of San Diego's summer theater festival (see *Events* in introductory copy).

The **San Diego Museum of Art** (*midway along El Prado* ☎ (619) 232-7931 ▨ *open Tues-Sun 10am-5pm, closed Mon, Jan 1, Thanksgiving, Dec 25*) is one of the most important museums in the state. It has permanent collections of European masters from the early Renaissance to the early 20thC, as well as early American decorative arts and Mexican paintings. A rental gallery has contemporary local works.

San Diego Zoo (★ *Park Blvd. at Village Pl.* ☎ (619) 231-1515 ▨ ✗ ▣ ✱ ➤ open July 1-Labor Day 9am-6pm; Mar 1-June 30 and Labor Day-Oct 31 9am-5pm; Nov 1-Feb 28 9am-4pm) has some 800 animal species, including one of two koala groups in the USA. Other collections of particular interest include primates and reptiles. Each animal lives in as exact a reproduction of its natural environment as climate and space will permit, except for the peaceable occupants of the children's zoo. For extra fees, tour buses and an overhead tramway help visitors to get around the often steep 128 acres, but even with these aids this is a place for walking shoes.

If possible, avoid weekends when the zoo is usually too crowded for comfort. The animals are most active early, before the heat of the day makes them drowsy. (See also **Wild Animal Park** under *Nearby sights*.)

The **Timken Gallery** (*near the middle of El Prado* ☎ (619) 239-5548 ▢ open Tues-Sat 10am-4.30pm, Sun 1.30-4.30pm, closed Mon, Jan 1, Sept, Thanksgiving, Dec 25) is a privately endowed small museum containing a collection of Russian icons. In addition, there are oil paintings by old masters, including Rembrandt, Rubens, El Greco and Brueghel.

Balboa Park has several small museums and cultural centers as well as outdoor recreation grounds. A visitor center near the corner of El Prado and Plaza de Panama has maps and informative leaflets.

Cabrillo National Monument

At the end of SR-209 ☎ (619) 293-5450 ▢ ➤ *Open 8.30am-7.45pm mid-June to Labor Day, 9am-5.15pm rest of year.*

At the tip of Point Loma this is among the most visited of all American national monuments or parks, preserving within 144 acres a micro-section of coastline little changed from the day Cabrillo landed. Also within the monument: a lighthouse built in 1854; a lookout point for watching migrating gray whales from Nov-Mar; an interpretive center; a statue of Cabrillo donated by Portugal; and some fine tidepools. Not least, the high ground affords magnificent views back to the city.

The Harbor

San Diego crowds the most interesting parts of its great harbor into a stretch reaching from Grape St. on the N side to the B St. Pier, encompassing within eight blocks its Maritime Museum and working piers for the tuna fleet. The Embarcadero runs right along the seawall. Seaport Village lies just s; the small boat harbors and marinas of **Harbor Island** and **Shelter Island** (see *Recreation*) are not far N, but are out of easy walking distance.

Three vessels are the heart of **The Maritime Museum** (*1306 N Harbor Dr., foot of Broadway* ☎ *(619) 234-9153* ▨ ⚓ *open 9am-8pm*). The centerpiece is the square-rigged *Star of India*, built in Great Britain in 1863 as the *Euterpe* and now the oldest merchant ship afloat and seaworthy. Berthed with her are the old San Francisco Bay ferryboat *Berkeley* and the British-built luxury steam yacht *Medea*. The vessels contain displays of local maritime history; women are requested to wear low heels for below-deck touring.

At Grape Street Pier the docks are built so that passers-by can watch tuna fishermen mending their nets.

La Jolla Museum of Contemporary Art

700 Prospect St., La Jolla ☎ *(619) 454-0267* ▨ *Open Tues-Fri 10am-5pm, Sat-Sun 12.30-5pm. Closed Mon, hols.*

The only art museum in the region focusing on modern art has both a permanent collection and traveling exhibitions. The building is itself of interest.

Mission San Diego De Alcalá ⛪ †

10818 San Diego Mission Rd., I-8 E to I-15/Murphy Canyon Rd., then N ☎ *(619) 283-7319* ▨ ⚓ *Open 9am-5pm. Closed Dec 25.*

The first of the 21-mission chain, now on a sharp knoll looking across to ultramodern **San Diego Stadium**, the mission chapel, a small museum and garden create a serene atmosphere, although not quite a sense of earlier times owing to overwhelming development around and about. Serra founded the mission in 1769, then moved it from its original location near Old Town to this site in 1774.

Old Town

Close to the intersection of I-5 and I-8, near the site of Gaspar de Portola's original presidio, Old Town preserves some of the earliest buildings in San Diego's first civil community. A **State Historic Park** encompasses about half of a 12-square-block area rescued from decay as part of the city's observance of the US bicentennial.

The park (☎ *(619) 294-5182* ⚲ *daily at 2pm*) and its surrounding area contain examples of adobes from the Spanish population and brick or frame buildings from the early Anglo settlers. Construction dates range from 1810-70. These buildings house an engaging mixture of museums, shops and restaurants. The main area is bounded by Juan St. and Congress St. and by the Pacific Highway and Twiggs St. Limited parking and some large open spaces mean a good deal of walking across fairly level ground.

Inside the park there are several small museums. One simply called **The Historical Museum** has a model of Old Town in 1870, plus displays of artifacts. The **San Diego Union Building** (*2626 San Diego Ave.* ☎ *(619) 297-2119* ▨ *open 10am-6pm, closed Jan 1, Thanksgiving, Dec 25*) is a reconstruction of the original offices and production plant of the city's major newspaper. **Seeley Stables** (*2648 Calhoun St.* ▨ ⚲ *open 10am-6pm summer, 10am-5pm rest of year, closed Jan 1, Thanksgiving, Dec 25*) houses a collection of horse-drawn vehicles including some stagecoaches. Other buildings include an early schoolhouse and several residences and small businesses. One of the most impressive structures, **Casa de Bandini**, is occupied by an elegantly furnished Mexican restaurant of the same name.

Outside the park's boundaries there are two more historic museums. To the E, **Whaley House Museum** (*2482 San Diego Ave.* ☎ *(619) 298-2482* ▨ *open Wed-Sun 10am-4.30pm*), San Diego's first brick house, is a restoration of a prestigious family's residence built in 1857. To the N, the San Diego Historical Society's **Junipero Serra Museum** (*2727 Presidio Dr., Presidio Park* ☎ *(619) 297-3258* ▨ *but donation requested, open Mon-Sat 9am-5pm, Sun noon-5pm, closed Jan 1, Thanksgiving, Dec 25*) houses important early documents and artifacts and a scholarly library.

Scripps Aquarium ☆

8602 La Jolla Shores Dr. ☎ *(619) 534-6933* ▨ ⚓ *Open 9am-5pm.*

One of the world's great institutions of oceanography, Scripps maintains an excellent aquarium-museum on the shore at La Jolla cove. Displays include tanks of rare fish from around the world, models of tidepools and depictions of oceanographic research work. Main feeding times for the animals are Sun and Wed at 1.30pm. A shuttle bus takes visitors from parking lot to aquarium.

Sea World ☆
1720 South Shores Rd., San Diego ☎ (619) 226-3901 ▨ *𝑲* ▣ *≉* ⇌ *Open 9am-dusk.*

At the s shore of Mission Bay, this first-rate theme park is built around spectacular shows by killer whales, porpoises and other sea mammals, but is hardly limited to them. The spacious grounds also have educational exhibits, a petting pool and recreation area called Cap'n Kids World.

Nearby sights

Two of San Diego's intriguing contributions to science are to the E and NE of the city in desert hills.

Palomar Observatory
Palomar, N of Escondido, 20 miles E of 1-15 via SR-76 ☎ (619) 742-3476 ▨ ⇌ *Open daily 9am-5pm. Closed Dec 25.*

One of the world's great optical observatories, Palomar has the 200in (5m) **Hale Telescope**, among others. In the same building, the **Greenway Museum** displays photos of the observatory's sightings.

Wild Animal Park
15500 San Pasqual Valley Rd., Escondido ☎ (619) 234-6541 or (619) 231-1515 ▨ ▣ ⇌ *Open mid-June to Labor Day 9am-9pm; Labor Day-Oct 31 and Mar 1 to mid-June 9am-5pm; Oct 31-Apr 30 9am-4pm.*

This 1,800-acre property belonging to the San Diego Zoological Society is a beautifully natural home for more than 2,200 free-roaming African and Asian animals. It is also both a reverse zoo (human visitors get around in monorail cars or other cages) and a pseudo-safari theme park complete with restaurants, live music shows and other diversions.

Recreation

For sensible reasons of safety, San Diego's ocean beaches are divided into swimming and surfing zones. Mission Bay and southern San Diego Bay have sheltered waters for swimming.

Fine ocean swimming beaches include **Coronado Municipal Beach** (the whole shore of the town), **La Jolla Shores**, w of La Jolla Shores Dr., via Vallecitos, and parts of **Pacific** and **Mission** beaches. **Silver Strand State Park**, s of Coronado, has a well-developed bayside beach. Several sections of shorelines in Mission Bay have sandy beaches.

Surfers have a choice of beaches all along the ocean shore. Favored among them are **Windansea**, off La Jolla Blvd. at Del Norte, **Tourmaline**, off Mission Blvd. at Loring, in La Jolla, and **Ocean Beach**, just s of the San Diego River mouth via Sunset Cliffs Blvd. to Niagara. Prime times are early morning and just before sunset.

Boating

Both sailboats and powerboats can be rented on San Diego and Mission Bays, and some marinas offer short courses in sailing. Jet skis are also available for rent. At the other extreme, every sort of paddleboat can be rented at Mission Bay. See telephone book Yellow Pages under *Marinas*. Note also that all of the major hotels on Mission Bay have boats for rent.

The E end of the South Pacific Passage section of Mission Bay is reserved for jet skis and high-speed water-skiers. The navy restricts skiing in some areas of San Diego Bay, but it is permitted in Glorietta Bay and in sheltered waters behind Harbor and Shelter Islands.

Fishing

Party boat companies operate from Quivira Basin on **Mission Bay**, **San Diego Bay** near Shelter Island, and from the northern suburb of **Oceanside**. All offer half-day trips.

Public pier fishing can be productive in San Diego. Bonito and halibut are the commonest catches from deep water; yellowfin and spotfin croaker feed at the breaker line. Piers in the area include **Ocean Beach Pier** and **Shelter Island Pier** in San Diego, and

Harbor Fishing Pier and **Oceanside Pier** upcoast at Oceanside. No fishing license is required. Tackle may not be available for rent at all of these piers, but may be obtained from nearby. See telephone book Yellow Pages under *Fishing Bait.*

Golf

San Diego County has a few more than 60 courses. About a third are open to the public; resort courses open to guests at affiliated hotels increase that number almost to half.

Public courses of particular interest include **Coronado Golf Course** (*2000 Visalia Row, Coronado* ☎ *(619) 435-3121*) 6,306yds, par 72, rated 70; **Cottonwood Country Club** (*3121 Willow Glen Rd., El Cajon* ☎ *(619) 442-9891*), Ivanhoe Course 6,719yds, par 73, rated 72.1, Monte Vista Course 6,100yds, par 72, rated 66; and **Torrey Pines Municipal** (*11480 N Torrey Pines Rd., La Jolla* ☎ *(619) 453-0380*), South Course 6,649yds, par 72, rated 71.5, North Course 6,317yds, par 72, rated 69.8.

Torrey Pines and Coronado are impossibly crowded on weekends; best time at both is weekdays from noon onward; the long drive E helps keep Cottonwood more available.

There are two grand golf and tennis resorts in the region: **La Costa Country Club** (*2 miles E of the beach town of Carlsbad via La Costa Ave.*) has 36 holes of fine golf available only to guests at the **La Costa Hotel and Spa** (*Costa del Mar Rd., Carlsbad* ☎ *(619) 438-9111*); and **Rancho Bernardo Inn and Country Club** (*17550 Bernardo Oaks Dr., San Diego, 2 miles NE of I-15 on the N side of Escondido* ☎ *(619) 487-0700*) is open to fee play, with guests at the Inn having priority for starting times.

Two less costly golf and tennis resorts: **Singing Hills Lodge** (*3007 Dahesa Rd., El Cajon* ☎ *(619) 442-3425*) has 54 holes of golf; **Whispering Palms Country Club** (*Rancho Santa Fe* ☎ *(619) 756-2471*) also has 54 holes.

Tennis

San Diego has scores of public courts. The most likely centers for players looking for an opponent are: **Morley Field** (*Balboa Park*), 25 courts; **Mission Bay Youth Field** (*at NE tip of Mission Bay*), 8 courts; and **Robb Field** (*just off Sunset Cliffs Dr., across the San Diego River from Mission Bay*), 12 courts. **Coronado Tennis Center** (*near the Hotel del Coronado*) has 8 courts. **La Jolla Recreation Center** (*615 Prospect at S side of town*) has 9 courts. Nonresidents must pay a daily court fee; all players must make reservations.

All the golf and tennis resorts noted under *Golf* have tennis facilities. **La Costa** has 25 courts, **Rancho Bernardo** 16, **Singing Hills** 12, **Whispering Palms** 11.

San Simeon

Map 14H3. On SR-1, 248 miles NW of Los Angeles.

San Simeon is essentially synonymous with the opulent, grotesque castle of newspaper baron William Randolph Hearst (1863-1951). Yet a whole village surrounds the main house, and a state beach and a cluster of motels and shops flank the hilltop monument.

Architect Julia Morgan and the master craftsmen who built San Simeon, the castle, high above the sea, began in the 1920s using walls, furnishings, sometimes entire rooms taken from historic buildings in Europe. A major purpose was to give Hearst a fit place in which to keep company with movie queen Marion Davies and many other Hollywood VIPs. The result is an astonishingly eclectic building; here a Roman pool, there a Gothic dining room, and everywhere fine pieces of art. The mix-and-match extravagance is overwhelmingly vulgar, but San Simeon is none the less fascinating as a result.

After Hearst's death, his family gave this residential core of their 275,000-acre estate to the state, to be used as a State Historical Monument open to the public. The **castle** (🏛 ★ ☎ *(805) 927-2020* 📷 ✗ *open 8.30am-3.30pm, closed Thanksgiving, Dec 25, Jan 1*) offers three separate tours, each beginning with a 5-mile bus ride up what Hearst called "Enchanted Hill." Tour One is of the main floor of the mansion plus gardens and guesthouse, Tour Two takes in several upper-story bedrooms, Hearst's libraries and the kitchen. Tour Three includes still more bedrooms, but focuses on art. The tours may be taken consecutively or on separate days, but each must be reserved and paid for separately. Each lasts about 2hrs and involves a substantial amount of walking and climbing. Some tickets are available at the Visitor Center (which also houses a permanent exhibit detailing Hearst's career), but advanced reservations are advised (☎ *(800) 444-7275, (619) 452-1950*). W.A. Swanberg's *Citizen Hearst* is recommended reading before visiting San Simeon.

Santa Barbara
Map 15l5. Straddles US-101, 96 miles N of Los Angeles. Served daily by American, United and commuter airlines, Amtrak and Greyhound Lines ℹ Conference and Visitors Bureau, PO Box 299, Santa Barbara 93102 ☎ (805) 965-3021; Santa Barbara Chamber of Commerce, 1 Santa Barbara St. ☎ (805) 965-3021.

Santa Barbara comes close to living up to the myth of California as earthly paradise. No climate is more benign in a state famous for benign climates. Even the sea is tempered here by a shield of offshore islands. In addition to these natural advantages, the small city has a rare civility owing in part to long-standing wealth, in part to one of the nine campuses of the University of California, and in part to well-remembered Spanish beginnings.

Santa Barbara started out as a Spanish presidio and mission in the 1780s. In every quarter, it still looks as if it has been transported lock, stock and barrel from some Spanish hillside. Subtropical gardens half hide villas with white walls and red-tiled roofs. Even the public buildings appear to have been designed in Seville or Jerez. Local feeling for a Mediterranean way of life goes beyond architecture: Santa Barbara awakens slowly, and does not hurry to bed at night.

Santa Barbara's particular charm as a resort city is that it has made no effort to be a resort city. The major hotels hide away from downtown traffic routes. Downtown stores and shopping centers serve local needs first, and visitors' needs only incidentally. The shops and restaurants are nevertheless excellent, partly owing to high standards, partly because of Santa Barbara's role as a principal escape for Los Angelenos. It is largely they who keep resorts and hotels sold out weeks in advance all summer long, and on weekends year round. But it is a different, slower-paced LA crowd than the one at Palm Springs.

Two last points: local public transportation is very good; and the orientation of the coast causes the sun to rise over the Pacific and set over the hills behind the town, which may at first bewilder newcomers.

Sights and places of interest
County Courthouse of Santa Barbara 🏛
1100 Anacapa St., at Figueroa St. 🖼 Open Mon-Fri 8am-5pm, Sat-Sun and hols 9am-5pm ✗ Wed and Fri 10.30am.
Spanish Colonial-style flourishes here in architect William Mooser's 1926 monumental collection of plain and fancy tiles, decorated beams, columns and arches. A clock tower, open weekdays only, gives fine views across the city. Pleasant gardens much used for pageantry fill a block-square site.

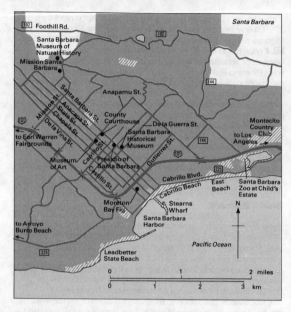

The Harbor

Santa Barbara's small boat harbor begins at the foot of State St., and has three main elements. **Stearns Wharf** is a refurbished collection of restaurants, tourist shops and bait stores for pier fishermen. Around to the w, the breakwater holds offices for operators of offshore cruises and charter boats, as well as boat sales agencies, tackle stores and marina offices. Between these extremities a smaller pier is the home base of a fleet of party fishing boats, which sail on half-day and full-day trips, mostly for calico and sand bass, rock cod and halibut.

Mission Santa Bárbara †

E Olivos St., at Laguna St., 4 blocks toward the mountain from State St., via Los Olivos St. ☎ *(805) 682-4713* 🔟 *Open 9am-5pm.*

Called the "Queen of the Missions" because of its comparatively refined Romanesque design and construction. Santa Barbara was founded in 1786. The present buildings date from 1812-20; they replaced earlier structures damaged in an earthquake. Tenth in the chain, the mission has a small museum of its founding era. Its church remains in active use, the only mission continuously in the hands of its founding order.

Moreton Bay Fig

Chapala St., near Santa Barbara's main beach.

Specimens of this gigantic New Zealand native tree exist elsewhere in southern California, but no other thrives as this one, which was planted in 1877. The canopy measures some 160ft (49m) in diameter.

Museum of Art

1130 State St. ☎ *(805) 963-4364. Donation expected. Open Tues-Sat 11am-5pm, Sun noon-5pm. Closed Mon, hols.*

A small museum, but local patrons have well endowed it with an impressive collection of Classical sculpture, Asian art and American paintings. Also an excellent doll collection.

Presidio of Santa Barbara State Historic Park

123 E Canon Perdido St. 🔟 *Open Mon-Fri 9am-noon, 1-4pm.*

Only two of the original buildings of the 1782 Spanish fort survive, El Cuartel, the guards' house, and La Caneda Adobe, a military residence, but they serve as a reminder of the plain, dusty lives lived by most early Californians. The Presidio Chapel is a re-creation of an early Spanish church.

Santa Barbara Botanic Gardens

1212 Mission Canyon Rd., 1.5 miles N of Mission ☎ *(805) 682-4726* 🔟 ✗ *Thurs 10.30am. Open 8am to sunset.*

The gardens occupy 75 acres laced by paths. Native plants cluster in groups defined by ecological zones from Santa Barbara Channel Island to desert. There is also a display showing how local Indians used plants.

Santa Barbara Historical Museum

136 E de la Guerra St. ☎ *(805) 966-1601* ⊡ ✗ *Wed 1.30pm. Open Tues-Fri noon-5pm, Sat-Sun 1-5pm.*

In a modern adobe built in the style of early structures, handsomely mounted displays of the city's Spanish and Mexican origins dominate, but Chinese and Anglo history receive equally attractive attention. Action-filled engravings and lithographs by Edward Borein give life to historic objects on display. Scholars may use the Gladhill Library.

Santa Barbara Museum of Natural History

2559 Puesta del Sol Rd., two blocks N of Mission ☎ *(805) 682-4711* ⊡ ✗ *Sun 2pm. Open Mon-Sat 9am-5pm, Sun 10am-5pm. Closed Thanksgiving, Christmas, New Year.*

Thoughtful displays in the Spanish-style museum building explain how a wide variety of life forms can thrive in the region. Two acres of gardens amplify the lessons.

Recreation

For all practical purposes, Santa Barbara has preserved all its white-sand beaches for public use. The city beach bears several names along its 3½-mile length. Running E from the city harbor they are **West**, **Cabrillo** and **East**. Equally sandy **Leadbetter State Beach** lies w of the harbor via an extension of Cabrillo Blvd. Families with small children will find the calmest waters in the harbor between the breakwater and **Stearns Wharf**, but all of these warm water beaches are safe for swimming. Volleyball nets are at the E end of the city beaches where Cabrillo Blvd. bends inland. Although there are public buildings, including a competition swimming pool adjacent to the harbor, the beaches have few amenities; dressing is best done at the hotel, picnics best prepared beforehand.

Secluded **Arroyo Burro** lies 2 miles w of town via Cliff Dr.

Golf

Santa Barbara and its suburbs have two public 18-hole courses and a third open to guests staying at many hotels. The public ones are **Sandpiper** (*7925 Hollister Ave., Goleta* ☎ *(805) 968-1541*), 7,066yds, par 72, rated 73.4 and **Santa Barbara Community** (*3500 McCaw Ave.* ☎ *(805) 687-7087*), 5,964yds, par 70, rated 65.5. The private course open to hotel guests is **Montecito Country Club** (*920 Summit Rd.* ☎ *(805) 969-3216*), 6,145yds, par 71, rated 68.6.

Tennis

The city of Santa Barbara maintains two fine complexes: **Municipal Courts** (*Salinas St., via Old Coast Highway*), 12 lighted courts, and **Lao Positas** (*1002 Las Positas Rd.*), six lighted courts.

San Francisco

This section is designed to help plan visits to San Francisco and adjacent areas of California. It gives ideas and information, addresses and telephone numbers, and contains a calendar of the most notable events, which are cross-referenced to the entries in the *A to Z*, where they are described in detail. (Up-to-the-minute information is available at the telephone numbers given with each calendar entry.) There is also advice on the best times to go, the places to visit, the best ways to get around, plus recommended tours. The city is broken down into more manageable areas — in much the same way that local citizens themselves understand and inhabit the city and neighboring areas.

This is followed by introductory guides to the information given in the *A to Z* sections; descriptions follow of sights and places of interest including parks, buildings, amusements and museums; types of hotels, with advice on finding and reserving accommodations; a guide to eating out in San Francisco, with advice on types of restaurant and where to find the best food; the best in nightlife and the performing arts; pointers on shopping, both window-shopping and the real thing; and details on when and where to exercise, and watch and participate in sports.

San Francisco telephone numbers have the area code **(415)**, which is not repeated in telephone numbers in this section. However, other area codes are given.

Calendar of events

See also *Sports and activities* and *Public holidays* in *Basic information*. Some dates vary yearly, so best check beforehand.

January

San Francisco International Boat Show, Moscone Center ☎521-2558.

Shrine East-West All Star Football Classic and Pageant, Stanford Stadium, Palo Alto ☎661-0291.

Chinese Lunar New Year celebration and parade, Chinatown ☎982-3000.

February

Golden Gate Kennel Club All-breed Dog Show, Cow Palace ☎530-1466.

Orchids by the Bay, orchid display, Fort Mason, Marina District ☎332-9100.

Crab Festival, Bay Area ☎981-8030.

Virginia Slims Women's Tennis Tournament, Oakland Coliseum ☎673-2016.

March

San Francisco International Film Festival, America's oldest, Bay Area movie theaters ☎931-FILM.

St Patrick's Day celebration and parade, Downtown ☎974-6900.

Annual Battle of Harmonicas, Palace of Fine Arts Theater ☎762-2277.

Bammies (Bay Area Music Awards), local talent on display at various locations ☎388-4000.

Grand National Junior Rodeo and Horse Show, Cow Palace ☎469-6000.

National Championship Cat Show, Cow Palace ☎469-6065.

Easter Sunrise Service, Mt. Davidson ☎974-6900.

April

Cherry Blossom Festival and parade, Japantown ☎922-6776.

Annual Golden Gate International Rugby Tournament ☎556-0560.

San Francisco Giants baseball season opens (through Oct), Candlestick Park ☎467-8000.

Yachting season opens, San Francisco Bay ☎(213) 974-6900.

Bay Meadows Thoroughbred Racing season opens, San Mateo ☎574-7223.

May

Cinco de Mayo Celebration and parade, Hispanic festival, Mission District ☎826-1401.

San Francisco Examiner Bay to Breakers race, annual run from Bay to Ocean ☎777-7770.

San Francisco Historic Trolley Festival, Market Street ☎974-6900.

San Francisco New Performance Festival of drama, dance, music and opera, at various locations ☎863-1320.

June

Friends of the San Francisco Public Library Annual Book Sale, Pier 2, Fort Mason ☎558-2200.

Union Street Festival of Arts & Crafts, Union St. ☎346-4446.

Carnival, Mardi-gras style festival/parade with music and dance, Mission District ☎826-1401.

Lesbian-Gay Freedom Parade ☎861-2404.

Kitemakers' Annual Father's Day Kite Festival, Marina Green ☎956-3181.

San Francisco Symphony Beethoven Festival, Davies Symphony Hall and Herbst Theater, Civic Center ☎431-5400.

Vaudeville Festival, San Francisco State University ☎338-2467.

New North Beach Fair, Upper Grant Ave. ☎346-4446.

July

Fourth of July Celebration & Fireworks, Crissy Field, Presidio ☎556-0560.

Summer Pops Concerts, San Francisco Symphony at Civic Auditorium ☎431-5400.

KQED International Beer Festival, Concourse Exhibition Center ☎553-2200.

Stern Grove Midsummer Music Festival, in a natural amphitheater, America's oldest free festival, Sunset District ☎398-6551.

San Francisco Marathon ☎681-2323.

Midsummer Mozart Festival, Herbst Theater, Civic Center ☎552-3656.

August

San Francisco 49ers football season opens (through Dec), Candlestick Park ☎392-7469.

Japantown Summer Festival, Japantown ☎563-7656.

San Francisco Hill Stride, 7-mile walk ☎546-6150.

San Francisco County Fair, Flower Show

and Arts Festival, County Fair Building, Golden Gate Park ☎558-7962.

Pacific States Craft Fair, Fort Mason, Presidio ☎896-5060.

September

American Indian Trade Fair and Exposition, intertribal pow-wow, arts and crafts, Civic Center Plaza ☎626-8122.

Ringling Brothers Barnum & Bailey Circus, Cow Palace ☎469-6000.

Youth Fair, carnival, skateboarding, contests, entertainment, Civic Center Plaza ☎557-8758.

San Francisco Blues Festival, Great Meadow, Fort Mason ☎762-BASS.

San Francisco Opera Season opens (through Dec), Opera House, Civic Center ☎864-3300.

Bridge-to-Bridge Run, 8-mile race and 5-kilometer fun-run, Ferry Building ☎951-7000.

Transamerica Men's Open Tennis Championship, Cow Palace ☎469-6000.

October

Columbus Day Celebrations, Italian community pageant and parade plus Blessing of the Fleet, North Beach and Fisherman's Wharf ☎434-1492.

Grand National Livestock Exposition, Rodeo and Horse Show, Cow Palace ☎469-6000.

Halloween and Pumpkin Festival, Clement St. ☎346-4446, and Halloween Costume Promenade, Polk, Castro and Market Sts.

American Conservatory Theater Season opens (through May), Geary Theater, Downtown ☎673-6440.

Castro Street Fair, Castro District ☎346-2640.

November

Folk Art Exhibition and Sale, Conference Center, Fort Mason ☎441-6100.

Annual KQED Wine & Food Festival, Concourse Exhibition Hall ☎553-2000.

San Francisco Automobile Show, Moscone Center, Soma ☎673-2016.

Dickens Christmas Fair, 19thC London re-created in northern California, Fort Mason ☎441-5705.

December

Sing-It-Yourself-Messiah, singalong with the San Francisco Symphony Chorus, Davies Symphony Hall, Civic Center ☎979-8098.

Pickle Family Circus, Palace of Fine Art Theater, Marina District ☎826-0747.

Nutcracker, San Francisco Ballet's annual performances, War Memoria Opera House, Civic Center ☎621-3838.

A Christmas Carol, seasonal Dickens from the American Conservatory Theater, Geary Theater, Union Sq. District ☎673-6440.

When and where to go

Forget the idealized picture of California, State of perpetual sunshine; that's the Southland. Mark Twain wasn't joking when he said the coldest winter he ever spent was one summer in San Francisco. The chills he experienced were, and are, a trick of fogs produced by cold ocean waters along the shore N of Santa Barbara. These summer fogs cover a very narrow band, just a few miles wide where there is coastal shelf; perhaps only a few hundred yards wide where hills rise rapidly from the surf. After the fogs lift in Aug, San Francisco enjoys its warmer, sunnier days, its temperate approximation of summer cooled by ocean breezes. The real imitation winter comes between Nov and Feb, when it is rainy rather than really cold. Winter rains do not restrict themselves to the coastal shelf, though there is a steady increase in the amount and frequency of rains from S to N. Broadly speaking, San Francisco has a temperate marine climate: Nov through Feb are wet, June through Oct are dry. In late summer the mercury seldom climbs above 70°F (21°C) or falls in winter below 40°F (5°C). Spring and fall are the most pleasant seasons.

Getting there

San Francisco International Airport, 14 miles S of downtown on US-101, is served by nearly all major national and international airlines and is the world's sixth busiest. The North Terminal and South Terminal handle domestic airlines; the International (Central) Terminal, completed in 1983, handles overseas flights. Arrival is at the lower level, departure at the upper level. A free shuttle service is available within the airport. There is information for disabled travelers (☎573-9688). The airport has protected short-term parking for some 7,000 vehicles, but it is often full. Valet parking is also

113

provided. Facilities within the airport include a communications center (*upper level International Terminal*) for long-distance calls, a choice of restaurants and bars, gift stores and newsstands. For reservations and up-to-date flight information most airlines have toll-free (*800*) numbers detailed under "Air Line Companies" in the Yellow Pages. For general flight information ☎555-1212.

Ground transportation to San Francisco and other Bay areas includes buses loading at the lower level outside baggage claim areas (reservations recommended before collecting baggage), taxis loading at stands on the lower level, and limousines by prior reservation. San Francisco is sufficiently compact to make taxis affordable in a way that they are not in Los Angeles.

Buses from the airport

Airporter   To downtown, every 20mins 5am-midnight, less often through the night ☎495-8404.

California Minibus   To downtown, every hour 5.30-10.30pm, reservations required ☎775-5121.

Francisco Adventure   24hr shuttle from downtown to San Francisco and San Jose airports, plus sightseeing tours throughout N California ☎821-0903.

Good Neighbours Airport Shuttle   Door-to-door throughout San Francisco ☎777-4899.

Lorrie's   To major hotels, every 30mins 6am-9.45pm ☎673-2432.

Marin Airporter   To Sausalito and Marin County destinations, every 30mins 6am-midnight ☎461-4222.

Supershuttle   Door-to-door throughout San Francisco, around the clock ☎871-7800, (415) 558-8500.

Yellow Airport Shuttle   To hotels and door-to-door throughout San Francisco and Bay area, around the clock, reservations recommended ☎282-7433.

Taxis

Allied (☎ *826-9494*); **City** (☎ *468-7200*); **Classic** (☎ *584-2756*); **De Soto** (☎ *673-1414*); **Luxor** (☎ *552-4040*); **Pacific** (☎ *776-6688*); **Sunshine** (☎ *776-7755*), with Chinese-speaking drivers; **Town** (☎ *285-1244*); **Veteran's** (☎ *552-1300*); **Yellow Cab** (☎ *626-2345*).

Taxis also maintain stands at most major hotels, and additional companies are listed in the Yellow Pages.

Limousines

Alternative Limousine   ☎421-LIMO
Chauffeured Limousines   ☎344-4400, (800) 338-8200
A Classic Ride   Vintage limousines ☎626-0433
Cloud 9 Limousine Service   ☎878-8668
First Class Limousine   ☎261-5213
Golden Gate Limousine   ☎487-0531
Limousine Experience   ☎668-5466
Milt's Livery Service   ☎952-0466
San Francisco Sightseeing & Tours Inc.   ☎777-0102
Visit USA Bureau Inc.   ☎391-0500, (800) 722-0872

Limousine services are available for sightseeing tours as well as transfers for individuals or groups.

Car rental

Alamo Rent-a-Car   Cars and vans at competitive rates ☎347-9911.
Autoexotica   Top-name sports and luxury cars ☎885-6655
Avis Rent-a-Car   75 locations in s California ☎885-5011, (800) 331-1212.

Budget Rent-a-Car   American and prestige European cars, convertibles ☎875-6850, (800) 527-0700.
Dollar Rent-a-Car   Late-model economy and luxury American and Japanese cars ☎692-1205, (415) 952-6200.
Hertz Corporation   Ford cars, with special group and convention rates ☎771-2200, (800) 654-3131.
Rent-A-Wreck   No airport pick-up, but used cars, vans, trucks at rates up to 50 percent below competitors ☎776-8700.
Thrifty Rent-a-Car   Convention rates ☎673-6675, (800) 367-2277.

Alternative airports

San Francisco International is the biggest but not the only airport in the Bay area. There are smaller airports that could be a more convenient alternative for flights within the United States.
Oakland International Airport   Doolittle and Airport Way ☎839-7488
San Jose International Airport   1661 Airport Blvd. ☎(408) 277-4759.

Other transportation

San Francisco is also served by **Amtrak** *(☎ (800) 872-7245: bus connection from 16th St. depot in Oakland to Transbay Bus Terminal, 1st St. and Mission St.)*, **Greyhound Lines** *(depot at 101 7th St., one block s of Market)* and **Trailways, Inc.** *(depot at 1st St. and Mission St.)*. And local transportation within San Francisco and the Bay area is excellent.

San Francisco Municipal Railway *(☎ 673-6864)* blankets the city with bargain-priced light rail, trackless trolley, bus and cable car lines. However, carry the exact fare, as drivers do not give change. For route information ☎673-MUNI; timetables available from Metro station booths, AC Transit booths, and on Muni trolleys and buses.

BART — Bay Area Rapid Transit *(☎ 788-2278)* is a modern light rail system with lines running s from Market St. to Mission district and Daly City and E to Oakland, Berkeley and other East Bay cities. The system runs 7 days, 6am-midnight, except Sun 9am-midnight. Excursion tickets are available. However, it is more useful for travel to and from the suburbs than within the city proper.

Other bus services: **AC Transit** *(☎ 839-2882)* operates bus services to East Bay cities Berkeley, Oakland, Treasure Island and other cities in Alameda and Contra Costa counties via the Bay Bridge; **Owl Service** buses take over from Muni Metro from midnight-6am; and **Golden Gate Transit** *(☎ 332-6600)* runs from the Transbay Terminal at First and Mission Sts. into Marin and Sonoma Counties.

Cable Cars run three routes: the Powell-Hyde line from Powell and Market Sts. to Victoria Park near the Maritime Museum; the Powell-Mason line from Powell and Market to Bay St. near Fisherman's Wharf; and the California line from Market St. to Van Ness Ave. All-day passes are available. Tickets should be bought before boarding.

Ferry services include **Golden Gate Ferries** *(☎ 332-6600)*, from the s end of the Ferry Building at the foot of Market St., crossing the Bay to Sausalito in about 30mins; **Red & White Fleet** *(☎ 546-2896)*, from Pier 43½ to Sausalito, plus tours from Pier 41; and **Blue and Gold Fleet** *(☎ 781-7877)*, running tours from Pier 39.

Tours

Agentours Inc.   157 West Portal Ave. ☎661-5200, half-day sightseeing with multilingual guides.
Alcatraz   ☎546-2896, (800) 445-8880, from Pier 41 from 8.45am, reservations recommended in summer.

American Express Travel Service Office   237 Post St. ☎981-5533, (415) 981-6293, 4hr narrated tours of Sausalito and Muir Woods, 8hr visit to wine country, all-day tours of Monterey Peninsula and Carmel.

Ami Tours   808 Post St., Suite 1430 ☎ 474-8868, city and out-of-town tours including Victorian houses, wine country and coastline, plus customized tours.

Bargain Bus   ☎533-0874, 7hr tour of garment district, designer-clothes at discount prices, hotel pick-ups.

Cable Car Charters Inc.   2830 Geary Blvd. ☎922-2425, narrated tours of San Francisco from Pier 39 and Pier 41.

Carriage Charter   Pier 41 at Powell and Jefferson Sts. ☎398-0857, horse-drawn carriages around Fisherman's Wharf, North Beach from 1pm.

Commodore Helicopters   240 Redwood Highway, Highway 101 ☎ 332-4482, city, Bay, bridges and wine country from the air.

Express Tours Unlimited   PO Box 77267, San Francisco 94107 ☎621-7738, (800) 535-3500, city tours plus Monterey, Reno, Yosemite (May-Dec), by reservation only.

The Gray Line Inc.   350 8th St. ☎558-9400, Bay area tours including Alcatraz, Sausalito, San Francisco-by-night, Monterey, Carmel, Marin County, wine country.

HMS Tours   1057 College Ave., Suite 206 ☎(707) 526-2922, (800) 331-6086, wine country tours and hot-air balloon rides, hotel pick-ups.

San Francisco Bay Tours Inc.   2690 3rd St. ☎550-8954, city, Berkeley, Monterey, Carmel, Yosemite, with Japanese-speaking guides.

San Francisco Gourmet Tour   1550 California St., Suite 6164 ☎781-TOUR, the city's best restaurants by limo.

Scenic Cycling Aventours   PO Box 583, Ross 94957 ☎453-0676, 4hr tours of San Francisco and Marin County, bicycles and picnics provided.

Sentimental Journeys Sky Tours   North Field, Oakland International Airport ☎667-3800, (800) 634-1165, 1hr tours by restored Douglas DC-3 with in-flight refreshments.

Super City Tours Inc.   2143 Powell St. ☎391-9805, multilingual tours of San Francisco and Bay area by day or night.

Ticketeasy   59 Joice St., Suite 7 ☎956-1765, unusual tours of San Francisco at affordable prices: churches, theaters, factories, private homes.

Driving

San Francisco proper is of such a manageable size that visitors may not wish or need to drive, and parking and rush-hour congestion can be a problem, for this is not an automobile city like Los Angeles. Taxis are relatively plentiful, distances unlikely to tax the wallet, and public transportation is excellent. But the grid system of streets does make the city reasonably easy to navigate, and only widespread one-way systems frustrate the simplicity of it all. The main thing to remember is to turn the wheels toward the street when parking uphill, and when parking downhill to turn the wheels toward the curb. This isn't just good advice to guard against runaway vehicles on the city's steep hills; it's required by law!

Independent excursions into neighboring counties are best undertaken by car, and many of the routes (especially the northbound Pacific Coast Highway) afford spectacular scenery. Within the city the only really compelling reason to be auto-mobile is the "49-Mile Drive." Originated for the 1939-40 International Exposition, the half-day drive snakes through the city past major points of architectural, historical and scenic interest, including the splendid Golden Gate Park. The route is well signposted, and the Visitor Information Center (see below) provides free maps.

Walking

Do walk. Although some of the steeper hills can be taxing, and a handful of neighborhoods, such as the Tenderloin, Mission district and the Haight-Ashbury, can be intimidating after dark, the city's compactness and climate make walking a pleasure. The best approach is to identify a few destinations and an approximate route, then just ramble; there are few streets without something to interest or delight, be it an unusual building, a dusty bookstore or a chic café.

Otherwise, structured walking tours — many of them free — are available: Civic Center, North Beach, Japantown, Market St. etc. by **Friends of the Library** (☎ 558-3981); Chinatown by the **Chinese Cultural Foundation** (☎ 986-1822); the **Chinatown Walk 'n Wok** guided tour, including kitchens (☎ 355-9656); Golden Gate Park by **Friends of Recreation and Parks** (☎ 221-1311); the Victorian and Edwardian mansions of Pacific Heights by **Foundation for San Francisco Architectural Heritage** (☎ 441-3004); and the **Maltese Falcon Tour**, which explores Dashiell Hammett's San Francisco (☎ 564-7021).

Useful information

American Express Travel Service Office   237 Post St., downtown ☎981-5533; 295 California St., financial district ☎788-4367.
i *San Francisco Convention and Visitors Bureau*   201 3rd St., Suite 900 ☎974-6900 Mon-Fri 9am-5pm; for recorded information any time ☎391-2001 (*English*), 391-2003 (*French*), 391-2004 (*German*), 391-2122 (*Spanish*), 391-2101 (*Japanese*).
i *San Francisco Visitor Information Center*   Hallidie Plaza, 900 Market St., at Powell St. ☎974-6900, open Mon-Fri 9am-5pm, Sat 9am-3pm, Sun 10am-2pm, longer hours in summer.
AAA-California   150 Van Ness Blvd. ☎565-2012, members only.
Travelers Aid Society   ☎781-6738.
Highway conditions   ☎557-3755.
Post Office   GPO, 7th St. and Mission St., just s of Market St.
i ☎556-2500.
General delivery   Main Post Office, San Francisco, CA 94103.
Telegram, Telex, Fax   Western Union ☎392-7785; International Telephone & Telegraph ☎(800) 922-0184.
Weather   ☎936-1212.

Emergency information

San Francisco Police Department (SFPD)   ☎911, nonemergency ☎553-0123.
Fire (including rescue)   ☎911, nonemergency (415) 861-8020.
Coast Guard   ☎556-5500
Emergency hospital/city ambulance   ☎911, (415) 931-3900.
Medical Society referrals   ☎567-6230.
Dental Society referrals   ☎421-1435.
Suicide Prevention   ☎221-1424.
Narcotics Anonymous   ☎621-8600.

Late-night

Pharmacies: **Walgreen Drugs** (*3201 Divisadero, at Lombard* ☎ *931-6417, open 24hrs; 135 Powell St., at Union Sq.* ☎ *391-4433, open Mon-Sat 8am-midnight, Sun 9am-8pm*); **Mandarin Pharmacy** (*895 Washington St.* ☎ *989-9292, free delivery, open Mon-Fri 10am-6.30pm, Sat 10am-6pm*); **Merrill's Drug Center** (*805 Market St.* ☎ *781-1669, open Mon-Fri 7am-10pm, Sat-Sun*

7.30am-8.30pm); **Botkia Pharmacy** (*3189 Mission St.* ☎ *648-5577, open daily 9am-midnight*).

Baby-sitters: **Temporary Tot Tending** (☎ *355-7377, 871-5790 after 6pm*).

Foreign exchange

Banks can sometimes be a problem, being often unwilling to change foreign currency and travelers cheques except for regular customers or with a hefty service charge. But there are alternatives. In addition to the **American Express Travel Service Offices** listed above, there are the **Bank of America Foreign Exchange Office** (*Central Terminal, San Francisco International Airport* ☎ *876-7055, open daily 7am-11pm*), **Deak International** (*100 Grant Ave., downtown* ☎ *362-3452, open Mon-Fri 9am-5pm*) and **Foreign Exchange Ltd** (*415 Stockton St., at Union Sq.* ☎ *397-4700, open Mon-Fri 8.30am-5pm, Sat 9am-1.30pm*).

Maps and publications

Guidebooks and maps available in bookstores: *San Francisco/Access* (Access Press); *Hidden San Francisco* (Ulysses Press); *San Francisco AM/PM*; *Thomas Brothers Road Atlas and Driver's Guide to California* (Thomas Bros Maps).

Local newspapers and magazines of interest to visitors: morning *Chronicle* and evening *Examiner*, especially Fri editions for weekend events, and "Datebook" section from combined Sun edition for coming week's events. Also free *San Francisco Bay Guardian* for weekly news, arts and entertainment, and free monthly *City Sports*. Monthly magazines: *California* and *San Francisco*. Advertiser-oriented periodicals free in hotel rooms: *Key* and *Guestinformant*.

San Francisco area planner

Unlike the unique mega-city Los Angeles to the s, San Francisco has the manageable, understandable, conventional characteristics most of us expect of a city. It is user-friendly. Above all, it owes its character to the 1849 Gold Rush, the event that turned a sleepy pueblo into a port city that was not merely cosmopolitan but chameleon-like. Today, still, Americans think of it as American, Europeans call it America's most European city, and Asians are reminded of Asia.

To know San Francisco in all its guises it is necessary to explore all its varied neighborhoods. With just 49 sq. miles, inhabited by 750,000 people, the goal is achievable. But the city proper, perched on its water-lapped peninsula, is not the entire story. San Francisco does not exist in splendid isolation; the Bay Area, including Berkeley and Oakland to the N, and San Jose to the s, begins to rival LA for almost continuous urban sprawl. However, the more than a dozen neighborhoods identified below are distinct. In addition to the detailed orientation sketches of San Francisco, the planner should help visitors to locate and get the flavor of neighboring areas.

The Avenues *(map 8 C2-3)*

The w side of the city is known as The Avenues, after N-S avenues numbered 2-48. Residents often speak more specifically of the Sunset (s of Golden Gate Park) and the Richmond (N of the Park). A considerable number of the city's treasures are to be found out here. **Golden Gate Park**, at 3 miles long by ½ mile wide one of the USA's greatest urban parks, has forest groves, gardens, playgrounds, lakes, sports fields, and four of the city's finest museums: the **M.H. de Young Museum of Art**, the **Asian Art Museum**, the **Morrison**

Planetarium and the **Steinhart Aquarium**. Also in the area: the 270-acre **Lincoln Park** (and another worthy art museum, the **California Palace of the Legion of Honor**, with Rodin's *Thinker* in the atrium), **Ocean Beach**, the **San Francisco Zoological Gardens** and **Sigmund Stern Grove**.

And there is Clement St., with its small shops and restaurants, almost 100 of them inside one mile, whose ethnic diversity also signals the gradual changes in what, traditionally, has been largely a residential white middle-class area. Clement St. between 1st and 11th Aves. is known as "New Chinatown," and the Richmond district has more Japanese residents than Japantown. More recently, people of Vietnamese, Thai, Khmer and Laotian origin have moved in. They don't yet rival the East Europeans, Irish or Jews in numbers; the two most notable buildings are an Orthodox church (the **Cathedral of the Holy Virgin**, on Geary Blvd. and 26th Ave.) and a Jewish temple (**Emanu-El**, on Arguello Blvd. and Lake St.). But they are giving the area a more cosmopolitan complexion.

The same is true of the Sunset district s of the Park, where the traditional white, middle-class conservatism is being enlivened by new waves of ethnic immigration. The residential architecture is uninspired, but the area is thought ideal for raising a family.

Civic Center (map *12 D3*)
A mile w of Union Sq. and downtown, the Civic Center is the heart of San Francisco's political and cultural life. Here, in an eight-block area regarded as the finest grouping of Beaux Arts architecture in the USA, are **City Hall**, the **San Francisco Opera House**, the **Louise M. Davies Symphony Hall**, the **War Memorial Building**, the **Main Library** and the **Civic Auditorium**, a huge hall used for basketball, boxing and conventions. In recent years several fine restaurants attuned to concert-goers' schedules have blossomed in the district. The only drawback for visitors: the city's burgeoning number of homeless people are also attracted. Panhandlers and muggers can be a problem, especially after dark.

Fisherman's Wharf/Northern Waterfront (map *12 B3*)
Once this was an industrial area with a working port; now it is almost entirely tourist country, containing the altogether predictable seaside entertainments of Fisherman's Wharf and **Pier 39**, along with two elegant shopping complexes, called **The Cannery** and **Ghirardelli Sq.** (once a wool factory, later a chocolate factory), the **San Francisco Maritime Museum**, and the diverse community center within **Fort Mason**. For recreation there is **Aquatic Park** and **Municipal Pier**. The Powell St. cable cars end their routes here, and the area is well served by buses. There are fast-food restaurants, less predictable fresh-seafood stalls, and sometimes excellent street theater and musicians. It is also the place to pick up sightseeing cruises around the Bay.

Grant Avenue/Chinatown (map *13 C4*)
For many years San Francisco's Chinese-origin inhabitants, among the city's earliest residents and now second only to the New York Chinese in numbers, lived in a veritable city of their own. To the N of downtown, its main artery was Grant Ave. from Pine to Broadway. Of late, the large and growing population of Chinese-Americans and newly immigrated Chinese have burst the old boundaries in all directions, with the more affluent moving away from the city center. But some 75,000 still live in Chinatown, and Grant Ave., with its imposing Dragon Gate (built in 1969), remains the heart of their community. It looks and sounds like an Asian street, and the

accommodations for residents are often as cramped and spartan as in downtown Hong Kong or Taipei.

In truth, the dedication to amusing foreign tourists with restaurants, bars and curio stores is secondary to the self-sustaining life of the community. The cross streets and Stockton St., which runs parallel to Grant St., are more authentically Asian, to the point that English is not much help in some shops. Here curio stores yield to workaday butchers, fish stores, bakeries and grocer shops. Waverly St., a narrow alley parallel to Grant St., is about as authentic as Chinatowns come, with traditional Chinese roofs and shops selling exotic herbs and dry goods. Two engaging places, the **Chinese Cultural Center** and the **Chinese Historical Society**, make useful starting points.

The Hills (maps *12 C3, 13 B4*)

San Francisco is a city known for its hills; Nob, Telegraph and Russian are the most famous. They are, first and foremost, residential areas, with some notable neighborhood restaurants and fine hotels. There are dramatic views and, for the out of condition, even more dramatic climbs.

Russian Hill is named for a cemetery for Russian fur-hunters and traders. A century ago it was vaguely bohemian, and the original Swensen's ice cream parlor is there, on Union St. But nowadays it is primarily old money and the upwardly mobile who live there, and on Union St. they sustain what is perhaps the city's chicest shopping.

Telegraph Hill has the city's best views, and in recent years an influx of affluent young residents has seen a flowering of fashionable new restaurants. The many interesting features include, on the harbor slopes down from Coit Tower, hillside wooden cottages that survived the great 1906 earthquake and fire, accessible via rickety wooden walkways and steps.

Nob Hill, derived from "nabob" and characterized by Robert Louis Stevenson as "the Hill of Palaces," has some especially good examples of classic San Francisco architecture. Some of the finest estates were leveled in the earthquake and fire. But, like the rest of the city, the bourgeoisie bounced back, rebuilt, and remain entrenched atop the hills to this day. Nob Hill also has the **Grace Cathedral**, built between the wars, and now the largest Gothic building in the western USA. Needless to say, many of the city's swankiest restaurants are to be found on the hills.

Japantown (Nibonmachi) (map *12 D2*)

Since the 19thC, members of San Francisco's sizeable Japanese population have resided, for the most part, in a compact area stretching three blocks N from Geary Blvd., between Franklin and Fillmore Sts. Only a small proportion are resident nowadays, but the infrastructure and ambience are a magnet for a wider-spread community, and the area remains their spiritual nexus.

The district, between Union Sq. and the Richmond, has distinctly Japanese hotels, stores, nightclubs, restaurants, Buddhist temples, shrines, festivals, movie theaters, traditional massage parlors, and even hardware stores, in and near a three-block-long commercial and cultural center, which forms the s boundary of the neighborhood. The center was designed by Professor Yoshiro Taniguchi, an expert on traditional architecture, with a tall 8thC-style pagoda as its centerpiece. Within it are an outstanding Japanese bookstore, a shop specializing in *koi* (carp) and a Japanese theater.

Japantown is spick, span, bustling and delightful by day. However, a note of caution. Gangs from the neighboring Western Addition have been known to prowl by night, so vigilance is recommended for after-dark pedestrians.

Marina/Golden Gate (map 8 B3)

The area toward the mouth of San Francisco Bay has some of the city's most rewarding scenery and some very pleasant places to play. The **Golden Gate Bridge**, **Fort Point** and the **Marina Green** (see *SF Sports and recreation*) are all here; so is the monumental **Palace of Fine Arts** and, inside it, the **Exploratorium**. Harborside Marina Green is a popular spot for strollers, joggers, kite-flyers and sunbathers. The chic shopping district of Union St. lies on the s side of Lombard St., the major link between downtown and the Golden Gate Bridge. In this most exclusive of neighborhoods, residents are the long-time elderly, old money or high-earners inhabiting a mix of Pacific Heights converted Victorian mansions, luxury apartments and the Marina's Mediterranean-revival houses. The cluster of brightly painted Victorians beloved of postcard photographers is to be seen on the s of Alta Plaza Park.

The Mission (map 9 D4)

Within this sprawling district centered at the intersection of 24th St. and Mission St. lives most of San Francisco's large population of Hispanics. Mexicans and Mexican-Americans are the largest group, but substantial numbers of Salvadorans, Chileans and others share the space. The city's oldest buildings, **Mission Dolores** (or, more correctly, Mission San Francisco de Asís), sixth in the 21-mission chain and the beginning of European civilization in San Francisco, is in the district, as is the **Mexican Museum**. Mission St. has galleries and shops specializing in Hispanic arts and crafts, and a galaxy of good, inexpensive restaurants. However, the Mission is essentially a residential community with a strong sense of Hispanic identity and, as one of the city's less prosperous areas, in not a recommended base for tourists. Visitors are best advised to go there during daylight hours.

Montgomery Street (map 13 C4)

Montgomery St., sometimes called "Wall Street West," is convenient shorthand for the city's long-established financial district, which is to the E of downtown and is concentrated on but not limited to Montgomery St. between Market and California Sts. On what had been mudflats, the city's banking and financial center grew, like so much else, from the Gold Rush. Nevada silver that followed quickened the momentum. The hulks of "ghost ships," abandoned by crews infected with gold fever, were used as foundations for building. It was here that A.P. Giannini founded the Bank of Italy, later to become the Bank of America.

As with similar districts worldwide, this isn't the liveliest place for after-dark entertainment. Aside from some lively after-work bars, the splendidly varied architecture of its banks and other financial institutions and the public art in and around them are the main attractions. Much of the public art is in the **Embarcadero Center**, three office towers between Sacramento and Clay Sts., two blocks E of Montgomery. Tucked away in office buildings in the area are three worthy if small museums of history, the **Bank of California Old Coin and Gold Exhibit**, the **Levi Strauss History Room** and the **Wells Fargo History Room**.

North Beach (map 13 B4)

Traditionally, Little Italy — better known as North Beach — faced Chinatown across Broadway and Columbus Ave. During the past few years Chinese businesses have edged across the unofficial boundary, and now one-third of the population is Chinese. But the skirts of Telegraph Hill remain a bastion of the city's older generation of Italians, as well as the descendants of early Irish, Basque and

Mexican families. It is not a beach at all, but it is a rewarding place to go for some fine examples of Edwardian domestic architecture, its coffee houses, serious bars, bakeries, superb Italian grocery stores and satisfying meals at bargain prices.

The area has always enjoyed a slightly "alternative" flavor. The infamous Barbary Coast of red light, gambling and "shanghaied" sailors was here. Jack London and Mark Twain lived here, and the bohemian Beat Generation was born here in the 1950s. Here and there echoes remain, most notably in the still-thriving **City Lights** bookstore, haunt of Ferlinghetti and Ginsberg, and the timeless **Caffe Trieste** coffee house. What was the Barbary Coast, s of Broadway between Montgomery St. and Kearny St., is now Jackson Sq., where some attractive pre-quake buildings survive.

North Beach is one of the city's liveliest quarters for nightclubs, including the sleazier variety whose garish neon and ever-optimistic barkers tend to dominate along the w stretch of Broadway, though, to be fair, they are intermingled with more worthwhile establishments. The centerpiece of the district is **Washington Square**, which, with the Romanesque **Church of Saints Peter and Paul** as a backdrop, is an excellent place to see North Beach in all its ethnic, linguistic and social diversity.

Presidio *(map 11 C4)*

San Francisco began as a Spanish military settlement under the name Yerba Buena. The original Presidio remains an army post, occupying much of the NW corner of San Francisco's peninsula. The **Army Museum** is within its confines, as are **Fort Point Historic Site** and **Sandy Baker Beach**, both part of the **Golden Gate National Recreation Area**.

Union Square and downtown *(map 13 D4)*

Hotels, theaters, grand department stores and upscale shops all cluster around Union Sq. in a ten-block area bounded on the s by O'Farrell St., on the N by Sutter St., on the w by Jones St. and on the E by Kearny St. If the city has a center, this is it. And the Square itself, around a 90ft (27m) Corinthian column, serves as a pleasant oasis of greenery and flowers amid all the conspicuous consumption: a pleasant spot to take the air, feed the pigeons and watch the street parade and the street performers. The **Geary** and **Curran** Theaters, side by side on Geary St. between Mason and Taylor Sts., are the home of the city's repertory company, the **American Conservatory Theater**, and touring companies (see *SF Performing arts*). Otherwise, the district is of interest primarily to shoppers.

Other city areas

The mostly commercial strip of Market St., particularly from Powell St. E to the Embarcadero, is trying to become a grand boulevard. So far hopes exceed performance, and s of Mason St. it degenerates somewhat into budget stores and porno theaters. But, moving N, the street has some large department stores and some impressive new architecture, and there is usually lively street entertainment around the Powell St. cable car terminus.

The traditionally industrial area called **South of Market** (or, more trendily, **SoMa**) is being redeveloped around the **George Moscone Convention Center**, built in 1981 and named for the city's assassinated mayor. Taking its lead from New York's artsy SoHo district, its converted warehouses are becoming a focus for restaurants and, even more, nightclubs with names as zany as the entertainment centered around Folsom and Harrison Sts.

Most of the city's substantial homosexual population lives on or near two commercial streets, Polk St. between Geary St. and Pacific Ave., and Castro St. s of Market St. to 19th St. or just beyond. Castro St. is the axis for male homosexuals, Valencia for lesbians. As the restored "gingerbread" Victorian properties testify, the Castro gays have done much to gentrify and prettify what was previously a somewhat run-down district. Clubs, bars and nightclubs cater to their tastes.

Not all of San Francisco is always safe for strangers, or even wandering residents. A district best avoided by pedestrians after nightfall is the Tenderloin, a triangle bounded by Ellis St. to the N, Market St. to the s and E, and Hyde St. to the w. However, moderately-priced restaurants and markets opened by recent immigrants from SE Asia are making it an increasingly attractive area to visit. An area called the Western Addition has seen particular violence against tourists, primarily because its location near Civic Center and between downtown and Golden Gate Park leads many unwitting strangers into it. The section bounded by Gough St. to the E, Masonic Ave. to the w, Geary Blvd. to the N and Duboce Ave. to the s should not be risked by visitors on foot by day or night. Passengers on municipal buses have also been subject to violence within this zone.

San Francisco environs

Much of San Francisco's charm comes from adjacent regions so different in character and climate that they offer a complete change of pace. Highlights of these regions are described in a separate section headed *Environs and excursions*. Among the major day-trip destinations are **Marin County** and **Point Reyes Peninsula** across the Golden Gate to the N, **Berkeley** and **Oakland** on the E side of San Francisco Bay, **San Francisco Peninsula** directly s of the city, the wine country of **Sonoma** and **Napa Valleys** to the N, and **Santa Cruz** to the s.

Public transportation from the city to these outlying areas: **Golden Gate Transit** (☎ 332-6600), a bus and ferry system, connects the city with Sausalito, Mill Valley, Point Reyes and some Sonoma cities. **BART** (see *Other transportation*, page 115) and **A-C Transit**, a bus system, connect the city with Oakland, Berkeley and other cities in the East Bay counties of Alameda and Contra Costa. **Caltrain** (☎ 557-8661 or (800) 558-8661) operates commuter trains between the city, the San Francisco Peninsula and Santa Clara Valley. **Sam Trans** (☎ 761-7000), a bus system, connects the city with the San Francisco Peninsula. For tours to the above areas, see the list of tour companies for San Francisco on pages 115-16.

Sights and places of interest

Alcatraz

On an island a mile offshore from San Francisco's northern waterfront. Map 9A4 🗺 *for expert guided tours by National Park Service rangers, but ferries from Pier 43 (Fisherman's Wharf) to the island are expensive. Reservations advised for boats in all seasons, but especially in summer when they may be reserved 2-6wks in advance. For information or reservations, Red and White Fleet, Pier 41, San Francisco 94133* ☎ *546-2833. Ferry crossings take about 20mins, guided tours last 2hrs. Open 9am-4.30pm.*

The formidable concrete hulks of the old federal prison buildings that once held Al Capone, Robert Stroud (the Birdman of Alcatraz) and other famous felons echo every day to the footsteps of as many visitors as scheduled tour boats can carry. The prison closed in 1963; no prisoner is known to have made a successful escape.

Anchor Steam Brewery

1705 Mariposa St. Map 13F5 ☎ 863-8350 ✗ (call for times).
A tiny independent brewery employing only 25 people but producing excellent beer that is sought after throughout the United States. There is a 1hr tour culminating in a sampling of the products.

Balclutha

Pier 43. Map 12A3 ⬚ Open 10am-10pm.
A typical iron-hulled, square-rigged ship from the end of the era of sail, the *Balclutha* was built in Scotland in 1886. Some below-deck areas look much as they did during the ship's days at sea, while others display memorabilia. (See also *Fort Mason* and *San Francisco Maritime Museum*.)

Bank of California Old Coin and Gold Exhibit

400 California St., lower level. Map 13C4 ⬚ Open Mon-Thurs 10am-3pm, Fri 10am-5pm. Closed Sat, Sun, bank hols.
In addition to rare coins, the display includes pieces of gold-bearing quartz showing how the precious metal looks to a miner.

Cable Car Barn

Washington St., at Mason St. ☎ 474-1887. Map 13C4 ⬚ ✽ Open 10am-6pm.
Since 1887 this building, now both powerhouse and museum, has moved San Francisco's cable cars. Prime exhibits are the working gear and cable-car-inventor Andrew Hallidie's prototype Car No. 8.

Cable cars

These were invented in San Francisco before the turn of the century to haul passengers up and down hills too steep for horse-drawn carriages. The number of lines has dwindled from eight to three: Powell-Mason and Powell-Hyde (the most scenic route) run from Powell St. at Market St. to the northern waterfront. The third line runs along California St. from Market St. to Van Ness Ave.

California Academy of Sciences

Golden Gate Park, via entrance road from 8th Ave. and Fulton St. ☎ 750-7145 for recorded schedule of events. Map 10E3 ⬚ ▣ ✽ Open 9am-9pm in summer, 9am-5pm fall to spring.
One of the five finest natural history museums in the USA. Some of its eight departments function on separate schedules.

The **Discovery Room** (*behind Morrison Planetarium ⬚ but attendance limited to 20 at a time, open Tues-Fri 1-4pm, Sat, Sun 11am-3.30pm, closed Mon*) was designed for children, who are encouraged to investigate boxes for everything from spices to seashells and animal skulls.

The **Morrison Planetarium** (*☎ 750-7141 for times ⬚ but separate from general admission*) has a domed ceiling screen that is used both for star and laser shows.

The most dramatic element of the **Steinhart Aquarium** (*✪*) is its fish merry-go-round, a sort of reverse theater-in-the-round where observers stand in an open central area to watch a 360° panorama of all the great Pacific coast sport fishes, including sharks, swimming into an induced current in a 100,000-gallon circular tank. A simulated tidepool is another major attraction. In all, the aquarium has more than two million fish specimens.

The **Wattis Hall of Man** displays aspects of vanishing cultures from Eskimos to Australian aborigines. Other halls display stuffed specimens of the world's great animals.

California Palace of the Legion of Honor Ⅲ
Lincoln Park, 0.4 miles NW of 34th Ave. and Clement St. entrance to park ☎ 750-3659 for recorded message. Map 8B2 ▨ (but ▣ first Wed of each month) 兆 ⬛ Open Wed-Sun 10am-5pm. Closed Mon, Tues, major hols.

In this magnificent copy of the 18thC Parisian palace where Napoleon chose to house his Legion d'Honneur, the great majority of space is devoted to exhibits of the art and culture of France, ranging from medieval tapestries to 20thC Post-Impressionist paintings. Of particular note is a collection of sculptures by Rodin.

In unison with the *M.H. de Young Museum*, the Legion of Honor recently revealed a major collection reorganization. In the latter's case this will amount to 15 new galleries by 1990, with the permanent collections covering and illustrating the relationship of eight centuries of European art from the medieval to the 20thC. Among numerous notable exhibits are 14th and 15thC works by Ugolino da Siena and Fra Angelico, a bust of Cosimo I by Benvenuto Cellini, superb El Grecos, Watteau's *The Foursome*, and varied works by Manet, Monet, Degas, Seurat and Cézanne. Individual galleries cover a wide variety of themes, such as the Renaissance in Germany and the Low Countries, Italian and Spanish art of the 16thC, 17thC Dutch and Flemish art, and decorative arts of the 18thC.

The **Achenbach Foundation for Graphic Arts**, one of the major collections of art on paper in the western USA, is also housed here. Continually changing exhibitions draw upon a huge collection of 3,000 drawings and 100,000 prints, including works by Dürer, Gauguin and O'Keefe. This museum and the M.H. de Young Museum are administered jointly; a single admission ticket entitles visitors to tour both on the same day.

California Pioneers Museum
456 McAllister St. Map 12D3 ☎ 861-5278 for opening times.
Pioneer history including the Gold Rush and the birth and growth of San Francisco. Also 19thC paintings, a Wells Fargo stagecoach and a research library for scholars.

Candlestick Park
On an access road between freeway US-101 and San Francisco Bay at the s city limits. Map 9E5.
The 55,000-seat stadium is the site of home games for the baseball **Giants** (☎ 467-8000) and football **49ers** (☎ 468-2249).

Chinese Cultural Center
750 Kearny St. (on the 3rd floor of the Holiday Inn-Financial District) ☎ 986-1822. Map 13C4 ▣ 兆 Open Tues-Sat 10am-4pm, Sun 1-5pm. Closed Mon.
Galleries of Chinese and Chinese-American art, historic exhibits and cultural exchange exhibits from Asia. The Cultural Center also sponsors heritage and culinary walking tours of old Chinatown.

Chinese Historical Society
17 Adler St. Map 13C4 ▣ Open Tues-Sat 1-5pm.
This jewel box of a museum documents the remarkable contributions of the Chinese to the Gold Rush, the building of America's transcontinental railroads and the development of agriculture in California. Other exhibits show how the Chinese have maintained their traditions in an alien land.

Civic Center 🏛

On Van Ness Ave., between McAllister and Grove Sts. Map 12D3.

One of the grandest groupings of municipal buildings in the USA. Begun immediately after the earthquake and fire of 1906, the principal structures are **City Hall**, the **War Memorial Opera House** and **Veterans Memorial Building**. The latter contains the *San Francisco Museum of Modern Art*. All these were designed by Arthur Brown Jr. Other buildings in the complex and in similar classic styles are the **Civic Auditorium**, the **Main Library** and the **State Building**. The **Louise M. Davies Symphony Hall** is also part of the complex (see *SF Performing arts*).

Coit Tower

At the peak of Telegraph Hill, E end of Lombard St. Map 13B4 🚇 ⬅ Open 10am-4.30pm. Closed Jan 1, Dec 25.

The tower is a memorial to volunteer firemen in early San Francisco. An elevator takes visitors to the top, to see a 360° panorama of the city. The lobby contains murals from the 1930s.

Cow Palace

Geneva Ave. and Santos St., Daly City, slightly less than a mile W of freeway US-101, directly S of the San Francisco city limits via the Old Bayshore exit. Map 9F4.

The home of the San Francisco Grand National Rodeo and Livestock Exposition, the Trans America tennis tournament (see *SF Sports and recreation*) and other annual and special events ranging from conventions to rock concerts.

Crookedest Street

One block of Lombard St., between Hyde St. and Leavenworth St. Map 12B3 ⬅

Carving the sort of track a timid skier might make, this street snakes its way down a steep hill. Throngs drive down it, so expect a wait at the top.

Exploratorium ★

In the Palace of Fine Arts, 3601 Lyon St. (off Marina Blvd. via Baker St.) ☎ 561-0360 for recorded information on exhibitions and events. Map 11B5 🚇 and valid for six months ✳ Open Wed 1-9.30pm, Thurs-Fri 1-5pm, Sat, Sun 10am-5pm. Closed Mon, Tues.

A huge cavern filled with first-rate lessons in science disguised as fun and games. Ingenious gadgets let children and adults measure their own eyes, ears and voices; others deal with broader questions of physics. Be prepared to spend hours here.

Filbert Steps

Filbert St., on E side of Telegraph Hill between Coit Tower and Sansome St. Map 13B4.

Starting from the top, just off Telegraph Hill Blvd., near Coit Tower, a series of walkways and steps lead down past some of the city's oldest, quaintest houses and prettiest small gardens. Many date from the Gold Rush era. The Steps have been and remain a much sought after address and are especially popular with artists, writers and entertainers. Joan Baez lived here.

Fort Mason

Entrance in Marina Blvd. at the foot of Laguna St. Map 12B2 🚇 for some events. Hours vary for each element. For scheduled activities, which include mushroom fairs and trade exhibitions but focus most heavily on plays, music and classes, check with Fort Mason Foundation, Laguna St. and Marina Blvd., San Francisco 94123; visitor center in Building A near main entrance, open 9am-5pm ☎ 441-5705.

Once a port of embarkation for American troops headed into the Pacific, Fort Mason now operates as a diverse and ever-lively community center within the *Golden Gate National Recreation Area*. Among the elements: GGNRA headquarters, a youth hostel, an extraordinary vegetarian restaurant called **Green's**, several theater companies and part or all of four museums:

African-American Historical and Cultural Society (*Building C* ☎ 441-0640 ▨ *requested, open Tues-Sat noon-5pm, closed Sun, Mon*) — art, artifacts and a research library.

Museo Italo-Americano (*Building C* ☎ 673-2200 ▢ *open Wed-Sun noon-5pm, closed Mon, Tues*) — Italian and Italo-American art and artifacts. Its most intriguing displays trace patterns of immigration from Italy and settlement in the USA.

Mexican Museum (*Building D* ☎ 441-0404 ▨ *requested, open Wed-Sun noon-5pm, closed Mon, Tues*) — Mexican and Mexican-American art and artifacts. The great muralist Diego Rivera's influence is much seen here.

SS Jeremiah O'Brien, part of the *San Francisco Maritime Museum*, is the last unaltered Liberty ship afloat. In 1941 American shipyards turned out 2,751 of the vessels, each completed in less than a week. Many sailed from Fort Mason. A footpath leads from the *O'Brien* to the main maritime museum building.

Fort Point �
Directly beneath the San Francisco end of the Golden Gate Bridge (access from Lincoln Blvd. 400yds N of bridge approach) ☎ 556-1693. Map 10A3▢ ⚹ ✱ ⦿ Open 10am-5pm.

The gloomily handsome brick structure of Fort Winfield Scott was completed in 1861. Decommissioned in 1914, it now provides instructive images of an earlier military life through its architecture and troop drills (including artillery practice) from its original period. The latter are staged by National Park Service personnel dressed in period uniforms.

The seawall alongside is excellent for fishing and wave-watching, and especially for watching surfers in perilously rocky shoals. The view of the bridge from below is awesome.

Golden Gate Bridge ☆
Stretches from San Francisco's N shore across to Marin County. Map 10A2.

The first truly great suspension bridge, and between 1937-59 the longest in the world, Golden Gate Bridge, a symbol for San Francisco, is an incomparable place from which to see the city skyline. The best view is at the Marin County N end of the bridge. Pedestrians and bicyclists can (and do in throngs) cross at a leisurely pace for no fee. Inexpensive toll for vehicles southbound only.

Golden Gate National Recreation Area
Along the city's shoreline, from Fort Funston to Aquatic Park. Map 8B2 ☎ 556-0560 ⦿ A small visitor center in Fort Mason is open 9am-5pm.

The GGNRA encompasses all of San Francisco's ocean beaches, and most of the city's waterfront from the Golden Gate E to Aquatic Park, adjoining Fisherman's Wharf. See separate entries in this section for *Alcatraz, Fort Mason, Fort Point* and *San Francisco Maritime*

Museum. (For details of beaches, see *SF Sports and recreation*.)
The GGNRA also includes much of the Marin County shore from the
Golden Gate w and N to Point Reyes National Seashore.

Golden Gate Park ☆

*Bounded by Stanyan St. to the E, the Great Highway to the w,
Fulton St. to the N and Lincoln Ave. to the s. Map 10E3.*
Four blocks wide and more than 40 blocks long, the park contains an
outstanding museum of natural history, the *California Academy of
Sciences*; the city's greatest museum of art, the *M.H. de Young
Museum*; the **Strybing Arboretum**; and a whole range of outdoor
and indoor sports facilities. Informally, it is a paradise for bicyclists
(especially on Sun, when cars are forbidden in some streets), roller
skaters and joggers.

Most of the developed areas are in the easterly third of the park,
between Stanyan St. and 10th Ave. These include:

The *California Academy of Sciences* (see separate entry).

A **children's playground** (*near Stanyan St. and Waller St.
entrance, open during daylight*), which has a fine merry-go-round
(🔄) and a children's zoo.

The **Conservatory of Flowers** (*Kennedy Dr., near Arguello Blvd.
and Fulton St. entrance* 🔄 *open 9am-6pm*), a copy of the Kew
Gardens conservatory. It contains especially fine collections of
orchids and other tropical plants, and the flower gardens fronting it
are kept in bloom much of the year.

The **Japanese Tea Garden** (*adjoining de Young Museum, near
6th Ave. and Fulton St. entrance* 🔄 ✗ *open 8am-5pm*), dating from
1894. It comprises fine gardens and carp ponds (complete with
photogenic moon bridge), surrounding an open-air teahouse.
Spectacular during cherry-blossom time in March.

The **Music Concourse** (*in a shallow depression between de Young
Museum and California Academy of Sciences*), the site of free
concerts in summer, on Sun.

Shakespeare's Garden (*W of the Academy of Sciences Buildings*),
containing labeled specimens of every plant mentioned in the works
of William Shakespeare.

Stow Lake (*directly w of the Japanese Tea Garden, also accessible
from Kennedy Dr. or South Dr. by a clearly signed loop road*), with
rowboats and canoes for rent, for leisurely trips around **Strawberry
Island**.

Strybing Arboretum (*on South Dr., near the 9th Ave. and
Lincoln Ave. entrance* 🔄 ✗ *open Mon-Fri 8am-4.30pm, Sat, Sun,
hols 10am-5pm*), a collection of plants from every part of the globe.
In it is the **San Francisco County Fair Building** used for
horticultural shows and other events. (*For schedules* ☎ *558-3622.*)

The **Tennis Center** (*off Kennedy Dr., opposite Conservatory of
Flowers*), 21 hard courts open to the public daily during daylight.
(See *SF Sports and recreation* for information on playing.)

The *M.H. de Young Museum* with the **Asian Art Museum of
San Francisco** (see separate entry).

In the more open, western parts of the park are a paddock with a
small herd of buffalo, a polo field, an equestrian field, fly-casting
pools, a par-3 golf green, and a perfectly restored Dutch windmill.
Alas, the park is not safe after dark, except near the museums when
events draw crowds.

Grace Cathedral 🏛 ✝

At the top of Nob Hill, at California and Taylor Sts. Map 12C3 ⇚
Seat of the Episcopal Bishop of California, the cathedral is an
impressive example of Neo-Gothic architecture, begun in 1910 and

not finished until after World War II. An undisguised concrete exterior gives the cathedral its air of enduring strength. Its treasures include an altar from 11thC France, a 16thC carved wooden Flemish reredos, stained-glass windows by Connick, and a carillon of 44 bells cast in Croydon, England.

Haas-Lilienthal House 血
2007 Franklin St. ☎ 441-3004. Map 12C3 ▨ X Open Wed noon-4pm, Sun 11am-4.30pm. Closed Mon, Tues, Thurs-Sat.

An immaculately maintained 1886 Victorian building in the Queen Anne style. The museum is the starting point for an excellent walking tour of grand homes of the Russian Hill district, directly w of Van Ness Ave.

Heart of the City Farmers Market
United Nations Plaza, Larkin and Fulton Sts. Map 12D3. Open Sun and Wed 8am-5pm.

Up to 90 stalls selling fresh produce, preserves, honeys, nuts, olives, herbs, flowers etc.

Jackson Square 血
Formed by Jackson, Montgomery, Gold and Sansome Sts. Map 13C4.

Not really a "square" at all, but a rectangular block of distinguished 19thC buildings that survived the 1906 earthquake. After slipping into disrepair, the block underwent painstaking restoration from the early 1950s. The Square is now a Historic District, with 17 of the 3-story brick houses designated as landmarks. Most are antique dealers, art galleries and gift stores, or offices of interior design companies, but are well worth viewing, even from the outside.

Levi Strauss History Room
2 Embarcadero Center (Sacramento at Front St.). Map 13C5 ▣ Open Mon-Fri 10am-4pm. Closed Sat, Sun, major hols.

This traces with wit and style the history of jeans (the first ones were brown, not blue) from the 1870s to the present day.

Mission San Francisco de Asís 血 †
Dolores St., at 16th St. Map 12F2 ▨ Open 10am-4pm. Closed Thanksgiving.

Its formal name was and is as given, but it is nearly always called **Mission Dolores**. Founded in 1776, the year of American independence, it was the sixth of the Franciscan missions. The mission moved to its present site in 1782. Now dwarfed by the adjoining Mission Dolores Basilica, the old mission chapel is the least changed of any of the original 21 missions. The graveyard is a roll call of San Francisco pioneers.

Moscone Center
Howard St., between 3rd and 4th Sts. Map 13D4 ☎ 974-4000 ◁E

The first stage of the Yerba Buena development, a billion-dollar scheme aimed at further revitalizing the SoMa district. The 650,000sq. ft. center, much of it underground, contains a 6-acre column-free exhibition hall, meeting rooms and grand ballroom. There are great city views from the glass-walled lobby. The entire project, which will include expanded exhibition space, 24 acres of landscaped promenade, a hotel, galleries, a theater, restaurants and recreational facilities, is due for completion in 1992.

Murals of the Mission

Between Mission, 20th, Potrero and Precita Ave. Map 9D4 ✗ every first and third Sat leave from Precita Eyes Mural Center, 346 Precita Ave., map 9D4 ☎ 285-2287.

Enlivening walls and doors of the Mission district are more than 200 murals, some big, some small, some political, some religious, some global, some parochial, all wonderfully vivid. By car, 24th St. offers the chance to view the larger ones. On foot, walk ten blocks along 24th St. between Mission and York Sts. Inexpensive guided tours are preceded by a slide show and historical talk.

Old San Francisco Mint

88 5th St. (downtown between Market and Mission Sts.) ☎ 974-0788. Map 13D4 ◙ ✗ Open Mon-Fri 10am-4pm. Closed Sat, Sun, major hols.

The 1874 stone building is now a federal museum devoted mainly to money. Among its exhibits are privately minted coins and a pyramid of gold valued at approximately $10 million.

"Painted Ladies"

Steiner St., between Fulton and Hayes Sts. Map 12E2.

The six matching homes set against the backdrop of the modern cityscape are a "must shoot" for visiting photographers. The best angle is from the edge of a neighboring park, Alamo Sq.

Palace of Fine Arts ▥

Baker St. and Lyon St., in the Marina. Map 12B2.

A legacy of the Panama-Pacific International Exposition of 1915. Designed by famed local architect Bernard Maybeck, it was made originally as a temporary structure of plaster on light framing, but has been rebuilt in concrete. Its Neoclassical columns, dome and reflecting pool are much photographed. Appearance aside, it is notable as the home — at its rear — of the *Exploratorium* and the San Francisco Film Festival.

St Mary's Cathedral of the Assumption ▥ †

Gough St., at Geary Blvd. Map 12D3. Open Mon-Fri 7am-5pm, Sat, Sun 7am-6.30pm, except during special Masses.

This replacement for the earlier, traditional cathedral of the Catholic Diocese of San Francisco, destroyed by fire in 1962, was controversial throughout its construction because of its radical style. Officially described as hyperbolic paraboloid, it resembles a washing-machine agitator from the outside, but its soaring, cruciform interior is more awesome. The pipe organ is a grand sculpture as well as a musical instrument.

San Francisco Art Institute

800 Chestnut St. (near Jones St.), on Russian Hill above Fisherman's Wharf ☎ 771-7020. Map 12B3 ◖ Open Tues-Sat 10am-5pm. Closed Sun, Mon.

This college of fine arts maintains three public galleries showing contemporary works. One has a Diego Rivera mural. The buildings — one Spanish colonial, the other ultramodern — are of interest for themselves and for the views across the city.

San Francisco Fire Department Museum

655 Presidio Ave. (between Pine and Bush Sts.) ☎ 558-3891. Map 11D5 ◙ ✗ Open Thurs-Sun 1-4pm. Closed Mon-Wed.

Among fascinating displays of the history of local firefighting, there are relics from the great earthquake and fire of 1906.

San Francisco Maritime Museum
Map 12B3.

The various elements of the museum are all controlled by the National Park Service, as part of the *Golden Gate National Recreation Area*. Together they explain much of San Francisco's complex maritime history, through a pleasing mixture of grand and humble vessels.

At the **Hyde Street Pier** (*at the foot of Hyde St., directly w of Fisherman's Wharf* ☎ 556-6435 🖃 ✗ *open 10am-6pm*) are moored the old San Francisco-Oakland car ferry *Eureka*, the lumber schooner *C.A. Thayer* (a common 19thC vessel), the scow *Alma* (a hay-hauler in the bay) and — quaint stranger — the side-wheel Thames River tugboat *Eppelton Hall*. Others ships in the museum fleet are the *Balclutha* and the World War II submarine USS *Pampanito* (berthed at Pier 45).

The **museum building** (*Beach St., at the foot of Polk St.* ☎ 556-8177 🖃 *open 10am-6pm*) houses models, artifacts, photographs and other memorabilia of local maritime history. Some of the most telling exhibits relate to the Gold Rush era. Linking the museum building and Hyde Street Pier physically is **Aquatic Park**, a patch of lawn and garden, a beach, and, hidden away in trees near the base of Municipal Pier, some big-league *bocce* courts. **Municipal Pier**, accessible from Aquatic Park or the end of Van Ness Ave., is a breakwater and heavily used fishing pier.

San Francisco Museum of Modern Art
Veterans Memorial Building, McAllister St., at Van Ness Ave. in the Civic Center ☎ 863-8800. *Map 12D3* 🖃 (*but* 🖃 *on Thurs 6-10pm*) ✗ 🖃 *Open Tues-Wed, Fri 10am-6pm, Thurs 10am-10pm, Sat, Sun 10am-5pm. Closed Mon, major hols.*

Permanent collections include most familiar modern names, including Picasso, Matisse and Kandinsky, but changing exhibitions are a major part of the museum.

San Francisco Zoological Gardens
Sloat Blvd., near 45th Ave. in the SW corner of the city ☎ 661-4844. *Map 8D2* 🖃 ✗ 🖃 *Open 10am-5pm.*

Primates, especially gorillas, are the big attraction. Of particular note are the **Primate Discovery Center**, a $7 million home for 16 rare and endangered species, and **Gorilla World**, at an acre said to be the world's largest gorilla habitat, with eight separate viewing areas for humans. All of the great animals are represented. Some enclosures are naturalistic; others are smaller. An elephant train saves walking.

A connected **children's zoo** (🖃 *open 10am-5pm weather permitting*) has animals that can be petted and gentle rides.

San Francisco Public Library
Larkin St. and McAllister St. (Civic Center) ☎ 558-3191. *Map 12D3. Open Tues-Thurs 10am-9pm, Mon, Fri-Sat 10am-6pm, Sun 1-5pm.*

The library's outstanding special holdings are the History of the Printed Book, the Richard Harrison Collection of Calligraphy and Lettering, the George M. Fox Collection of Early Children's Books, the Schmulowitz Collection of Wit and Humor, and Norman H. Strouse's collection on the Panama Canal.

Sigmund Stern Grove
Sloat Blvd., at 19th Ave. in the Sunset. Map 8D2.

A beautiful, natural amphitheater hidden in a little valley below street

DE YOUNG MUSEUM FLOOR PLAN,
SAN FRANCISCO

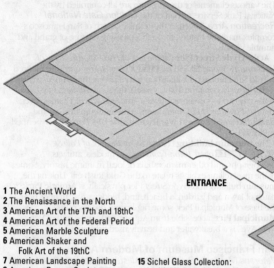

ENTRANCE

1 The Ancient World
2 The Renaissance in the North
3 American Art of the 17th and 18thC
4 American Art of the Federal Period
5 American Marble Sculpture
6 American Shaker and
   Folk Art of the 19thC
7 American Landscape Painting
8 American Bronze Sculpture
9 Landscapes of the American West
10 American Trompe l'Oeil
    and Still-Life Painting
11 American 19thC Genre Painting
12 18thC English Room
13 British Decorative Arts
14 Costumes

15 Sichel Glass Collection:
    drinking vessels from the 16thC
16 American Art from the 20thC
17 American Art from the late 19thC
18 British 18th and 19thC Art
19 McCoy Jones Gallery: textiles
20 American Decorative Arts
21 Traditional Arts of Africa,
    Oceania and the Americas

level. Here, on selected summer Sun afternoons, the city gives its
citizens free concerts.

Temple Emanu-El 🏛
Arguello Blvd., at Lake St. Map 11D4.
The cultural and religious center of Reform Judaism in San Francisco.
The architect, Arthur Brown Jr., also designed City Hall (see *Civic
Center*). The contrast between these two massively domed buildings
is a tribute to Brown's versatility.

Transamerica Pyramid 🏛
600 Montgomery St., at Columbus Ave. Map 13C4.
The sharp pyramid, 853ft (260m) tall, wasn't greeted with universal
rejoicing when built in 1972. Some San Franciscans wryly observe
that the Los Angeles architects William Pereira and Associates
designed it.... Still a remarkable landmark that's well worth seeing.

Twin Peaks
Via Twin Peaks Blvd. Map 9D4 ⇜
A scenic drive leads to the 910ft (227m) summit. On a clear day or
night, there is a breathtaking 360° panoramic view of the city.

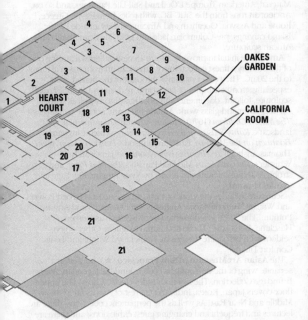

OAKES GARDEN

CALIFORNIA ROOM

HEARST COURT

Washington Square   ■ Closed to the public
Columbus Ave., at Union St. Map 13B4.

This is not a "square" at all and has nothing to do with Washington, which makes North Beach, which is not a beach, the perfect home for it. It is a good place to sit and watch locals bask in the sun beneath the graceful spires of **Saints Peter and Paul**.

Wells Fargo History Room
420 Montgomery St., between California St. and Sacramento St. Map 13C4☺ ✳ Open Mon-Fri 10am-3pm. Closed Sat, Sun, bank holidays.

With a genuine Wells Fargo stagecoach as its centerpeice, this one-room museum of California, 1849-1906, contains memorabilia of legendary stagecoach drivers and robbers.

M.H. de Young Museum ★
Golden Gate Park (two blocks s of park entrance at 8th Ave. and Fulton St.) ☎ 558-2887. Map 10E3☒ (but ☺ first Wed of each month) ☀ ⚷ ⚑ Open Wed-Sun 10am-5pm (closed Mon, Tues), except Asian Art Museum (☎ 558-2993), open Tues-Sun 10am-5pm (closed Mon).

The de Young is among the West Coast's leading cultural institutions. In 1989 it enhanced its status when it unveiled the first phase of a $1 million collection reorganization. Exhibits date from ancient times through the 19thC and come from Europe, America, Africa and Oceania. Of the great masters, specific galleries show El Greco, Rubens and his contemporaries, the age of Rembrandt, and Gainsborough and British art. There is an important textile collection.

The galleries are arranged by period, genre, theme and discipline: American Art of the Federal Period, American Folk Art and Shaker Material, American Trompe L'Oeil and Still-Life Paintings, and so on. Ancient art runs from the 3rdC BC, with relics from Egypt, Greece, Rome and Assyria. Oceanian and African exhibits include Pacific Island carvings, pre-Columbian jade and gold, Mexican murals and African sculpture.

Among the initial improvements are 15 new galleries featuring one of the country's finest collections of American art from colonial times to the 20thC. They cover paintings throughout the period, with especially strong examples of landscape, realism and *trompe l'oeil*, sculpture, folk art, documents and photographs, as well as wood carving, silver and glass work. Among the many notable paintings are *The Mason Children* (1670), Frederic Church's monumental 19thC landscape *Rainy Season in the Tropics*, George Caleb Bingham's *Boatmen on the Missouri*, Eastman Johnson's *Pension Claim Agent*, Thomas Anshutz' *The Ironworkers' Noontime*, James McNeill Whistler's *The Gold Scab*, Maxfield Parrish's *The Pied Piper*, and a strong collection of Surrealist works by Yves Tanguy, Kay Sage and Charles Howard.

Sculpture includes the work of 19thC artists such as Herbert Powers and William Wetmore Story, Augustus Saint-Gaudens and Arthur Putnam. The 20thC is represented by artists such as Herbert Haseltine, Boris Lovet-Lorski and Isamu Noguchi. Other objects seldom seen before are designs by Frank Lloyd Wright and Louis Comfort Tiffany.

The **Asian Art Museum of San Francisco** (✮), housed in a separate wing of the de Young, is built around the legendary Avery Brundage Collection. The first floor is devoted to China. The upper floor covers Japan, Korea, India and the rest of Asia as far as the Middle and Near East. As well as the permanent collections, there are lectures and frequent and changing guest exhibitions; and there are further improvements in the pipeline.

See also *California Palace of the Legion of Honor*.

Where to stay

From glamorous old grand hotels and newer luxury establishments to handsome little Victorian bed-and-breakfast inns and inexpensive motels, San Francisco lodgings cater to all tastes and budgets. Only to be expected, perhaps, of a city with a long history of playing host to travelers and one which has more recently busied itself with conventions and tourists. At the top end of the market, geographically as well as figuratively, are Nob Hill's **Fairmont Hotel & Tower** and **Mark Hopkins Inter-Continental**. Around Union Sq. the **Westin St Francis** and **Four Seasons Clift** share the 5-star billing. However, they are not alone in providing comfort or luxury. The alternatives are small downtown hotels and less well-known inns in refurbished mansions, many distinguished by an almost European intimacy and ambience, plus others with service and decor that owe more to Asian traditions.

In addition, there are plainer downtown hotels, and motor inns and motels, the latter suitable for visitors requiring parking space in a city where it is hard to find or expensive, and usually both. The Fisherman's Wharf area has a cluster of larger motor inns, but the greatest concentration of medium-size and small motels ranges from Van Ness Ave., westward along Lombard St. toward the Golden Gate Bridge. (Every quarter has at least one motel.)

San Francisco has numbers of 8- to 30-room inns in luxuriously restored early-day mansions and small hotels scattered about the city in which prices range from expensive to very expensive. For a $1 fee, **Bed & Breakfast Innkeepers of Northern California** (*PO Box 766, Calistoga, CA 94515*) will send a brochure listing its San Francisco members.

Hotel reservations are advised and, although there are a few exceptions, most hotels require a reservation deposit. San Francisco's 11 percent hotel tax is added to quoted room rates.

If there is difficulty in finding a room in town, contact the **Convention and Visitors Bureau** (see *Useful information*, p117) or the **San Francisco Hotel Association** (*323 Geary St., Rm 611* ☎ *392-7860*).

Hotels classified by area

Fisherman's Wharf/Northern Waterfront
Howard Johnson's Motor Lodge |||||
Ramada Inn-Fisherman's Wharf |||||
The Hills
Bedford |||||
Fairmont Hotel & Tower |||||
The Huntington ||||| *to* |||||
Mark Hopkins Inter-Continental |||||
to |||||
Stanford Court |||||
Vintage Court |||||
York |||||
Japantown
Best Western Kyoto ||☐
Miyako |||||
Montgomery Street
Hyatt Regency |||||
SOMA
Hotel Meridien |||||

Sheraton Palace |||||
Tenderloin
Phoenix Inn |☐
Union Square and downtown
Beresford ||☐
Campton Place |||||
Canterbury/Whitehall |||||
Cartwright |||||
Chancellor ||☐ *to* |||||
Diva |||||
Four Seasons/Clift |||||
Galleria Park |||||
Hotel California ||☐
Hyatt on Union Sq. |||||
Inn at Union Sq. ||||| *to* |||||
Parc Fifty Five |||||
The Raphael ||☐ *to* |||||
Sir Francis Drake |||||
Westin St. Francis ||||| *to*
|||||

Bedford ♣
761 Post St., San Francisco 94109
☎ *673-6040 or (800) 652-1889.*
Map 12D3 ||||| *144 rms* ☐ ⬛ ☐
⬛
Location: 3½ blocks w of Union Sq.
With its white-painted modern furniture and bright decor, the Bedford is stylish as well as comfortable. Rooms near the top of the 17-story building are the quietest and have fine and interesting urban views. Some suites. The lobby is a pleasant place to sit and watch the world go by.
⬛ ☐ ☐ ☐ ⬛ ⬛ ⬛ ⬛

Beresford
635 Sutter St., San Francisco
94102 ☎ *673-9900. Map 13C4*
||☐ *114 rms* ☐ ⬛ ⬛ ☐
Location: Two blocks w of Union Sq.
A sense of well-being pervades this old hotel. It has good-sized rooms furnished with plain but tasteful old furniture. Bathrooms are a little time-worn, but impeccably clean. (**Beresford Arms**, the sister establishment a block s, has 90 similar rooms, many with kitchens.) The Beresford's **White Horse Tavern** is a replica of the original in Edinburgh.
⬛ ☐ ☐ ⬛

Best Western Kyoto
1800 Sutter St., San Francisco
94115 ☎ *921-4000. Map 12D2*
||☐ *125 rms* ⬛ ☐ ⬛ ⬛
⬛ ⬛
Location: Near Japan Center, a mile w of Union Sq. To meet the tastes of Japanese guests, many rooms have steam baths. Reservation deposit required.
☐ ☐

Campton Place ⬛
340 Stockton St., San Francisco
94108 ☎ *781-5555. Map 13D4*
||||| *126 rms* ⬛ ☐ ⬛ ⬛ ☐ ⬛ ⬛
Location: Union Sq. An old building refurbished into a luxury hotel with near-residential comforts. Its restaurant was a legend the week it opened.
⬛ ☐ ☐ ☐ ⬛ ⬛

Canterbury/Whitehall
750 Sutter St., San Francisco
94109 ☎ *474-6464 or (800)*
652-1614. Map 13C4 ||||| *250 rms*
⬛ ⬛ ☐ ⬛ ☐ ⬛
Location: One block N and one w of Union Sq. The hotel occupies two buildings. Although it is a little worn and some of the rooms are quite small, the original Canterbury remains reasonably comfortable. The

recently acquired Whitehall section (its rooms identifiable by 4-digit numbers) has large, well-furnished rooms with new baths. Some suites.

✹ ☐ ☞ ☕

Cartwright
524 Sutter St., San Francisco 94102 ☎ *421-2865. Map* **13C4**
▥ *119 rms* AE ⊙ ⊛ VISA
Location: One block N of Union Sq. An old hotel with small rooms, it is frequently renovated to keep it comfortable and tasteful. The lobby is a fair advertisement.

✹ ☐ ☞ 🗞

Chancellor ✿
433 Powell St., San Francisco 94102 ☎ *362-2004. Map* **13C4**
▥ *to* ▥ *140 rms* ⇥ AE CB ⊙ ⊛ VISA
Location: Half block N of Union Sq. A comfortable, well-staffed, quiet old hotel. A few of its cheerfully decorated rooms are small, but all are kept fresh and immaculately clean.

✹ ☐ ☞ 🗞 ☕

Diva
440 Geary St., San Francisco 94102 ☎ *885-0200. Map* **13D4**
▥ *125 rms* ⊙ ⊛ VISA
Location: Two blocks W of Union Sq.. Brushed metal, glass, VCRs, and other high-tech surfaces and gadgets are its hallmarks.

✹ ☐ ☞ 🗞

Fairmont Hotel & Tower ⬚ ▥
950 Mason St., San Francisco 94106 ☎ *772-5000. Map* **13C4**
▥ *596 rms* ☞ ⇥ AE CB ⊙ ⊛ VISA
Location: At the top of Nob Hill. The original turn-of-the-century lobby, with its towering marble columns and staircases, is a grand place for people-watching. Big-name entertainers stay at the Fairmont; politicians and other celebrities favor it as well. There is a choice between luxuriously spacious rooms in the old building and more up-to-date comforts in the 24-story tower added in 1962.

✹ ☐ ☞ 🗞 ☽ ☕ ♫ ☕ ☰

Four Seasons/Clift ⬚
495 Geary St., San Francisco 94102 ☎ *775-4700 or (800) 828-1188. Map* **13D4** ▥ *329 rms* ⇥ AE CB ⊙ ⊛ VISA
Location: Two blocks W of Union Sq. Known simply as The Clift until its acquisition a few years ago by a Canadian company, the hotel was for years almost an overseas club for well-heeled Britons. Its clientele has grown more international, but its

traditional, pale-hued elegance survived a recent renovation intact, and its staff performs all the old functions of grand luxury hotels with undiminished skill. A bar and restaurant, the **Redwood Room**, is a splendid demonstration of finely finished redwood. The **French Room** is among the city's most esteemed restaurants.

✹ ☕ ☐ ☞ ☽ ☕ ♫

Galleria Park
191 Sutter St., San Francisco 94104 ☎ *781-3060. Map* **13C4**
▥ *177 rms* ☰ ☞ ⇥ AE CB ⊙ ⊛ VISA
Location: Between financial district and Union Sq.. One of the most comfortable of almost a score of renovated, renamed older hotels in the downtown. Its oyster bar is worth knowing.

✹ ☕ ☐ ☞ 🗞 ☕

Holiday Inns   See page 138.

Hotel California
405 Taylor St., San Francisco 94102 ☎ *885-2500 or (800) 622-0961. Map* **13D4** ▥ *242 rms* ☞ ⇥ AE CB ⊙ ⊛ VISA
Location: Two blocks W of Union Sq.. Less spartan by miles than its prices suggest.

✹ ☐ ☞ 🗞 ☕

Hotel Meridien
50 3rd St., San Francisco 94103 ☎ *974-6400 or (800) 223-9918. Map* **13D4** ▥ *700 rms* ☰ ☞ ⇥ AE CB ⊙ ⊛ VISA
Location: Just off Market St. Air France's outpost in San Francisco looks far better from inside than it does from without. One modern tower hotel among many, it distinguishes itself with excellent public rooms and good restaurants.

✹ ☕ ☐ 🗞 ☽ ☕ ♫

Howard Johnson's Motor Lodge at Fisherman's Wharf
580 Beach St., San Francisco 94133 ☎ *775-3800. Map* **12B3** ▥ *128 rms* ☞ ⇥ AE ⊙ ⊛ VISA
A conventional modern motor inn.

✹ ☕ ☐ ☞ 🗞

The Huntington ⬚
1075 California St., San Francisco 94108 ☎ *474-5400. Map* **13C4** ▥ *to* ▥ *143 rms* ⇥ ⇥ AE ⊙ ⊛ VISA
Location: At the top of Nob Hill. This small hotel in the grand tradition is almost a club for local society because of its restaurants: the lobby-level **Big Four** (for good-value lunches and an after-work bar) and the downstairs

L'Étoile. The rooms are quietly luxurious. The staff is impeccable. There is even an elevator operator.

‡ □ ▧ ♨ ♀ ♪

Hyatt Regency

5 Embarcadero Center, San Francisco 94111 ☎ 788-1234. Map **13C5** ▥▥ 806 rms ▤▤ ▭ ⇌ ⊂ᴮ ⊙ ⊙ ₥₥

Location: At the foot of California St. near Market St. This hotel has one of those Hyatt trademark lobbies — a soaring atrium with giant welded-steel sculpture and a reflecting pool visible from the door of virtually every room. Afternoon tea dances and Sun brunches enliven interior views still further. Rooms are functional and modern.

‡ □ ▧ ♿ ♨ ♀ ♪ ♥

Hyatt on Union Square

345 Stockton St., San Francisco 94108 ☎ 398-1234. Map **13D4** ▥▥ 693 rms ▤▤ ⇌ ᴬᴱ ⊂ᴮ ⊙ ⊙ ₥₥

Location: As name — on Union Sq. A tower hotel built in 1972, it has conventionally comfortable rooms of generous size by the standards of its era. The decor and furnishings add some touches of luxury.

‡ ♿ □ ▧ ♀ ♪

Inn at Union Square

440 Post St., San Francisco 94102 ☎ 397-3510. Map **13C4** ▥▥ to ▥▥ 27 rms ᴬᴱ ⊙ ₥₥

Location: Four doors w of Union Sq. An instant success with celebrities and business travelers, the inn has a tiny lobby on each of its six floors where guests have continental breakfast, tea and hors d'oeuvres. Large rooms are elegant with Georgian furnishings, yet lightened with whimsy. For example, most beds have gaily designed half-canopies, and the high ones have brass footstools. The staff is hospitable.

⌂ ‡ □ ▧ ⚡

Mark Hopkins Inter-Continental
▥

1 Nob Hill, San Francisco 94108 ☎ 392-3434. Map **13C4** ▥▥ to ▥▥ 406 rms ▭ ⇌ ᴬᴱ ⊂ᴮ ⊙ ⊙ ₥₥

Location: At the top of Nob Hill. Every Hollywood movie set in the Pacific in World War II had its obligatory scene shot in The Top of the Mark. Today San Francisco's skyline looks quite different, but the great bar still sets the tone for the hotel, which remains as traditional as a grand tradition should. The skilled staff avoids any feeling of hurried bustle.

⌂ ‡ ♿ □ ▧ ⚡ ♨ ◄ ♀ ♪ ♥

Miyako

1625 Post St., San Francisco 94115 ☎ 922-3200. Map **12D2** ▥▥ 208 rms ▤▤ ▭ ⇌ ᴬᴱ ⊂ᴮ ⊙ ⊙ ₥₥

Location: At Japan Center, a mile w of Union Sq. In a modern 14-story building, the hotel caters to a Japanese clientele with Japanese-influenced decor in the rooms, and authentic Japanese decor and furnishings in the suites, many of which have saunas. Japanese guests dominate, but are far from alone.

‡ □ ▧ ♿ ◄ ♀ ♪

Parc Fifty Five

55 Cyril Magnin St., San Francisco 94102 ☎ 392-8000 or (800) 228-9898. Map **13D4** ▥▥ 1,005 rms ▤▤ ▭ ᴬᴱ ⊂ᴮ ⊙ ⊙ ₥₥

Location: Near Market and Powell. The largest modern tower hotel in the city underwent a name change in mid-1989. Previously it was the Ramada Renaissance. Its decor remains stylish, its staff excellent.

‡ ♿ □ ▧ ⚡ ◄ ♀

Phoenix Inn

601 Eddy St. San Francisco 94109 ☎ 776-1380. Map **12D3** ▥ 44 rms ▭ ⇌ ⊂ᴮ ⊙ ⊙ ₥₥

Location: Two blocks e of Van Ness Ave. Don't let the Tenderloin location put you off: the Phoenix is a gem. Service is friendly; the rooms, all overlooking the large central courtyard garden, are spacious, comfortable and decorated with modern art; there's complimentary breakfast from the lobby; and the parking lot is free. A special feature is the in-house video system showing movies set in San Francisco, e.g., *The Maltese Falcon.* The motel is a favorite with visiting musicians and younger, fashionable travelers. Get a copy of The Phoenix's San Francisco insider's guide, *Beyond Fisherman's Wharf.*

♿ ⚡ ≋ □ ▧ ♀

Ramada Inn-Fisherman's Wharf

590 Bay St., San Francisco 94133 ☎ 885-4700 or (800) 228-2828. Map **12B3** ▥▥ 231 rms ▤▤ ▭ ⇌ ᴬᴱ ⊂ᴮ ⊙ ⊙ ₥₥

Location: Two blocks s of Fisherman's Wharf. Conventional modern motor inn.

‡ ♿ □ ▧ ♀

The Raphael

386 Geary St., San Francisco 94102 ☎ 986-2000 or (800) 821-5343. Map **13D4** ▥ to ▥▥ 151 rms ▤▤ ▭ ᴬᴱ ⊂ᴮ ⊙ ⊙ ₥₥

Location: One block w of Union Sq. Extensively remodeled within the past few years, The Raphael is extremely comfortable, verging on luxurious. All rooms are cheerfully light and comfortably modern. Bathrooms are particularly spacious. Some rooms on the upper floors of this 14-story building are quite large, and those away from the street are quiet. Multilingual desk staff are helpful.

✥ ◻ ⌧ ♀

Sheraton Palace ⌾
639 Market St., San Francisco 94119 ☎ *392-8600 or (800) 325-3535. Map* **13**D4 ▮▮▮▮ *528 rms*
▭ ▱ ⬜ AE CB ◉ ◎ VISA
Location: Four blocks E of Union Sq.
Mark Twain was dazzled by the lobby clock in the days when the hotel had a carriage entrance, both long since gone. Guest rooms in the impressive old pile of bricks still show signs of the grand era, but remain comfortable only in a faded way. The one undimmed treasure in the hotel has occupied the old carriage entrance since 1909: the **Garden Court**, a magnificent atrium with leaded glass canopy, crystal chandeliers and Italian marble columns.

✥ ◻ ⌧ ⚅ ⚌ ♀

Sir Francis Drake
450 Powell St., San Francisco 94102 ☎ *392-7755. Map* **13**D4 ▮▮▮▮
415 rms ▭ ⇌ ⬜ AE CB ◉ ◎ VISA
Location: One block N of Union Sq.
The towering lobby is as big as a railroad station, and not much warmer, but guest rooms in this aging hotel are conservative in furn ishing and decor, and most are spacious. The Sir Francis is easy to spot: in tribute to the name, doormen wear Beefeater uniforms.

✥ ◻ ⌧ ⚌ ⚔ ♀

Stanford Court ⚅
905 California St., San Francisco 94108 ☎ *989-3500. Map* **13**C4
▮▮▮▮ *402 rms* ▭ ▱ ⇌ ⬜ AE CB ◉
◎ VISA
Location: At the top of Nob Hill.
Converted from an apartment building into a hotel in 1972, Stanford Court is the standard by which San Francisco's luxury hotels are measured. Rooms are spacious. In addition to telephones in the

bathrooms and similar practical amenities, decor and furnishings are of a style and quality hard to find in private homes. Cosseting by skilled staff helps make the price a bargain. **Fournou's Ovens** French restaurant adds luster.

◉ ✥ ◻ ⌧ ⚌ ♀

Vintage Court
650 Bush St., San Francisco 94108 ☎ *392-4666. Map* **13**C4 ▮▮▮▮ *106 rms*
▭ ⇌ AE CB ◉ ◎ VISA
Location: On Bush St., just off Powell St. Another genuinely comfortable small downtown hotel, brought about by renovation. **Masa's** restaurant is here.

✥ ⚅ ◻ ⚘ ♀

Westin St Francis ⚅ ⌾
335 Powell St., San Francisco 94119 ☎ *397-7000 or (800) 228-3000. Map* **13**D4 ▮▮▮▮ *to* ▮▮▮▮ *1,200 rms* ▭ ▱ ⇌ AE CB ◉ ◎ VISA
Location: Overlooking Union Sq. The staggering number of rooms is split between 600 in the handsome original stone building, rebuilt directly after the great earthquake and fire of 1906, and 600 in a soaring 32-story tower behind it. The new rooms are luxurious and modern. The best of those in the old structure, refurbished in 1980, are palatial. The main lobby and an adjoining wine bar, **The Compass Rose**, are exquisitely finished in traditional styles. In the new tower, a disco called **OZ** is phantasmagoric in ways that only modern materials could achieve. **Victor's**, a tower-top restaurant that is reached on vertiginous outdoor elevators, has one of the best chefs in the city.

✥ ◻ ⌧ ⪍ ⚌ ♀ ◉ ♫ ⚘

York
940 Sutter St., San Francisco 94109 ☎ *885-6800. Map* **12**C3
▮▮▮▮ *95 rms* CB ◉ ◎ VISA
Location: On Sutter near Leavenworth. Renovated as an Art Deco period piece, the York is comfortable, though some rooms are small. Its **Plush Room** books big-name entertainers.

✥ ◻ ⌧ ⚘ ♀ ♪

⌘ **Holiday Inns**: The choice includes **Holiday Inn-Civic Center** (☎ *626-6103* ▮▮▮▮), at Market St.; **Holiday Inn-Financial District** (☎ *433-6600* ▮▮▮▮ *to* ▮▮▮▮), one block E of Chinatown, at N boundary of Financial District; **Holiday Inn-Fisherman's Wharf** (☎ *771-9000* ▮▮▮▮ *to* ▮▮▮▮), three blocks S of Fisherman's Wharf; **Holiday Inn-Golden Gateway** (☎ *441-4000* ▮▮▮▮), three-quarters of a mile N of Civic Center; and **Holiday Inn-Union Square** (☎ *398-8900* ▮▮▮▮), at Sutter and Powell St. All of these are conventional, modern towers, save for the 5-story hotel at Fisherman's Wharf, which rambles.

✎ The **Cow Hollow Motor Inn** (*2190 Lombard St., San Francisco 94123* ☎ *921-5800* ⬛ *60 rms*) is a comfortable motor inn. Standard motels include **Beck's Motor Lodge** (*2222 Market St., San Francisco 94114* ☎ *621-8212* ⬛ *56 rms*) and **Rancho Lombard** (*1501 Lombard St., San Francisco 94123* ☎ *474-3030* ⬛ *34 rms*).

Where to eat

From its earliest days San Francisco has welcomed expatriates from every country with a cuisine worth considering, and some without, and has fed them all to their satisfaction. Although there is every degree of luxury and a striking variety of national and ethnic cookery, the pure San Francisco-style restaurant has its base in the pioneer ethic, which has it that money spent on decor cannot be spent in the kitchen. Plain tables, plain walls, bare wood floors and aging waiters in black are the hallmarks of **Jack's**, **Sam's Grill** and **Tadich Grill**, originals which have begun to spawn a new generation of similar restaurants in which the main difference is younger waiters in blue aprons instead of black. Even such in-vogue places as **Chez Panisse** in Berkeley, with a culinary reputation approaching the legendary, would strike a Spartan as bare. Still, these may be the places to find the best food in San Francisco.

In a city with so many cultural cross-currents, pinning down a local cuisine defies both imagination and logic. The old San Francisco restaurants pay expert attention to the grilling of fresh fish, but may add anything from a Slavic to a French touch. Traditional French cookery is widely available in the city; there is an excellent choice of Chinese places, and Italian restaurants are plentiful. Solid communities of Armenians, Basques, Russians, Greeks, Japanese, Mexican and Central Americans and a newer wave of Vietnamese, Thais and Khmers maintain echoes of home, mainly faithful, some innovative. Most of the city's famous restaurants are within the quarter bounded by Market St. to the s, Van Ness Ave. to the w, and the Bay on the other sides. However, for adventurous eaters, some of the most intriguing restaurants hide away in neighborhood shopping streets.

Finally, San Francisco is a city in love with ice cream. A separate list of ice cream parlors ends this section.

Restaurants classified by area

The Avenues
Alejandro's ⬛
Angkor Wat ⬛
Khan Toke Thai House ⬛ *to* ⬛
Yet Wah ⬛ *to* ⬛
Civic Center
Hayes Street Grill ⬛
Modesto Lanzone-Opera Plaza ⬛
Stars ⬛ *to* ⬛
Fisherman's Wharf/Northern Waterfront
Gaylord India ⬛ *to* ⬛
Mandarin ⬛
Lanzone and Son ⬛
Paprikas Fono ⬛
Scoma's ⬛ *to* ⬛
Grant Avenue/Chinatown
Empress of China ⬛ *to* ⬛
Imperial Palace ⬛ *to* ⬛
Nam Yuen ⬛
The Hills
Café Bedford ⬛
L'Étoile ⬛

Fournou's Ovens ⬛ *to* ⬛
Japantown/Marina/Golden Gate/Presidio/Pacific Heights
Balboa Café ⬛ *to* ⬛
Green's ⬛
Scott's Seafood Grill ⬛
Vivande Porta Via ⬛
Montgomery Street
Blue Fox ⬛ *to* ⬛
Gaylord India ⬛ *to* ⬛
Harbor Village ⬛ *to* ⬛
Iron Horse ⬛ *to* ⬛
Jack's ⬛
Sam's Grill ⬛ *to* ⬛
Tadich Grill ⬛ *to* ⬛
Waterfront ⬛ *to* ⬛
North Beach
Amelio's ⬛ *to* ⬛
Alfred's ⬛ *to* ⬛
Caffe Sport ⬛ *to* ⬛
Chez Michel ⬛ *to* ⬛
Ernie's ⬛
Fior d'Italia ⬛ *to* ⬛

139

Fog City Diner *///* to *////*
Hunan *//*
Square One *//* to *////*
Vanessi's *//*
Washington Square Bar & Grill *////*
SOMA
Le Piano Zinc *//* to *////*
Tenderloin
California Culinary Academy *//*
Thai Binh Duong *☐* to *//☐*
Union Square and downtown
Campton Place *////*
Le Central *//* to *////*
Donatello *////*
Fleur de Lys *////* to *////*
Harris' *//* to *////*
Les Joulins *//* to *////*
Kinokawa *//*
Masa's *////*
Trader Vic's *//* to *////*

Amelio's

1630 Powell St. ☎ 397-4339. Map 13C4 //// to //// ☐ ■■ Open 6-10pm.
One-time speakeasy and Italian restaurant turned French. A favorite with well-to-do locals. **Specialties:** *Fish baked in a crust, plume de veau.*

Alejandro's ☙

1840 Clement St. ☎ 668-1184. Map 13C4 //// ☐ ☿ ☐ Open Sun-Thurs 5-11pm, Fri-Sat 5pm-midnight.
Alejandro's — sometimes Alejandro's Sociedad Gastronomica — is where the city's Central and South American chefs gather to compare notes. The Peruvian owner-chef has an affinity with Mexican and Spanish cuisines as well as his own. The eclectic results are spectacular. Reservations vital.
Specialties: *Conejo in salsa de mani (rabbit in peanut sauce), sopa 7 mares-paribuela, and, above all, paella.*

Alfred's

886 Broadway ☎ 781-7058. Map 13C4 //// ☐ ■■ AE CB ☐ ☐ VISA Open Mon-Fri 11.30am-2pm, 5.30-11pm, Sat 5.30-11pm, Sun 5.30-10.30pm.
Alfred's is both an Italian restaurant and a great steakhouse. Consensus opinion is that its mesquite charcoal-grilled steaks are the best in town, but the rack of lamb and osso bucco (lunch only) ought not to be overlooked. The decor is San Francisco plush-red banquettes, red wallpaper, big chandeliers, waiters in tuxedos — but relieved by a big glass case full of aging beef. **Specialties:** *Antipasto, porterhouse and Delmonico steaks.*

Angkor Wat

4217 Geary St. ☎ 221-7887. Map 10D3 //// 𝄞 ✿ AE ☐ ☐ Open Tues-Sat 5-10.30pm, Sun 5-10pm.
French-trained chef/owner Keau Ty opened San Francisco's first Cambodian restaurant. He now runs two, and this is the swankier one. The decor recalls the ancient Khmer monument, and excellent food is enhanced by traditional music and dance. **Specialties:** *Broiled chicken, beef with lemon soup.*

Balboa Café ☙

3199 Fillmore St. ☎ 922-4595. Map 12B2 //☐ to //// ☐ ■■ ☿ ☐ VISA Open 11.30am-2.30pm, 6-10pm.
There are those who believe that most of the imaginative cooking in San Francisco is being done in Berkeley. If so, the imagination is being reimported. Jeremiah Tower, previously a guiding light of Chez Panisse, created a menu of extraordinary dishes for this classic, old-fashioned bar and café. In season (Dec-Jan) Monterey Bay prawns turn stoics into rhapsodists. **Specialties:** *Hamburgers, fritattas, fettucine.*

Blue Fox ⌂

659 Merchant St. ☎ 981-1177. Map 13C4 //// to //// ☐ ■■ ⚊ by valet AE CB ☐ ☐ VISA Open Mon-Sat 6-11pm.
The rooms have a formal elegance — paneling, old oil paintings, crystal chandeliers — that brings people back year after year for anniversary dinners. A veteran staff and a conservative continental menu keep the celebrants content. Reservations advised; jacket and tie required.
Specialties: *Gamberi alla livornese, mousseline de poisson, frog's legs.*

Café Bedford ☙

761 Post St. ☎ 928-8361. Map 13C4 //☐ ☐ AE CB ☐ ☐ VISA Open Tues-Sat 6-9.30pm, Sun 10am-1pm.
The food in this small, quiet restaurant in the **Bedford** (see *SF Hotels*) is California with French touches: imaginative without challenging the loopier frontiers of flavor and fuss. **Specialties:** *Smoked salmon pasta, chicken in Pommery sauce.*

Caffe Sport

574 Green St. ☎ 981-1251. Map 13B4 //☐ to //// ☐ ☐ VISA Open Tues-Sat noon-2pm, 6.30-11pm.
It takes real concentration to notice that the garlicky food is good in this Neapolitan kitsch palace and general tower of babble. Reservations

are required, although they do not guarantee exactly when you will eat, or with whom. The waiter may overrule a diner's choice, and will be right. *Specialties: Pasta alla vongole, scampi al'Antonio, calamari.*

California Culinary Academy
625 Polk St. ☎ *771-3500. Map 12D3* ▥ ▯ ⊡ ✗ AE ⊙ ⊡ VISA *Open Mon-Fri: lunchtime seatings noon, 12.30pm, dinner seatings 6pm, 6.45pm, 7.30pm. Academy shop open Mon-Fri 8.30am-6pm.*
Students of the West Coast's best cooking school prepare and serve classic French cuisine with some Californian touches. The food is first-rate and reasonably priced, and service is friendly. Reservations, well ahead, are essential for the main dining room and recommended for the lighter brasserie lunches served on the balcony. There is a small coffee shop/bakery/culinary shop/bookstore next door. Tours by reservation Mon-Fri at 3pm.

Campton Place △
340 Stockton St. ☎ *781-5155. Map 13D4* ▥ ▯ AE CB ⊙ ⊡ VISA *Open 8am-10pm.*
In the hotel of the same name (see **SF Hotels**), an altogether original chef presents an altogether original menu drawn from old American resources. Astonishing renewals of old familiars include — *Specialties: Grilled quail, spring lobster, blue corn cakes.*

Le Central
453 Bush St. ☎ *391-2233. Map 13C4* ▥ ▯ to ▥ ▯ ⊡ ✓ AE ⊙ VISA *Open Mon-Fri 11.45am-10.15pm, Sat 6-10.15pm.*
A bustling brasserie has the city's longest-cooking *cassoulet* among other entries on a properly simple and tasty menu. The place is a lunchtime favorite with some of the city's movers and shakers. Reservations advised. *Specialties: Boudin noir, cassoulet.*

Chez Michel
804 North Point St. ☎ *771-6077. Map 12B3* ▥ ▯ to ▥ ▯ ▦ ▬ ⊙ VISA *Open Tues-Sun 6pm-12.30am.*
The decor is somewhere between Art Deco and modern and has almost as many straight-edged Scandinavian touches as French ones, but the menu is pure, innovative French, simple and fresh without being *nouvelle*. Pleasant bar. *Specialties: Brains in black butter, rack of lamb.*

Donatello △
505 Post St. ☎ *441-7182. Map 13C4* ▥ ▯ ⊡ ✓ AE CB ⊙ ⊡ VISA *Open 11.30am-2.30pm, 6-10.30pm.*
On a mezzanine floor flanking the Pacific Plaza hotel lobby, the Donatello uses marble and silk to achieve a light, refined, original appearance in each of two long, narrow rooms. The northern Italian menu follows suit, giving San Francisco by far its most elegantly prepared and served Italian cuisine. *Specialties: Lo scrigno di Venere, quaglie farcite alla Bolognese.*

Empress of China
838 Grant Ave. ☎ *434-1345. Map 13C4* ▥ ▯ ▦ ▬ ⊙ ⊡ VISA *Open Mon-Sat 11.30am-3pm, 5-11pm, Sun 12.30-11pm.*
The food is good, but it is the luxurious decor and attentive service that set this restaurant a little apart from several other Grant Ave. institutions. Pleasant bar. *Specialties: Flaming young quail, Szechuan spiced beef.*

Ernie's △
847 Montgomery St. ☎ *397-5969. Map 13C4* ▥ ▯ ▦ ▬ ✓ AE CB ⊙ ⊡ VISA *Open 6.30-10.30pm.*
Decor at Ernie's outglitters and outplushes San Francisco's most famous Gold Rush bordellos. Jackets and ties are required, as are reservations, sometimes several days in advance.

L'Étoile △
1075 California St. ☎ *771-1529. Map 13C4* ▥ ▯ to ▥ ▯ ▦ ▬ ✓ *by valet* AE CB ⊙ ⊡ VISA *Open Mon-Sat 6-8.30pm.*
An austerely beautiful room and a well-prepared traditional French menu are maintained downstairs in **The Huntington** (see **SF Hotels**) for a clientele dominated by San Francisco socialites. Reservations required, usually a day or two ahead. The same clientele fills a luxurious lounge, where pianist Peter Mintun dotes on Cole Porter and his peers. *Specialties: Quenelles, rack of lamb, tournedos.*

Fior d'Italia
621 Union St. ☎ *986-1886. Map 13B4* ▥ ▯ to ▥ ▯ ⊡ ✓ AE CB ⊙ ⊡ VISA *Open 11am-11pm.*
The great winemaker Louis M. Martini was a regular customer because he liked to be surrounded by a discriminating clientele. At a new address, and with plusher decor, it remains a quiet, comfortable

141

restaurant for those who appreciate northern Italian food and excellent wine. **Specialties:** *Veal Stelvio, chicken Mascotte, zabaglione Montecarlo.*

Fleur de Lys

777 Sutter St. ☎ *673-7779. Map 13C4 ▥▥ to ▥▥ ⬚ ▦ ☕ ▦ by valet* ▦ ▦ ▦ ▦ ▦ *Open Tues-Sun 6-11pm.*

Fleur de Lys is an entirely happy place to have dinner. The principal decoration is a vast red and green floral fabric draped to form, more or less, a tent inside the room. The food is traditional French, with an occasional Algerian nuance, well prepared and skillfully served. **Specialties:** *Moules marinière, coq au vin, duckling with figs.*

Fog City Diner ✿

1300 Battery St. ☎ *982-2000. Map 13B4 ▥▥ to ▥▥ ⬚ ▦ ▦*

In this architectural tribute to a 1950s diner, the menu offers full meals, but also a sort of American equivalent to *dim sum* — small plates that can be ordered by the half-dozen. The crowd is half the fun. Reservations mandatory. **Specialties:** *Crab cakes, Buffalo chicken wings, black bean chili.*

Fournou's Ovens ⌂

905 California St. ☎ *989-1910. Map 13C4 ▥▥ to ▥▥ ⬚ ▦ ☕ ▦ by valet* ▦ ▦ ▦ ▦ *Open Mon-Fri 11.30am-2.30pm, 6.30-10.30pm, Sat-Sun 6.30-10.30pm.*

In the **Stanford Court** (see *SF Hotels*), the restaurant descends from a bar to a conservatory overlooking Powell St. and the cable cars, then through several terraces to a bank of tile-fronted ovens from which it draws its name. Although the decor remains tastefully plain from top to bottom, there is no more elegant a dining room in the city. The menu is tried-and-true French, and without a failure. **Specialties:** *Rack of lamb aux aromates, James Beard's duckling with kumquat sauce.*

Gaylord India

Ghirardelli Sq. ☎ *771-8822, map 12B3; also at 1 Embarcadero Center* ☎ *397-7755, map 13C5 ▥▥ to ▥▥ ⬚ ▦ ▦ ☕ ▦ ▦ ☕ ▦ ▦ Open 11.30-2pm, 5-11pm.*

The restaurants are part of a national chain, but maintain rigorous standards. San Francisco offers no better tandoori cooking, nor do many other places. Reservations required. **Specialties:** *Chicken tikka, sag gosht, navratan korma.*

Green's

Building A, Fort Mason (Laguna and Mason Sts. entrance) ☎ *771-6222. Map 12B2 ▥▥ ▦ ▬ ▦ ▦ Open Tues-Sat 11.30am-2.15pm, 6-8.30pm, Sun 10am-2pm.*

Owned by a Zen community with lofty culinary standards, Green's elevates vegetarian meals to memorable stature. Superb breads come from an affiliated bakery. A short but thoughtful California wine list is one bonus; sterling views of the Golden Gate are another. Reservations always required. **Specialties:** *Salads, fritattas, pizza.*

Harbor Village

4 Embarcadero Center, Lobby Level ☎ *781-8833. Map 13C5 ▥▥ to ▥▥ ⬚ ▬ ▦ ▦ Open Mon-Fri 11am-9.30pm, Sat-Sun 10.30am-9.30pm.*

Cantonese cuisine and seafood in smart surroundings with fine views across the harbor. Lunchtime *dim sum* may be the best in town, so you may wait for a table on weekends. **Specialties:** *Minced pigeon, steamed crab with ginger and garlic.*

Harris'

2100 Van Ness Ave. ☎ *673-1888. Map 12C3 ▥▥ to ▥▥ ⬚ ☕ ▦ ▦ ▦ Open Mon-Fri 11.30am-11pm.*

Dark, handsome wood paneling and uniformed waiters lend elegance, and the menu provides fish and other diversions (especially at lunch); but at heart this is a steak house, and a good one. **Specialties:** *Dry-aged steak, prime rib.*

Hayes Street Grill

324 Hayes St. ☎ *863-5545. Map 12D3 ▥▥ ⬚ ▬ ▦ ▦ Open Mon-Thurs 11.30am-10pm, Fri 11.30am-11pm, Sat 6-10pm.*

Tucked behind the San Francisco Opera House, this restaurant follows the fine San Francisco tradition of bare wood floors, unadorned walls and bentwood chairs as a properly informal environment for serious attention to grilled fish; but here the touch is French rather than Slav. A choice of fresh fish (halibut, sole, sea bass, angler, shark, trout) is cooked to taste, and served with any of several fine sauces (*beurre blanc*, sorrel butter, caper sauce Grenobloise). **Specialties:** *Grilled fish, Monterey Bay prawns in season.*

Hunan

924 Sansome St. ☎ *956-7727. Map 13C4 ▥▥ ⬚ ☕ ▦ ▦ ▦ Open Mon-Fri 11.30am-9.30pm.*

Hunan is a much lionized source of hot, spicy north Chinese cookery. The place looks like a decorated gymnasium, but for connoisseurs of fiery peppers, decor is beside the point. Knowledgable locals take their meals in the relatively intimate bar. *Specialty: Spicy chicken salad.*

Imperial Palace

919 Grant Ave. ☎ *982-4440. Map 13C4 |||] to |||| ▢ ☂ ⚱ CB ⊙ ⊚ VISA Open Sun-Thurs 11.30am-1pm, Fri-Sat 11.20am-2am.*

One of Chinatown's grand bastions of Cantonese-style cookery has left it to others to chase after the recent fashion for north Chinese dishes. The room is so softly lighted that museum-quality art objects make their presence felt only slowly. Even the bar is subdued to the point of serenity. Jacket and tie advised; reservations required. *Specialties: Minced squab Imperial, barbecued lamb with Chinese zucchini, lobster Imperial.*

Iron Horse

19 Maiden Lane ☎ *362-8133. Map 13D4 |||] to |||| ▢ ▰ ⚍ ☂ AE CB ⊙ ⊚ Open Mon-Sat 11.30am-4pm, 5.30-10.30pm. Closed Sun.*

Conveniently located, and elegant without being over-formal, the Iron Horse is a good Italian/continental restaurant and has one of the busiest after-work bars in town. Reservations advised. *Specialties: Medallion of veal Ruggero, chicken sauté Mascotte.*

Jack's

615 Sacramento St. ☎ *986-9854. Map 13C4 |||] to |||| ▢ ☂ Open Mon-Sat 11.30am-9.30pm, Sun 4.30-9.30pm.*

This is the quintessential San Francisco-style restaurant, complete with white tiled floors, plain wood chairs, bare walls and utilitarian lighting. The waiters are more permanent than the fixtures, and the clientele is more permanent than the waiters. To the complete satisfaction of regulars and waiters alike, Jack's menu is just as durable in all its quirky bounty. Jacket and tie required; reservations advised. *Specialties: Sorrel soup, English mutton chops, fillet of sole Marguery.*

Les Joulins

44 Ellis St. ☎ *397-5397. Map 13D4 |||] to |||| ▢ ▰ AE ⊙ VISA Open Mon-Sat 7.30am-3pm, 5.30-10pm.*

In a useful location for downtown shoppers, Les Joulins falls somewhere between brasserie and bistro for atmosphere; but the skillfully prepared conventional French menu reaches beyond the decor. Adjoining the dining room is a superior pâtisserie and charcuterie. Reservations advised for lunch and dinner. *Specialties: Salmon en croûte, roast duckling in orange and fig or peach sauce.*

Khan Toke Thai House

5937 Geary Blvd. ☎ *668-6654. Map 10D2 |||] to |||] ▢ ▰ ☂ AE ⊙ VISA Open 5-11pm.*

Widely regarded as among the best of the city's growing number of Thai restaurants. Choice of Thai-style dining reclining on cushions at low tables, or upright Western-style. Either way, waitresses wear traditional dress, and there's classical Thai dancing on Sunday. On top of this, the food is reasonably authentic, though less fiery than old Bangkok hands may wish. Tell the staff you want it hotter. *Specialties: BBQ chicken, chicken coconut soup, curry.*

Kinokawa

347 Grant Ave. ☎ *956-6085. Map 13C4 |||] ▢ ☂ ⚲ AE CB ⊙ ⊚ VISA Open Mon-Fri 11.30am-2.30pm, 5pm-11pm, Sushi bar to 3am.*

Sushi has not become a civic religion in San Francisco as it has in Los Angeles, but it has caught on, and Kinokawa does very well at this combined sleight-of-hand show and feast of fish and rice. *Sashimi* and *hibachi* on offer also.

Mandarin △

Ghirardelli Sq. ☎ *673-8812. Map 12B3 |||] ▢ ▰ ⚍ VISA Open Mon-Fri noon-11pm, Sat-Sun 12.30-11.30pm.*

Cecilia Chiang pioneered N Chinese cookery in San Francisco, and her breathtakingly opulent restaurant at the top of the Woolen Mill building remains a treasure. The food is always fine, sometimes stunning. Impeccable service, and the decor and grand views of the Bay count for almost as much. *Specialties: Minced squab in lettuce leaves, smoked tea duck (one day's notice), beggar chicken.*

Masa's △

648 Bush St. ☎ *989-7154. Map 13C4 |||| ▢ ▰ ⚍ ☂ AE CB ⊙ ⊚ VISA Open Tues-Sat 6-9.30pm.*

The late founder, Masa Kobayashi, was one of the first to marry Japanese presentation with French ingredients and techniques. His successors continue the tradition of producing dishes too beautiful to touch and too

Modesto Lanzone-Opera Plaza
601 Van Ness Ave. ☎ *928-0400. Map 12D3* 🞑🞑🞑🞑 ⬚ ⮑ ⧖ ⮝ ⒜Ⓔ ⒸⒷ ⊙ ⓒ ⓥⓢⓐ *Open Mon-Fri 11.30am-midnight, Sat 4pm-midnight.*

Lanzone and Son
Ghirardelli Sq. ☎ *771-2880. Map 12B3* 🞑🞑🞑🞑 ⬚ ⮑ ⮑ ⮝ ⒜Ⓔ ⒸⒷ ⊙ ⓒ ⓥⓢⓐ *Open Tues-Fri 11.45am-11pm, Sat-Sun 4pm-midnight.*

In Opera Plaza, Modesto's is a sleek, modern art gallery as well as a fine restaurant for northern Italian food. Lanzone and Son in Ghirardelli Sq. is Rococo in decor, but serves the same menu. **Specialties:** *Pansotti (little pasta stuffed with ricotta and covered with walnut sauce), cima di vitello.*

Nam Yuen
740 Washington St. ☎ *781-5636. Map 13C4* 🞑🞑🞑 ⬚ ⮑ ⓒ ⓥⓢⓐ *Open Tues-Sat 11.30am-11pm.*

This pleasantly understated restaurant has an unofficial reputation for having trained many of the well-regarded Cantonese chefs in town. True or not, it is an excellent middle ground between grand Chinese restaurants and those with formica-topped tables where the Chinese truck drivers eat. Reservations accepted. **Specialty:** *War won ton.*

Paprikas Fono
900 North Point St. ☎ *441-1223. Map 12B3* 🞑🞑🞑 ⬚ ⮑ ⓒ ⓥⓢⓐ *Open Mon-Thurs 11am-11pm, Fri-Sat 11am-11.30pm, Sun 11am-10.30pm.*

Laszlo and Paulette Fono, the ingenious pair who invented The Magic Pan crepe cooker, have now turned their talents to running a Hungarian restaurant on one of the upper levels of Ghirardelli Sq. Reservations advised. The *palacintas* that made them famous are on the menu, joined now by a broad range of their native dishes. **Specialties:** *Chicken paprika, veal paprika, gulyas with fried langos.*

Le Piano Zinc
708 14th St. ☎ *431-5266. Map 12E2* 🞑🞑🞑 ⬚ ⮑ ⒜Ⓔ ⓒ ⓥⓢⓐ *Open Tues-Sun 6pm-midnight.*

Resident and visiting Parisians adore this chic brasserie-style restaurant, which reminds them of home. Classic French cuisine, plus jazz piano on a white baby grand and singers. Reservations recommended. **Specialties:** *Game, breast of duck with peaches.*

Prego
2000 Union St. at Buchanan. ☎ *563-3305. Map 12B3* 🞑🞑🞑 *Open 11.30am-midnight.*

A trendy spot with a lively bar, wood-burning pizza oven, good Italian food and friendly service. Expect to wait for a table even with a reservation. **Specialties:** *Tortelloni di Magro al Burro, Trittico di Gnocchi, Pizza.*

Sam's Grill
374 Bush St. ☎ *421-0594. Map 13C4* 🞑🞑 to 🞑🞑🞑 ⬚ ⓒ ⓥⓢⓐ *Open Mon-Fri 11am-10.30pm. Closed major hols.*

Another of the old San Francisco no-frills good fish restaurants with bare floors and veteran waiters that used to abound downtown but have dwindled to a precious few. This one even has a row of curtained booths for secluded gluttony. Arrive before 11.30am for lunch or wait until after 2pm. A long menu has the faintest Italian flavor. **Specialties:** *Charcoal broiled fillet of petrale, clams Elizabeth, deviled crab à la Sam.*

Scoma's ✿
Pier 47 ☎ *771-4383. Map 12B3* 🞑🞑🞑 to 🞑🞑🞑🞑 ⬚ ⒜Ⓔ ⒸⒷ ⊙ ⓒ ⓥⓢⓐ *Open 11.30am-11.30pm.*

Tucked into a corner of Fisherman's Wharf, behind the row of buildings fronting Jefferson St., Scoma's offers traditional San Francisco-Italian fish cookery in abundance. The restaurant does not accept reservations, but deals with its customary mixed mob of locals and tourists efficiently and in good humor. **Specialties:** *Cioppino alla pescatore, sautéed calamari and scampi.*

Scott's Seafood Grill
2400 Lombard St. ☎ *563-8988. Map 11B5* 🞑🞑🞑 ⬚ ⮝ ⒜Ⓔ ⓒ ⓥⓢⓐ *Open 11am-11pm.*

One of the new generation of San Francisco fish houses, Scott's is comfortable but looks as frill-free as uncurtained windows and bare wood floors can make it. The cooks grill fresh fish in full view of the diners. Scott's does not accept reservations. Be ready to wait, and wait, and, on weekends, wait some more. (A branch downtown at Embarcadero 3 serves similar fare in slightly flashier, more modern surroundings.) **Specialties:** *Blue-point oysters on ice, Pacific salmon with hollandaise, fisherman's stew.*

Square One
190 Pacific at Front St. ☎ *788-1110. Map 13C4* 🞑🞑🞑 to 🞑🞑🞑🞑 ⬚ ⮑

SF Restaurants

🍴 ▣ 𝚅𝙸𝚂𝙰 Open Mon-Fri
11.30am-2pm, Mon-Sat 6-10pm.
Owner-chef Joyce Goldstein has
plowed a lot of new ground since
graduating from Chez Panisse and
shows no sign of slowing down in her
search for yet another heartily
flavorful bread, soup, casserole, stew,
whatever. The atmosphere in a bright,
modern room is always energetic.
Menu changes daily.

Stars
150 Redwood Alley ☎861-7827.
Map 12D3 ▥ to ▥▥ ☐ ❦ 𝚅𝙸𝚂𝙰
Open Mon-Fri 11.30am-2.30pm,
nightly 5.30-10 or 11pm.
Jeremiah Tower had a strong hand in
the early days of Chez Panisse and an
equally strong hand in developing
restaurants of like temperament. This
one is his own, and his inventiveness
has not flagged. Great for lunch or
after-the-show. Menu changes
regularly, but always has fish, pasta,
grilled meats as anchors.

Tadich Grill
240 California St. ☎391-2373.
Map 13C4 ▥ to ▥▥ ☐ ❦ Open
Mon-Sat 11.30am-10.30pm.
Closed major hols.
The full name of this old San
Francisco eating house is Tadich's
Original Cold Day Restaurant. It
doesn't make much sense, but has
stuck with the place through at least
two moves, as has an atmosphere full
of comfort and free of frills. A no-
reservations policy means a long wait
for booths or small tables, but the
long counter usually has vacant
places soon if not immediately. Most
of the clientele goes to have fresh fish
grilled by veteran cooks to the
magnificent standards of Adriatic
Slavs; but casseroles cannot be
overlooked. **Specialties:** Snapper,
sand dabs, crab, prawns à la Monza.

Trader Vic's △
20 Cosmo Pl. ☎776-2232. Map
12C3 ▥ to ▥▥ ☐ ❦ ❦ by
valet 𝙰𝙴 𝙲𝙱 ▣ ▣ 𝚅𝙸𝚂𝙰 Open
Mon-Fri 11.30am-2.30pm, 5pm-
midnight, Sat-Sun 5pm-midnight.
Polynesia is only one influence in a
richly varied menu served with
flourishes by the European and Asian
staff. The decor is whimsically tropical
in the main room, but severely
nautical in the Captain's Cabin, a
gathering place for San Francisco
society, especially after the theater.
Reservations required. Men must
wear jacket and tie; trouser suits for
women are tolerated. In the bar, the
unwary will learn the perils of tropical
rum drinks. **Specialties:** baked crab

(Dec-Feb), Indonesian lamb, salmon
in red caviar sauce.

Thai Binh Duong (Pacific Restaurant)
607 Larkin St. Map 12D3 ☐ to ▯
☐ Open Mon-Sun 8.30am-8pm.
A neighborhood Vietnamese
restaurant with a pleasant no-frills
decor and a predominantly Asian
clientele, who know a thing or two
about Vietnamese food. The staples
are well done and inexpensive.
Specialties: Beef noodle soup,
imperial rolls.

Vanessi's
498 Broadway ☎421-0890. Map
13C4 ▥ ☐ 𝙰𝙴 𝙲𝙱 ▣ ▣ 𝚅𝙸𝚂𝙰 Open
Mon-Sat 11.30am-1am, Sun
4.30pm-midnight.
In this ever-thrumming hive of eaters
and drinkers, cooks working behind a
long counter are one of the great
long-running shows in town. Flames
do not move half as fast. Reservations
advised but guarantee little. San
Francisco is full of places famous for
Joe's Special, but this is the best place
for these cousins to *fritattas*, made
with minced meat, spinach and eggs.
Grilled meats also good. **Specialties:**
Ravioli, calamari (fried or sautéed in
tomato sauce), zabaglione, abalone
(when available).

Vivande Porta Via
2125 Fillmore St. ☎346-4430.
Map 12C2 ▥▥ ▭ 𝙰𝙴 ▣ ▣ 𝚅𝙸𝚂𝙰
Open 11.30am-4pm.
Carlos Middione's nearest rival for
splendid Italian lunches is somewhere
in Tuscany.

Washington Square Bar & Grill
1707 Powell St. ☎982-8123. Map
13B4 ▥▥ ☐ ❦ ❦ ♪ ▬ by valet
𝙰𝙴 ▣ 𝚅𝙸𝚂𝙰 Open Mon-Sat
11.30am-2.30pm, 6-11pm, Sun
10am-3pm, 6-11pm.
A haven for local newspaper people
and other writers and for jazz piano
players, who may be interested in
good Italian food or may be there just
to drink real whiskey in preference to
vodka and other timid stuff. The
menu has some set pieces and some
daily specials, but the inclination is
always toward fish, veal and pasta.
Brunch dishes keep an Italian flavor,
too. Everything is good, and much is
imaginative. Reservations advised.
Specialties: Fisherman's salad, fried
calamari with anchovy sauce.

Waterfront
Pier 7, The Embarcadero ☎391-
2696. Map 13C5 ▥ to ▥▥ ☐ ❦ by
valet 𝙰𝙴 𝙲𝙱 ▣ ▣ 𝚅𝙸𝚂𝙰 Open Mon-

145

*Fri 11.30am-2.30pm, 5-10.30pm,
Sat-Sun 11am-3pm, 5-10.30pm.*
This, one of the new generation of
fish houses, leans toward understated
decor (although not as far as Tadich's
or Sam's Grill) and grilling or
sautéeing rather than frying in batter.
Tables are on several levels inside a
glass wall, with views of city fireboats
and the Bay beyond. Many locals —
and visitors — think SF's best brunch
is served here. ***Specialties:*** *Grilled
fish, seafood salads.*

Yet Wah
2140 Clement St. ☎ *387-8040.
Map* **10D2** ▥▯ *to* ▥▥▥ ⊡ ▦ ☒ AE

CB ⊙ ⊚ VISA *Open 11.30am-
11.30pm.*
Yet Wah is a small, family-owned
chain, which maintains consistently
high standards. But the dining room
in the outrageous purple building on
Clement St. is emphatically the
flagship. The decor is gilt and
crimson, but softened by plants in an
atrium and by pleasantly dim lighting.
Reservations accepted. A menu with
as many as 200 items has most north
Chinese dishes that will be familiar to
most Americans. Every dish is
prepared to order. ***Specialties:***
*Potstickers, mushu pork, hot pepper
prawns.*

Also recommended

Inexpensive North Beach Italian **Gold Spike** (*527 Columbus Ave.*
☎ *986-9747*); **La Pantera** (*1234 Grant Ave.* ☎ *392-0170*); **New Pisa** (*550
Green St.* ☎ *362-4726*); **The US Restaurant** (*431 Columbus Ave.*
☎ *362-6251*). Also **Basta Pasta** (*1268 Grant Ave.* ☎ *434-2248*), which
children really love.
Inexpensive Chinatown For *dim sum,* **Asia Garden** (*772 Pacific Ave.*
☎ *398-5112*) and **Hang Ah** (*1 Pagoda Pl., off Sacramento St. near Stockton St.*
☎ *982-5686*); for full menu, **Sam Wo** (*813 Washington St.* ☎ *982-0596*).
Inexpensive Mission District Central American **Frutilandia** (*3007
24th St.*) for Cuban beef and black beans; **Las Guitarras** (*3274 24th St.,*
☎ *824-1027*); **Roosevelt Tamale Parlor** (*2817 24th St.* ☎ *648-9899*); **El
Trebol** (*3324 24th St.* ☎ *285-6298*) for *pupusas* and other Salvadoran
specialties.
Soup, salads and sandwiches **Clown Alley** (*42 Columbus Ave.*
☎ *421-2540*) for hot dogs and burgers that can be eaten there or taken out;
Perry's (*1944 Union St.* ☎ *922-9022*) offers sandwiches and more, in
conjunction with a great bar; **Salamagundi's** (*442 Geary St.* ☎ *441-0894*) has
especially fine soups.
Kosher delicatessen **David's** (*474 Geary St.* ☎ *771-1600*).
Breakfast **Sear's Fine Foods** (*439 Powell St.* ☎ *986-1160*), where there's
always a long line, usually out of the door.

Ice cream parlors

Bud's (*1300 Castro St.*); **Double Rainbow** (*1653 Polk St. and 3933 24th St.*);
Gaston's Ice Cream of San Francisco (*3277 Sacramento St.*); **Gelato** (*2211
Filbert St. and 201 Parnassus St.*); **Joe's** (*5351 Geary Blvd.*); **St Francis Ice
Cream Parlor** (*2001 24th St.*); **Swenson's** (*Hyde St. at Union St.*), the original
of a vast chain; **Uncle Gaylord's** (*55 Vermont St., 721 Irving St. and 1900
Market St.*).

Nightlife

San Francisco paid a price for inaugurating topless, and later bottomless,
dancing. In recent years the city's reputation for nightlife rested primarily
on near-naked jiggling and an ever lively rock music scene. An earlier
interest in and reputation for cabaret, comedy, folk, jazz and show music
seemed to dwindle away under the weight of these two. Still, none of
the latter forms died and, lately, diversity has made a comeback.
    Many of the trendiest new hot-spots are to be found in the fast reviving
SoMa district. What follows is a brief taste of what's on offer. Consult
Datebook, the supplement of *The San Francisco Chronicle,* as well as

the free-sheets *Calendar* magazine, *San Francisco Key* and *The San Francisco Bay Guardian* for detailed week-by-week information on acts and times.

Most nightclubs sell tickets at the door. Of course, the bigger the name, the wiser it is to reserve in advance. Some clubs work through ticket agencies, especially **BASS** (☎ *835-3849*) and **Ticketron** (☎ *495-4088*). Many sell advance tickets directly.

Bars/Cocktails/Cafés

Act IV Lounge
Inn at the Opera, 333 Fulton St.
☎ *863-8400. Map 12D3* 🍴 ⊟ ♀
♪ *nightly 5pm-midnight.*
Crackling fireplace, tasteful decor and easy-listening piano playing make this ideal for a romantic evening.

Blue Light Café
1979 Union St. ☎ *922-5510. Map 12B3* ♀ *Nightly 4pm-1am.*
1970s musician Boz Scaggs' place attracts an affable yuppie crowd with good recorded music, tasty southwestern snacks and excellent cocktails.

Buena Vista
2765 Hyde St. ☎ *474-5044. Map 12B3* 🕭 ♀ *Mon-Sat 9am-2am, Sun 8am-2am.*
They claim to have introduced Irish Coffee to the USA. True or not, the bar is famous for it. Usually it's crowded, with great views of the Bay and passing scene.

Caffe Trieste
601 Vallejo St. ☎ *392-6739. Map 12C3* ⊟ ♪ *early till late.*
Favorite of beatnik poets, writers, artists and intellectuals. The Giotta family, who run the place, stage sing-songs on weekends.

Perry's
1944 Union St. ☎ *922-9022. Map 12B3* ⊟ *until midnight* ♀ *Daily 9am-2am.*
The city's best-known young and fashionable singles bar.

Redwood Room
495 Geary St. ☎ *775-4700. Map 12D3* ♀ ♪ *nightly 4.30pm-1am.*
Wood-paneled Art Deco elegance; soothing piano music; dress formal.

San Francisco Brewing Company
155 Columbus Ave. ☎ *434-3344. Map 13B4* ⊟ ♀ ♪ *Mon-Thurs 11.30am-midnight, Fri 11.30am-1.30am, Sat 3pm-midnight, Sun noon-midnight.*
Excellent beers made on the spot, a friendly atmosphere and plenty of history. The bar and its period interior date from 1907. The location was once the waterfront Barbary Coast, celebrated for its anything-went exuberance, and boxer Jack Dempsey was a bouncer here.

Top of the Mark
Mark Hopkins Hotel, California St. at Mason ☎ *392-3434. Map 13C4* 🕭 🍴 ♀ ♪ *nightly 4pm-2am.*
The 360° view from the legendary 19th floor is as spectacular as when it opened in 1939 — maybe more so. The decor is refined, dress formal. However, there's no need to dress up for drinks — and the view, available any time of day or evening.

Tosca Café
242 Columbus Ave. ☎ *986-9651. Map 13B4* 🖳 ♀ *Nightly 7pm-2am.*
Another North Beach institution, Tosca's is cordial, crowded and noisy. Check out the opera-playing jukebox and the speciality cappuccino coffee. Movie fans might spot Francis Ford Coppola, who is a regular; his office is across the street.

Vesuvio Café
255 Columbus Ave. ☎ *362-3370. Map 13B4* 🖳 ♀ *Daily 6am-2am.*
A landmark North Beach bar and haven for Beat Generation poets and artists. Little changed, it is still popular with the San Francisco artistic and literary crowd.

Cabaret and comedy

Beach Blanket Babylon Goes to .... (new destinations from time to time)
Club Fugazi, 678 Green St.
☎ *421-4222. Map 13B4* 🍴 *Nightly at 8pm.*

A long-running, locally topical revue with enough tall hats and funny dances to appeal to out-of-towners almost as much as San Franciscans. Reservations are definitely recommended.

SF Nightlife

City Cabaret

401 Mason St., near Union Sq.
☎ *441-7787. Map 13C4 ⬛ or*
⬛ *for ♪ or ⬛, (on a variable schedule depending on reservations).*
Chameleon-like City Cabaret has music, cabaret or improvisational comedy, depending on who or what is hot at the moment.

Cobb's Comedy Pub

2069 Chestnut St. ☎ 563-5157. Map 12B2 ⬛ but drink minimum for ⬛. Sun-Thurs at 9pm, Fri-Sat at 9 and 11pm.
In the unlikely environs of the Marina, Cobb's books a fairly set rotation of local comedians most nights, but spices up its roster with an occasional nationally-known out-of-towner.

Finocchio's

506 Broadway ☎ 982-9388. Map 13C4 ⬛ for ⬛. Tues-Sat 9, 10.20, 11.40pm, 1am.
Female impersonators do their thing at one of San Francisco's longest-running tourist attractions.

Holy City Zoo

408 Clement St., ☎ 386-4242. Map 10D3 ⬛ to ⬛ plus two-drink minimum for ⬛. Sun-Thurs 8.30pm, Fri-Sat 8.30, 11pm.

Robin Williams is the greatest graduate of this tiny club where novice stand-up comics encourage audience participation.

The Other Café

100 Carl St. (off Cole St. in the Haight-Ashbury) ☎ 681-0748. Map 11F4. Tickets available from BASS ⬛ for ⬛, nightly from 9pm.
Local comedians try out new material. Food available.

Plush Room

940 Sutter St., in the York Hotel ☎ 885-6800. Map 12C3 ⬛ plus two-drink minimum for ♪ Sun, Tues-Thurs at 8.30pm and 10.30pm.
Just when it seemed like all the solid old lounge and cabaret performers had run out of anywhere to go other than the Venetian Room ... along came the Plush Room.

Punch Line

444 Battery St. ☎ 474-3810. Map 13C4 ⬛ to ⬛ plus two-drink minimum for ⬛. Wed-Sun 9, 11pm. Closed Mon-Tues.
An intimate bar and club which books established comedians and rising locals Wed-Sat, and lets anybody take a crack on Sun.

Dancing/Nightclubs

Cesar's Latin Palace

3140 Mission St. ☎ 648-6611. Map 9D4 ⬛ but no minimum for ♪ and ⬛ Wed-Sat 8pm-6am.
All-star salsa band plus ● between sets, and tango on Sun.

Club DV8

55 Natoma St. ☎ 777-1419. Map 13D4 ⬛ ⬛ ☯ ♪ ⬛ Wed-Thurs 9pm-3am, Fri-Sat 9pm-4am.
Part of the hip SoMa scene; live entertainment and disco.

Firehouse-7

3160 16th St., ☎ 621-1617. Map 12F3 ⬛ ⬛ ☯ ♪ ⬛ late till later.
Mostly dancing to rock, punk, reggae, heavy metal etc., with some live performances. The clientele is cool, so wear your shades.

I-Beam

1748 Haight St. ☎ 668-6006. Map 11E5 ⬛ ☯ ♪ ⬛ ⬛ Nightly 9pm-2am.
Rock and New Wave both live and recorded by local and visiting

upcoming bands. Impressive lights and lasers.

Last Day Saloon

406 Clement St. ☎ 387-6343. Map 10D3 ⬛ ⬛ for ♪ and ⬛ Tues-Sun from 9pm.
Amid photographs of the 1906 earthquake and its aftermath, dancing on a big floor to bands of every kind from classic rock and country and western to rhythm and blues.

Le Montmartre

2125 Lombard St. ☎ 563-4618. Map 12B2 ⬛ to ⬛ for ♪ and ⬛ nightly 9.30pm-2am.
Styled after Parisian nightclubs, it books Brazilian and continental bands that appeal to European visitors.

The Oasis

11th St., at Folsom ☎ 621-8119. Map 13E3 ⬛ ⬛ ⬛ ☯ ♪ ⬛ ⬛
Upscale dance club with top-40 disco and live bands playing jazz, R&B, rock etc. Dancing over the pool under the stars or indoors. "Egyptian" decor.

Greek

Greek Taverna
256 Columbus Ave. ☎ *362-7260. Map 13B4* 🖃 *for* ♪ 🍷 *Mon-Sat from 6pm.*
Bouzouki bands and belly dancers. Food available.

Jazz

Great American Music Hall
859 O'Farrell St. (near Larkin) ☎ *885-0750. Map 12D3* 🖃 *to* 🖃 ♪ *show times variable* 🍷 *sometimes.*
In a splendidly rococo room, the club offers rock, folk and sometimes comedians, but is best known as the number-one place in town for big band jazz. Food available.

Kimball's
300 Grove St., near Civic Center ☎ *861-5555. Map 12D3* 🖃 *but two-drink minimum for* ♪ *Wed-Sat from 8.30pm.*
Kimball's is the city's front-line, full-time jazz club. Most of the players are local, or out-of-towners on the way up, but some of the great names and faces from the days of bop onward get on the stand here when they are in town.

Milestones
376 5th St., in SoMa ☎ *777-9997. Map 13D4* 🖃 *but two-drink minimum for* ♪ *nightly from 8.30pm.*
One of the earliest nightspots to open during the gentrification of SoMa is now its most durable jazz club and one of the district's most orderly night spots. Most of the players are locals.

New Orleans Room
Fairmont Hotel, California St. at Mason St. Map 13C4 🖃 *but minimum on drinks. Wed-Sun from 9pm.*
Honest-to-goodness, San Francisco-style Dixieland.

Pier 23
Embarcadero (two blocks N of Ferry building) ☎ *362-5125. Map 13B5* 🖃 *for* ♪ *Wed-Thurs 9pm-1am, Fri-Sat 9pm-2am, Sun 4-9pm.*
A bastion of house-band Dixie (except for jam sessions on Sun). It is decorated in the style of a waterfront saloon, which it also is. Food available.

Rock, Country, Folk

Mabuhay Gardens
443 Broadway ☎ *956-3315. Map 13C4* 🖃 *plus one-drink minimum* 🍷 *nightly from 9.30pm* ♥ *from 11pm.*
A Filipino restaurant by day, but a perfectly decorated palace of punk by night, with punk theater preceeding punk rock.

Paul's Saloon
3521 Scott St. ☎ *922-2456. Map 11B5* 🖃 *but minimum of one drink (beer and wine only) during each set* ♪ *(nightly from 9pm).*
This is the one, true home of

bluegrass in town. Even your aged aunt would feel at ease.

Wolfgang's
901 Columbus Ave., in North Beach ☎ *474-2995. Map 13B4* 🖃 *But two-drink minimum for* ♪ *or* 🍷 *nightly at 8 and 10pm.*
This is 1960s pioneering rock promoter Bill Graham's place, which means good sound systems, good sightlines, and tasteful acts of almost any sort, but mostly rock and jazz. Occasionally it means comedy, now and again something altogether surprising. Dinner is served before or between shows.

Supper club

Venetian Room
950 Mason St. ☎ *772-5163. Map 13C4* 🖃 *for* 🍷 *Tues-Sun at 9.30pm, midnight.*
A beautiful nightclub at the **Fairmont Hotel & Tower** (see *SF Hotels*), the

149

Venetian Room is a year-round cornucopia of show-business greats from Ella Fitzgerald to Joel Grey. Dancing to Ernie Hecksher's local big band before and between shows.

Topless

On the whole, the topless/bottomless scene is confined to a string of charmless and tacky joints, with barkers trying to attract clients through entrances on Broadway or Columbus Ave. Equally sleazy, though slightly less tacky and better value for money, is **Mitchell Brothers' O'Farrell Theater** (*corner Polk St. and O'Farrell* ☎ *776-6686* ✖ *daily from 11.45am*), where gonzo journalist, *Rolling Stone* magazine contributor and political commentator Dr Hunter S. Thompson was once night manager. But be warned! The live acts and movies leave nothing to the imagination.

Performing arts

The city is oriented more to music and dance than to theater, but all three scenes are fairly lively, and audiences are as hungry for the experimental and avant garde as for time-honored classics. Most music and ballet is at the Civic Center, and most theater is Downtown. For current performances, consult the *Datebook* section of the *San Francisco Chronicle*, known as "The Pink Pages" because of its color.

Ticketing agencies include **BASS** (☎ *762-2277*), **Ticketron** (☎ *392-7469*) and **STBS** (*Stockton St., between Post St. and Geary St.* ☎ *433-7827*), which sells half-price tickets Tues-Sat noon-7.30pm (cash only).

Ballet

The **American Ballet Theater** (*War Memorial Opera House, Van Ness Ave. and Grove St.* ☎ *864-6696*) has a 16-performance season from Feb-March. Its recent successes include Mikhail Baryshnikov's *Swan Lake*. Also at the War Memorial Opera House, the **San Francisco Ballet** (☎ *621-3636*) holds its Jan-May season and July summer festival.

The **New Performance Gallery** (*3153 17th St.* ☎ *863-9834*) stages modern and contemporary dance by various companies, including the **San Francisco Jazz Dance Company** (☎ *898-4113*).

Cinema

The city has some 50 movie theaters, not including the porno variety. A great majority of first-run houses showing American, European and Australian films are in residential neighborhoods, especially on Geary Blvd. and Clement St. in the Richmond, on Union St. and Fillmore St. in or near Pacific Heights, and on Van Ness Ave. N of Civic Center. The Financial District and Northern Waterfront have a sparse scattering. Downtown has only one regular first-run house. Chinatown has a small number of theaters featuring movies from Hong Kong and Taiwan.

Music

The **San Francisco Opera** (☎ *864-3330*) is at the War Memorial Opera House (see above) for its Sept-Dec season and June-July summer festival. The **San Francisco Symphony** (*Davies Symphony Hall, Van Ness Ave. and Grove St.* ☎ *431-5400*) has a Sept-May season, and major orchestras and recitalists on tour also play at Davies Hall.

The city has a near-limitless supply of chamber music societies and recitalists. Some of the finest recital programs are presented at the

California Palace of the Legion of Honor (*Lincoln Park, California St. and 33rd Ave.* ☎ *221-4811*).

Theater

The classic-oriented **American Conservatory Theater** is a nationally known repertory company with an Oct-May season in the 1,354-seat Geary Theater (*415 Geary St., near Mason* ☎ *673-6440*).

The **Curran Theater** (*445 Geary St., near Mason* ☎ *673-4400*), with 1,000 seats, is used by touring companies. So is the 1,200-seat **Golden Gate Theater** (*25 Taylor St., at Market St.* ☎ *775-8800*), by touring companies performing mostly musicals, and the 2,500-seat **Orpheum Theater** (*1192 Market St., near Civic Center* ☎ *473-3800*).

The **Lamplighters-Opera West Foundation** (*at Presentation Theater, 2350 Turk St., near Masonic Ave.* ☎ *752-7755*) is a Gilbert and Sullivan repertory company with a June-Apr season. The theater has 498 seats.

The **Magic Theater** (*Building D, Fort Mason Center, Laguna St., at Marina Blvd.* ☎ *441-8822*) shows new and contemporary plays by writer-in-residence Sam Shephard and others, year-round in two 99-seat theaters.

The **One-Act Theater Company of San Francisco** (*430 Mason St., near Geary St.* ☎ *421-5355*), a local repertory company, presents a year-round season of classic and contemporary one-act plays in a 99-seat theater.

Shopping

A background of wealth, a cosmopolitan population, and tourism combine to make San Francisco an excellent city for shopping; but compact size is what puts it in a class by itself. There are fewer of the custom-built malls that characterize shopping in Los Angeles, but they are every bit as attractive, and there is no shortage of fine individual retailers or upscale department stores. Opportunities are noted first by neighborhood, followed by specifics and special interests.

Union Square/downtown

Most of the city's department stores and many luxury shops are on and around Union Sq. Modeled after Milan's Galleria Vittorio Emmanuelle, the 3-level **Crocker Galleria** (*Union Sq., between Post, Kearny, Sutter and Montgomery Sts.*) contains some 50 shops and restaurants, with the emphasis on designer fashion and gifts. For more chic boutiques check out **Maiden Lane**. Nearly all are open Mon-Sat 9.30am-5.30pm. Some are open Thurs evening and Sun.

Department stores **Emporium-Capwell** (*835 Market St., at Powell St.*); **Gumps** (*250 Post St.*), especially for decorative and fine arts; **Liberty House** (*Stockton St. and O'Farrell St.*); **Macy's** (*entrances on Geary St., Stockton St. and O'Farrell St.*); **I. Magnin** (*Geary St. and Stockton St.*), which includes **Laykin et Cie** jewelry and **Narsai's Market**; **Neiman-Marcus** (*Geary St., at Stockton St.*); **Nordstrom** (*865 Market St.*), opened in Oct 1988; **Saks Fifth Ave.** (*Post St. and Powell St.*).

Fabrics **Britex** (*146 Geary St.*); **Pierre Deux** (*532 Sutter St.*).

Fine kitchenware and cutlery **Exclusive Cutlery Shop** (*110 Grant Ave.*); **Williams Sonoma** (*576 Sutter St.*).

Florists **Kalman & Belli** (*653 Market St.*); **Hoogasian Flowers** (*250 Post St.*).

Jewelers **Shreve & Co.** (*210 Post St.*); **Tiffany & Co.** (*252 Grant Ave.*); **Tom Wing and Sons** (*190 Post St.*).

Men's fashions   **Wilkes Bashford** (*375 Sutter St.*); **Banana Republic** (*224 Grant Ave.*); **Brooks Brothers** (*201 Post St.*); **Cable Car Clothiers/Robert Kirk Ltd.** (*150 Post St.*).
Sporting goods   **Eddie Bauer** (*220 Post St.*); **Orvis** (*166 Maiden Lane*); **Okabe Sports** (*355 Sutter St.*).
Women's fashions   **Banana Republic** (*224 Grant Ave.*); **Jaeger International** (*272 Post St.*); **Jessica McClintock** (*353 Sutter St.*); **Justine** (*3263 Sacramento St.*); **MAC** (*812 Post St.*) — Madonna shops here; **Stella Volvo** (*3424 Sacramento St.*); **Victoria's Secret** (*395 Sutter St.*).
Other specialists of interest   **Crate and Barrel** (*125 Grant Ave.*), good affordable stuff for the home; **Alfred Dunhill Ltd.** (*290 Post St.*), pipes, tobacco, men's wear, gifts; **Gucci** (*253 Post St.*), signature leather goods; **FAO Schwartz** (*180 Post St.*), toys; **Selix Formal Wear** (*123 Kearny St.*), rent-a-tux; **Godiva Chocolatier** (*50 Post St.*), luxury candies; **Spectacles at Union Square** (*177 Maiden Lane*), designer eyewear in a hurry.

Financial District
The numbered buildings of Embarcadero Center, between Sacramento St. and Clay St., and on Battery St. and Drumm St., have several floors of shops. Others are on nearby streets.
Cameras   On Kearny St. — **Brooks** (*no. 45*); **Camera Boutique** (*no. 250*); **Cameras Unlimited** (*no. 33*). In Embarcadero Center 3 — **Pacific Camera**.
Computers and software   **Computer Connection** (*3 Embarcadero Center*); **Radio Shack Computer Center** (*One Market Place*); **Computercraft** (*225 Kearny St.*).
Fashion and accessories   **Galletti's** (*1 Embarcadero Center*), for shoe repair; **Little Daisy** (*1 Embarcadero Center*); **Livingston Bros.** (*2 Embarcadero Center*).
Other specialists of interest   **The Nature Company** (*4 Embarcadero Center*), unusual treasures for nature students; **See's Candies** (*3 Embarcadero Center*), fine chocolates.

Northern Waterfront
The area is schizophrenic, divided between exclusive shops in the Cannery and Ghirardelli Sq. (two pioneer examples in the US of handsome industrial buildings being reclaimed from obsolescence for shopping galleries) and curio and trinket places on Fisherman's Wharf and Pier 39.
   In the Cannery (*bounded by Jefferson St., Beach St., Leavensworth St. and Hyde St.*) — **Black Sheep Needleworks**; **Gourmet & Liquor Market**; the **Print Store**; **Upstart Crow Bookstore**.
   In Ghirardelli Sq. (*bounded by Beach St., North Point St., Hyde St. and Polk St.*) — **Almond Plaza** (the nut in every form); **Bebe Pierrot Children's Wear**; **J.D. Browne** (travel accessories); **The Kite Store**; **Don Conard Mobiles**; **Ghirardelli Bookstores**; **The Hammock Way**; **Jeffrey's Toys**; **Richter's Music Boxes**.
   Fisherman's Wharf area — **The Anchorage Shopping Center** (*bounded by Beach, Jefferson, Jones and Leavenworth Sts.*), galleries, boutiques, craft, gift and jewelry stores, plus restaurants and fast food; **Cost Plus** (*2552 Taylor St.*), a colorful two-building bazaar of low-cost imports.

Chinatown
Grant Ave. from Bush St. to Broadway is another bazaar. From the street it looks as though it is all gimcrackery, but many of the shops have outstanding Asian art and artifacts amid the curios, and there are excellent outlets for Chinese medicines (notable is **Superior**

Trading Company (*837 Washington St.*) for ginseng), kitchen goods and Asian foodstuffs.

Pacific Heights/Union Street

Between Fillmore St. and Larkin St., **Union St.** is the city's axis for yuppie shoppers, packed with retailers of fashion, art, antiques, books and home accessories. Many are in old Victorian houses. Pubs, cafés and pastry shops are plentiful. Not far away, **Clement St.** (*from Arguello to 10th Ave.*) is a potpourri of Asian, Russian and Japanese restaurants and shops. **Japan Center** (*bounded by Geary Blvd., Post, Maguna and Fillmore Sts.*) is a 5-acre "village" designed by architect Minoru Yamasaki, with art, books, gifts, pearls from Asia, plus *sushi* bars and restaurants. **Sacramento St.** (*five blocks centered on Presidio Ave.*) has small shops among vintage houses.

Haight-Ashbury

The historic and emotional crossroads of Flower Power, Haight St. is now the place for hippie memorabilia: clothes, records, books, comics, paraphernalia. Also second-hand "antique" clothing, hand-made jewelry, arts and home accessories.

SoMa

Not yet so relentlessly arty as New York's SoHo district, but getting there, with a scattering of trendy boutiques and galleries, and the best outlet discount stores in town (see individual entries below).

Art galleries

Such household names as Picasso, Calder, Wyeth and Disney only begin to suggest the range of art in all mediums in San Francisco's art galleries, which number more than a hundred. Typical hours are Tues-Sat 9.30am-5.30pm, but some specialists are open only two or three days a week, or by appointment. For a complete listing, see Yellow Pages under *Art Galleries, dealers and consultants*. Downtown has the greatest concentration of galleries, especially on Sutter St. between Kearny St. and Jones St. Other focal points include the Civic Center area, Union St. and, to a lesser extent, SoMa.

For early western paintings by Dixon, Hill, Remington and their peers — **Maxwell** (*551 Sutter St.*), also American and European periods.

For contemporary American and Californian painters and sculptors including Diebenkorn, Neri, de Forest, Holland, Thiebaud and Wiley, see the following — **Allrich** (*251 Post St., 4th fl.*), also Asian; **John Berggrueb** (*228 Grant Ave., 3rd fl.*), also Europeans and photographers; **Braunstein** (*254 Sutter St., 2nd fl.*); **Hansen-Fuller Goldeen** (*228 Grant Ave., 5th fl.*); **Ivory Kimpton** (*55 Grant Ave., 2nd fl.*); **John Pence** (*750 Post St.*); **Dana Reich** (*278 Post St., Suite 506*); **Rorick** (*637 Mason St.*); **Janet Steinberg** (*315 Sutter St.*); **Stephen Wirtz** (*345 Sutter St.*), also Europeans and photographers. Civic Center — **Vorpal** (*393 Grove St.*), also European and American paintings and African and pre-Columbian artifacts. Union St./Pacific Heights — **Artists' Cooperative** (*1047 Bush St.*); **Grapestake Gallery** (*2876 California St.*), also photography; **William Sawyer** (*3045 Clay St.*); **Thackery & Robertson** (*2266 Union St.*), photography and fine art. SoMa — **Crown Point Press Gallery** (*871 Folsom St.*), etchings.

For American and European paintings and prints: downtown — **Circle Gallery** in Frank Lloyd Wright's model for the Guggenheim Museum (*140 Maiden Lane*), also jewelry; **Harcourt** (*535 Powell St.*); **Pasquale Ianetti** (*575 Sutter St.*); **Erika Meyerovick** (*231 Grant Ave.*); **Worstman-Stewart** (*516 Sutter St., 2nd fl.*).

For Asian artists: downtown — **Nong** (*433 Sutter, Hyatt-Union Sq. mezzanine*). Union St./Pacific Heights — **Satori** (*2124 Union St.*). Miscellaneous locations — **Soker-Kaserman** (*1457 Grant Ave.*); **Triangle Gallery** (*99 Minna St., off 2nd St. near Market St.*), also contemporary American paintings, sculpture and ceramics.

For Latin American artists: downtown — **Moss Gallery** (*111 Maiden Lane, 4th fl.*). The Mission — **Galeria de la Raza** (*2851 Mission St.*).

For botanical prints: downtown — **Henry Evan** (*555 Sutter St., Rm 306*), Fri-Sat noon-5pm only.

Bookstores

Hours for these shops are generally Mon-Sat 9am-5.30pm, but you may find exceptions.

Antiquarian booksellers   **Argonaut Book Shop** (*786 Sutter St.*); **Holmes Book Store** (*22 3rd St., near Market St.*), a branch of an Oakland store, also general second-hand books; **The Bookstall** (*708 Sutter St.*); **Acorn Books** (*740 Polk St.*).

Special interest shops   **City Lights** (*261 Columbus Ave., North Beach*), Ferlinghetti's mecca of the beat goes on; **European Book Co.** (*925 Larkin St., and branch at 500 Sutter St.*), French, German and other European-language books; **Gourmet Guides** (*1767 Stockton St., North Beach*), cookery and travel; **Green Apple** (*506 Clement St., the Richmond*), paperback and general second-hand books; **Sierra Club Bookstore** (*730 Polk St.*), outdoorsman books, maps and gifts; **Stacey's** (*581 Market St.*), medical, technical and business books.

Music and records

A few special and unusual shops: **San Francisco Opera Shop** (*199 Grove St., Civic Center*), everything but live singers; **Pacific Coast Music** at **Sherman & Clay** (*141 Kearny St.*), huge stocks of sheet music and piano rolls; **Tower Records** (*Columbus Ave. at Bay St., North Beach/Fisherman's Wharf*), mind-boggling selection of records and tapes, 365 days a year.

Wine

Shops convenient to downtown with unusual stocks: **Connoisseur Wine Imports** (*462 Bryant St.*), primarily European; **Draper & Esquin** (*655 Davis St.*), European and rare California wines; **London Wine Bar** (*415 Sansome St.*), some tastings of European and Californian selections.

At the **Liquor Barn** (*550 North Point St., near Fisherman's Wharf*) there are thousands of Californian and other wines and a wide range of liquor and beers of the world at discount. A tasting bar offers selected wines by the glass.

Outlet discount stores

Aca Joe Outlet (*915 Front St.*), casual and sportswear; **Eileen West** (*61 Bluxome St.*), dresses and sleepwear; **Esprit Factory Outlet** (*16th and Illinois Sts.*), name-brand leisure-wear at knockdown prices; **Gunne Sax Outlet** (*35 Stanford St., off Brannan and Townsend Sts.*), party dresses and gowns, including Jessica McClintock; **New West Designs** (*425 Brannan St.*), European fashions; **Rainbeau Factory Outlet** (*300 4th St.*), aerobic, exercise and dancewear; **Sister Max Outlet** (*70 Grant Ave., at Geary St.*), designer wholesale, including evening dresses; **660 Center** (*660 3rd St.*), discount mall selling children's and women's clothes, jewelry and more; **Van Heusen Factory Store** (*601 Mission St.*), bargain shirts and sweaters.

Sports and recreation

San Francisco offers varied outdoor recreation. Tennis and golf head the list of specific sports, but running is enormously popular, and health clubs and gyms are plentiful. Because of sea fogs and cold ocean waters, the beaches are more for strolling and fishing than for swimming.

Beaches

San Francisco's principal beach, **Ocean**, stretches from the W end of Geary Blvd. S to the city limits and beyond. It can be used along its whole length by walkers and joggers. At the N end, waves are good for surfing. Along the bluffs directly S of San Francisco Zoo, perfect upwelling breezes draw large numbers of hang gliders. The Great Highway runs directly behind the shore for nearly the entire length of the beach.

A smaller, more secluded GGNRA beach called **Baker** stretches away S from the Golden Gate Bridge. Popular with surf fishermen and strollers, and in fair weather with picnickers, it can be reached by a clearly marked road turning W off Lincoln Blvd. However, waves and currents at both beaches are too rough for swimming. **Aquatic Park**, at the foot of Hyde St., has a sandy beach and sheltered but chilly waters.

Fishing

San Francisco has ample pier and deep-sea fishing. The former is done mainly from Municipal Pier at the foot of Van Ness Ave., the Fort Mason piers, accessible from Marina Blvd. and Laguna St., and the seawall adjoining Fort Point, accessible from Lincoln Blvd. on the bay side of the Golden Gate Bridge. Bait is available near **Municipal Pier** (*Muny Bait Shop, 3098 Polk St. at Bay St.* ☎ *673-9815*); tackle can be rented at the shop.

Many party boats operate from Fisherman's Wharf. See telephone book Yellow Pages under *Fishing parties*.

Golf

There are two municipal 18-hole courses in the city and a third just S. **Lincoln Park Golf Course** (*Clement St. at 34th Ave.* ☎ *221-9911*), 5,081yds, par 68, rated 64.3, has some holes overlooking the Golden Gate. **Harding Park Golf Course** (*off Skyline Blvd./SR-35 on Harding Rd.* ☎ *664-4690*), 6,637yds, par 72, rated 70.8, occupies a peninsula thrusting into Lake Merced due E of San Francisco Zoo. **Sharp Park Golf Course** (*on SR-1 at Sharp Rd., Pacifica* ☎ *355-2862*), 6,398yds, par 72, rated 70, is an oceanside course S of the city. Mail concerning any of these should be addressed c/o: McLaren Lodge, Golden Gate Park, San Francisco 94117.

Jogging/fitness courses

Beneath the freeway at Drumm and Clay Sts., **Marina Green** (*Marina Blvd., from Buchanan St. W*), has a 2½-mile track for joggers, and a fitness course alongside it. **Golden Gate Park** has an infinity of paths for joggers.

Tennis

The largest facility is a center with 21 hard courts in **Golden Gate Park** (*off Kennedy Dr., opposite the Conservatory of Flowers*). Reservations are required on weekends (☎ *556-4800*), or reserve at the tennis shop. There is a small fee for hourly play.

For locations of other hard courts in the municipal park system ☎ 558-4054.

Environs and excursions

San Francisco is so manageable, especially for walkers, that it is tempting to stay put and enjoy its variegated delights. By all means enjoy the compact city, but resist the temptation not to venture farther afield. There is plenty to attract and interest within easy striking distance.

Berkeley
*Map **14**E3. From San Francisco, E across the San Francisco-Oakland Bay Bridge, then N on I-80 to University Ave. exit. Served regularly from San Francisco and Oakland by BART (☎ (415) 788-2278 from San Francisco or (415) 465-2278 from Oakland) and A-C Transit (☎ (415) 653-3535).*

Home of the original University of California campus, and California's self-elected social laboratory. In some ways its moods swing with the day, while in others the city remains steadfastly true to itself. In any season, it shows every sign of a highly educated, politically active citizenry. It has superior museums within the university. There are splendid views back across the bay to San Francisco and the Golden Gate. However, to discover the temper that has made Berkeley famous requires aimless wandering on UC's campus and in the streets near it, especially on Bancroft Way and Telegraph Ave. Start at **Cody's Bookstore** (*2454 Telegraph Ave.*).

See also *Oakland*.

Sights and places of interest
Berkeley Marina
A man-made peninsula thrusting w into San Francisco Bay from the foot of University Ave., the Marina has a 3,000ft (924m) public fishing pier (with bait and tackle shop, catering both to pier and party boat fishermen), sailboat rentals, yacht moorings, picnic parks, a hotel and several restaurants, all with unimpeded views of San Francisco's skyline and the Golden Gate.
Berkeley Municipal Rose Garden
At Euclid Ave. and Bayview Pl., the park contains 4,000 rose varieties. Open daily during daylight hours.
Tilden Regional Park
On Grizzly Peak Blvd. in the steep hills behind UC's campus, Tilden is one of several large parks in the East Bay Regional Parks System. It has a relentlessly rolling championship golf course (6,301yds, par 70, rated 69.6), a splendid carousel, picnic lawns and paths for walking.
University of California campus
At the E end of University Ave. between Hearst Ave. and Bancroft Way.

One of America's largest and most prestigious universities, UC-Berkeley offers a veritable cornucopia of worthy sights and events. A few examples indicate the possibilities.

The **Lawrence Hall of Science** (*on Centennial Dr., just downhill from its intersection with scenic Grizzly Peak Blvd.* ☎ *open 10am-4.30pm, Thurs till 9pm*), a child's paradise of science displays, lays the emphasis on computers and physics. Check at the information desk for special daily programs.

The **University Art Museum** (*Bancroft Way near College Ave.* ☎ *open Wed-Sun 11am-5pm, closed Mon, Tues, major hols*) is particularly known for its collection of Hans Hofmann paintings. Also housed here is the **Pacific Film Archive**, which regularly shows classic movies. A sculpture garden adjoins the museum building, which is a sculptural statement in itself. Just across the street, in Kroeber Hall, is the **Loewy Museum of Anthropology** (☎ *open Mon-Fri 10am-4pm, Sat-Sun noon-4pm*) where major collections of North, Central and South American artifacts can be seen.

The **Botanical Garden** (*along Strawberry Creek between the football stadium and Lawrence Hall of Science, open 9am-5pm*) contains rare plants gathered into ecological communities.

Maps for self-guiding campus tours may be obtained at the **Student Union Building** (*Bancroft Way, opposite the end of Telegraph Ave.*). Guided tours depart from this building Mon-Fri at 1pm. Parking in the area is difficult.

〓 **Chez Panisse** ✿
1517 Shattuck Ave., Berkeley 94709 ☎ *(415) 548-5525* ⫻⫻⫻ ▬▬ ▆▆
Downstairs open Tues-Sat 6-10pm, upstairs Mon-Sat 11.30am-midnight.
Some consider this California's best restaurant. The decor throughout is simple in the extreme, but the small main dining room stages a perpetual quest by perfectionists for yet another flawless expression of New California cuisine, which was developed here by founder and chef Alice Waters as a more flavorful, regionalized counterpart to *nouvelle cuisine.* Upstairs is a café for lighter, less expensive dishes such as *calzone*, pasta and salads. The main dining room's fixed-price menu changes nightly as well as seasonally. Most ingredients are organically grown. Reservations are required downstairs; it can be difficult to get a table.

Marin County
Map 14E3. Across the Golden Gate from San Francisco. US-101 is the axis. Region served daily from San Francisco by Golden Gate Bridge district commuter ferries and buses.
The current national image of Marin County does not cover all of the territory within its formal political boundaries. It covers only the mythical part of Marin County, the part where citizens in measurable numbers learn self-awareness in salad-making classes, or loll in hot tubs drinking wine and fanning themselves with peacock feathers.

This mythical county has woven itself into real Marin towns, especially **Mill Valley** and **Tiburon**, and, to a lesser degree, **Sausalito** and **San Rafael**. It does not include areas to the N and W, hence the divided definition here.

Each of the four towns named has specialty shops and restaurants in beautiful natural surroundings. Marin has some of the Bay Area's greatest natural scenery, especially on the headlands of the **Golden Gate** and above them on **Mt. Tamalpais**.

This part of Marin County exaggerates the San Francisco Bay area's range of summer micro-climates. On an Aug afternoon, temperatures in the eastern skirts of Mt. Tamalpais can reach 105°F(40.5°C) while Sausalito stays at 58°F(14°C) under a blanket of fog, although the two points are hardly 10 miles apart. The only advice for roving tourists is to dress lightly and take a heavy sweater.

Marin Headlands
Part of the *Golden Gate National Recreation Area* (see *SF Sights*), these steep hills offer superb views back through the **Golden Gate Bridge** to San Francisco's skyline.

At the outer end of the headlands, the beautifully situated **Point Bonita Lighthouse** is one of the best spots in all of California for wave-watching.

Visitors coming from San Francisco should turn off from US-101 at the Sausalito exit, then turn left into a tunnel after traveling less than 500yds, to get to a road leading onto the headlands. Once on the headlands, it is possible to drive to an ocean beach at **Fort Cronkhite**, also part of the Golden Gate NRA.

Mill Valley
In and around this affluent commuter suburb there are some fine shops and restaurants. From San Francisco, the SR-1 exit three miles N of the Golden Gate Bridge leads directly to Miller Ave., a main road running N into town.

Mount Tamalpais State Park
Occupying the upper flanks of conical Mt. Tam nearly all the way to its 2,586ft (788m) peak, this park is a favorite with hikers for its mixture of grassy meadows and redwood-shaded gullies. The

6,200-acre park surrounds **Muir Woods National Monument** and abuts open lands of the Marin Water District, extending hiking possibilities far beyond its own borders. Trails lead W all the way to the Pacific shore at Stinson Beach, or NE into water district lands in the warm-weather zone. Park headquarters is on The Panoramic Highway, which, 3 miles W of US-101, branches off from SR-1.

San Rafael

Marin's largest city and county seat is a spruce commercial center of interest to visitors primarily for two buildings that date from opposite ends of California's history.

Sights and places of interest
Marin County Civic Center 🏛
At the juncture of US-101 and N San Pedro Rd. on the N side of San Rafael 🖭 *Open Mon-Fri 9am-5pm.*
One of Frank Lloyd Wright's last great public buildings. The repeated use of arches and an ingenious metal-skinned tower that hides cooling equipment dominate the building's external appearance. Inside, a towering central court has hanging gardens. There are no guided tours of the building, which houses government offices, but surrounding gardens offer delightful strolls.
Mission San Rafael Arcángel ✝
1104 5th Ave. ☎ *(415) 454-8141* 🖭 *Open 6.30am-5.30pm.*
A reconstruction of the mission that was founded in 1817, 20th of the Franciscan chain. It was designed to be no more than a sun-blessed sanitarium for converts whose health had declined in the fogs at Mission Dolores in San Francisco.

Sausalito

Sausalito plummets from steep hills to a long, curling shoreline that looks back across the Golden Gate to San Francisco. A great majority of the town's shops, restaurants and other attractions are on or near its waterside main street, Bridgeway, 2 miles from where a road turns down into town at the N end of the Golden Gate Bridge.

A vast concrete shell called **Village Fair** houses a score of specialty shops. Opposite Village Fair and immediately N of the Sausalito-San Francisco ferry pier, a small boat harbor makes a pleasant place for yachtsmen to wander. A little fleet of party boats operates from piers in this harbor, going outside the Golden Gate for salmon, striped bass or bottom fish, depending on the season (see Yellow Pages under *Fishing parties*). Sausalito's famous community of houseboats is anchored some 2 miles N, where Bridgeway joins US-101.

Sights and places of interest
US Army Corps of Engineers Bay Model
2100 Bridgeway ☎ *(415) 332-3871* 🖭 *Open Tues-Sat 9am-4pm. Closed Sun-Mon, major hols.*
This is an enchanting show. Using brilliantly dyed water, tests are carried out on a vast model of San Francisco Bay, San Pablo Bay and the Sacramento River delta, to show everything from the path of the Sacramento River flow to the movement of oil spills. Call ahead to find out if any tests are scheduled. A lively visitor center displays bay flora and fauna and man's effect on the whole.

Tiburon

One block of the original waterside main street has a tight cluster of bars and restaurants with outdoor terraces much patronized by yachtsmen. Seafood is the best choice. Shops and galleries lend variety. On a narrow, steep-sided peninsula, Tiburon and neighboring **Belvedere** have some of northern California's most dramatic residential architecture. Main St., Tiburon, is 4 miles from freeway US-101 via SR-131 (Tiburon Blvd.), or 8 miles from Sausalito by road (but only 2 miles by boat). Red and White Fleet tour boats from San Francisco call here.

Monterey Peninsula

*Map **14G3**. From San Francisco, 94 miles s via US-101, SR-156 and SR-1. Served daily by PSA, United and commuter airlines and Greyhound Lines i Monterey Chamber of Commerce and Visitors and Convention Bureau, PO Box 1770, Monterey 93940 ☎ (408) 649-1770; office at 380 Alvarado St., Monterey.*

Three peninsula towns — Monterey, Carmel-by-the-Sea and Pacific Grove — attract some 6.5 million visitors each year: 105 for each permanent resident. Seascapes from Pacific Grove down to Point Lobos rank among the most beautiful in the world. This is a mecca for golf. But variety is what puts the Monterey Peninsula in a class by itself. Seascapes range from wild to settled. Golf comes on a fog-shrouded shore or in sun-baked valleys. The three towns are completely unalike, and their hotels and restaurants excel in different ways.

Monterey looks like a typical, all-business American town, but it is more. It has the region's car dealers, supermarkets and convention hotels. But it has also developed its economically obsolete **Fisherman's Wharf** and **Cannery Row** districts into compelling tourist attractions and created a townwide museum of historic buildings.

Pacific Grove has a prim, Victorian appearance. More purely residential than its neighbors — partly because it sits at the outer tip of the peninsula and partly because a Presbyterian majority kept alcohol and thus tourist development out of the community until the 1970s — Pacific Grove attracts visitors because of the sheer beauty of its rocky shoreline.

Carmel is pure storybook in its quaint prettiness. Buffered from Monterey by the golf greens and great homes of **Del Monte Forest**, the town has managed to keep the scale of everything small, save perhaps the reflected fame of its one-time Mayor, actor/director Clint Eastwood, who legalized take-out ice cream cones and Frisbees in public parks. (Eastwood's pub/restaurant, **The Hog's Breath Inn** (*on San Carlos between 5th and 6th Sts.* ☎ *(408) 625-1044*), is worth a visit.) Streets without sidewalks or lights dodge around old trees. There are no street numbers for houses or businesses.

Although many residents deplore the fact, Carmel is the most commercial community on the peninsula, its 6-block center packed solid with quiet hostelries, varied restaurants and galleries and stores carrying everything from tourist kitsch to jewels fit for a crown.

Carmel also has advantages of location. It has a long sandy beach, the implausible beauties of **Point Lobos** and **Del Monte Forest** flank it on either side and share their bracing seaside climate, and, just inshore, narrow **Carmel Valley** refuses admission to summer sea fogs. Thus its tennis and golf resorts enjoy dry warmth while sea fogs sweep across Monterey and Del Monte Forest.

For all that there are differences, the Peninsula makes a cohesive whole. A good local transportation system is only the most obvious example of the fact.

The toll road called **17-mile Drive** loops through the private enclave of Del Monte Forest, which separates Monterey and Pacific Grove from Carmel. Along the route are some fine rocky headlands, including **Cypress Point**, three splendid golf courses that delight even touring professionals, and a few over-the-wall glimpses of splendidly grandiose homes built between World Wars I and II.

Sights and places of interest
Cannery Row

When there were sardines, it was Cannery Row. Now it is a hotel, restaurant and souvenir stores row. Monterey's spectacular aquarium (see below) is here also.

Carmel Mission ☆ †

*w of SR-1 via Rio Rd., or s of Ocean Ave. in Carmel via Junipero St.
Open Mon-Sat 9am-5pm, Sun 1-5pm. Donation expected.*

The Basilica of Mission San Carlos Borromeo de Carmelo has few peers and no
superiors among the Franciscan missions in California for grace of proportion
and refinement of architectural detail. Once badly decayed, it has been
restored to excellent condition. Padre Junipero Serra began construction of the
second mission in 1771. He lived and worked at Carmel until his death in 1784
and is buried in the chapel here. Two small religious museums adjoin the
mission church.

Fisherman's Wharf

Much of the Old Wharf has been converted into restaurants, galleries and curio
stores. A small fleet of party boats puts out daily.

Monterey Bay Aquarium

886 Cannery Row 🔄 ☎ *(408) 649-6466, (408) 375-3333 for recorded
information. Open 10am-6pm. Closed Christmas* ⚌ ✗ ⟨ ✱

Just a couple of doors up from Doc Rickett's old marine laboratory, celebrated
in John Steinbeck's *Cannery Row*, sits the startlingly original Monterey Bay
Aquarium. Monterey Bay is one of the most diverse ecosystems in the world,
and exhibits in this one-time fish cannery celebrate every aspect of it from
forests of towering kelp to a little bubble full of sand dollars. Much of the
aquarium is hands-on (pet a stingray!), and even the most formally educational
aspects are lively. Highlight of the day is probably the feeding of sea otters at
11am, 2pm and 4.30pm. A note of caution: entrance can be difficult on
holidays and weekends without advance reservations and tickets.

Monterey Path of History

Monterey played a pivotal role in California's development from Spanish to
American territory. In tracing a rough oval around downtown Monterey,
well-preserved buildings illustrate each major era.

    Colton Hall (*Pacific St. near Jefferson St.* 🔄 *open Tues-Sun 10-noon,
1-5pm, closed Mon, hols*) is where settlers framed American California's first
constitution. This is where to begin a tour and where to pick up an explanatory
map showing the way to other stops along the path: **Customs House, Allen
Knight Maritime Museum, Larkin House, Stevenson House** and the
Royal Presidio Chapel.

Pacific Grove Museum of Natural History

Forest Ave. at Central Ave. 🔄 *Open Tues-Sun 10am-5pm. Closed
Mon, hols.*

Just uphill from the beach and butterfly trees at Lovers Point, here are well-
arranged displays of local geology and animal life.

Pacific Grove shoreline

The **Great Tidepool**, immortalized in Steinbeck's *Cannery Row*, is the biggest
of a long series of rocky shoals rich in sea life. It is almost due w of Point Pinos
Lighthouse. The whole **Pacific Grove** shore w of Lovers Point gives good
vantages for watching sea otters, sea lions and scores of shorebirds. It and the
adjoining sandy cove of **Asilomar State Beach** are nature reserves where all
collecting of life forms is strictly forbidden.

Point Lobos State Reserve

w of SR-1, 3½ miles s of Carmel 🔄 *Open daily during daylight hours.*

The reserve protects an almost unchanged primitive ecological system
containing 300 plants and 250 animal species on 1,250 acres of land and
uncounted other species in 750 underwater acres. Of principal interest are
groves of Monterey cypresses, sea otters, sea lions and, from Nov-Feb,
migrating gray whales.

    Cars must stay on one long looping road, leaving the richest rewards to
visitors who walk the network of trails. When summer crowds overrun parking
facilities, latecomers must await their turn at the entry gate.

Oakland

*Map **14E3**. On the E shore of San Francisco Bay at the
intersection of I-80, I-580 and SR-17. Served daily by AirCal,
PSA, United, Western Airlines, Amtrak and Greyhound Lines.
From San Francisco, served by BART light rail trains and A-C
Transit buses i Oakland Convention & Visitors Bureau, 1330
Broadway, Suite 1105, Oakland 94612 ☎ (415) 839-9000.*

Sandwiched between San Francisco and Berkeley both physically
and psychologically, Oakland has been hard put to establish a
singular identity. It is still primarily an industrial city and not at all a

center of tourism. In the 1989 earthquake Oakland was very severely hit.

For visitors, interest comes mainly in the form of an engrossing museum, a vital waterfront and some pleasant parks.

Sights and places of interest
Lake Merritt
Three blocks away from Oakland Museum, at end of 14th St. ✱
The city park's children's fairyland, bird sanctuary and rental boats make it a respite for restless youngsters who have seen too many paintings at the museum (see below).
Oakland Museum
100 Oak St., Oakland 94607 ☎ *(415) 834-2413* ⊡
On its two lower levels, the museum has a fine permanent exhibition of California's natural and human history. The natural history section approximates a walk from Pacific shore to Sierra ridge line; the human history begins with Native Americans and carries forward to World War II. On the top level a chronology of California art progresses from the certain views of 19thC landscapists to the misty visions of contemporary painters. The museum also hosts major traveling exhibitions.
Oakland Waterfront
Oakland has a busy deepwater port with some of the most advanced container-ship operations on the Pacific Coast. Each Thurs, the Port of Oakland conducts four free boat tours of its harbor. Tours depart from a pier at **Jack London Square**, a bustling collection of waterfront restaurants and shops at the foot of Broadway. For tour information and reservations, contact **Public Relations, Port of Oakland** (☎ *(415) 444-3188*).

See also *Berkeley*.

San Francisco Peninsula
*Map **14F3**. Extends 35 miles s from San Francisco along US-101 and I-280. Served daily from San Francisco by Southern Pacific commuter trains* ☎ *(415) 981-4700 and Sam Trans buses* ☎ *(415) 761-7000.*
Although there is a long, lightly populated slope facing the Pacific, most locals think only of the narrower San Francisco Bay side when they say "Peninsula." Along the bay shore is a string of towns packed side by side from San Francisco to the Santa Clara Valley. For a place so small, with so few gaps between towns, it is curiously diverse.

Some of the towns are industrial, some middle-class commuter communities, some wealthy enclaves, some a mixture of any or all of the above. For visitors the most interesting districts are **San Mateo-Burlingame**, near San Francisco International Airport, and **Palo Alto**, adjoining Stanford University. Business travelers flock to electronics and space companies in the geographically imprecise but altogether real Silicon Valley, which extends s from Palo Alto to San Jose in the Santa Clara Valley.

Sights and places of interest
Bay Meadows Race Course
PO Box 5050, San Mateo 94402, adjoining US-101 at the Hillsdale exit 5 miles s of San Francisco International Airport ☎ *(415) 574-7223.*
The track is open much of the year for thoroughbred, harness and quarter-horse racing with pari-mutuel betting.
Coyote Point Museum ✩
Coyote Point Dr., San Mateo 94010, s of San Francisco International Airport, 4 miles to Poplar Ave. exit from US-101, then follow signs ☎ *(415) 342-7755* ⊠ ✗ *by appointment* ✱ *Open Wed-Fri 10am-5pm, Sat-Sun 1-5pm. Closed Mon, Tues, Jan 1, Dec 25.*
In recent years the decline of San Francisco Bay as a natural environment has been reversed. In a fine bayside park, Gordon Ashby's museum realizes brilliantly what is being saved. One huge room contains demonstrations of the bay area's six biotic communities arranged to approximate a walk from ridgetop to tide line, or vice versa. Visitors see living insect communities and films, and games-playing computers that explain what has to be done in nature

to assemble the ingredients of a hamburger and how to load Noah's Ark to keep the passengers from eating one another. (See *Oakland* for **Oakland Museum**, another Ashby design.)

Filoli 🏛

Canada Rd., adjacent to I-280 N of Woodside ☎ (415) 364-2880 💷
Open Tues-Sat 10.30am or 1pm, by reservation only, mid-Feb to mid-Nov. Closed Sun-Mon, hols, mid-Nov to mid-Feb.

In 1916, on a 750-acre estate, a locally famous architect named Willis Polk designed a grand house in the style of one built for the Duke of Devonshire by Christopher Wren and Inigo Jones. He surrounded it with Dutch, Spanish and Persian gardens, a knot garden and a stained-glass window garden.

National Aeronautics and Space Administration/Ames Research Center

Moffett Field, adjoining US-101 at Mountain View ☎ (408) 965-6497
💷 *Open Mon-Fri at 9.30, 10.30am, 1 or 2.45pm by appointment only.*

Tours include a wind tunnel, flight simulators and the airfield's flight line, all more exciting than the name promises.

Stanford University

General tours by students begin at the Palm Dr. entrance to Main Quad, Mon-Sat 11am, 2.15pm, Sun 2.15pm ☎ (415) 497-2862 💷

One of the great private universities in the USA, Stanford occupies a sprawling campus directly w of Palo Alto. The handsome main campus is reached most easily via the Embarcadero Rd. exit from US-101.

The **Stanford Linear Accelerator** (*2575 San Hill Rd., Menlo Park 94025, just over ½ mile E of San Hill Rd. exit from I-280, 29 miles s of San Francisco ☎ (415) 854-3300, ext. 2204 💷 open daily by appointment only, closed major hols*) offers a tour lasting about 2hrs that explains Stanford's mile-long nuclear research facility.

The **Stanford University Museum of Art** (*Lomita Dr. at Museum Way 💷 ✘ open Tues-Fri 10am-4.45pm, Sat-Sun 1-4.45pm*) contains an important Rodin collection. Other exhibits include ancient Oriental, Egyptian and primitive art, and early Californiana. The museum also has Stanford family memorabilia.

Sunset Magazine's Demonstration Garden

Willow Rd. at Middlefield Rd., Menlo Park 94025, 1 mile w of Willow Rd. exit from US-101, 26 miles s of San Francisco ☎ (415) 321-3600 💷
Open Mon-Fri 9am-4.30pm. Closed weekends, hols.

One of the Western US's most important publishers of magazines and books on travel, food, gardening and the home maintains a 7-acre show garden open to the public. Along a meandering path, there is a slow shift from groups of plants common to the sw deserts (anchored by a Joshua tree) to those of the Pacific NW (a grove of Douglas firs marks the spot). Tours include editorial offices and demonstration kitchens as well as the garden.

Santa Clara Valley

*Map **14F3**. From San Francisco, 46 miles s on US-101 or I-280. Served daily by AirCal, American, Continental, PSA, Republic, United and Western Airlines, Greyhound Bus Lines, Amtrak, and from San Francisco, by Southern Pacific commuter trains i San Jose Visitors Bureau, Paseo de San Antonio, San Jose 95113 ☎ (408) 998-7000.*

San Jose has been growing since the 1950s. Now, as the undeclared capital of Silicon Valley, this erstwhile sleepy farm town has passed San Francisco in population. With its companion communities it is double the size. San Jose used the Los Angeles formula of annexing huge swathes of grasslands, then filling them in with new houses and commercial developments. Where old towns existed, San Jose surrounded them. Some capitulated and joined. Some clung to their legal existence. A handful maintained their real identities.

The result of all this is northern California's nearest approximation of the LA style. The vitality is beginning to produce some quality to go along with the ugly and nasty. San Jose and its companion communities have the endless mediocre commercial streets, bewildering traffic jams and smog typical of fast, sprawling, car-oriented growth. But they also have a fine symphony orchestra, excellent shopping areas, attractive wineries and a grand theme park.

Sights and places of interest
Great America
PO Box 1776, Santa Clara 95052. The theme park adjoins US-101 at Great America Parkway exit, 45 miles s of San Francisco ☎ (408) 988-1800 ◼◼ ✱ AE 🏧 VISA *Open daily 10am-10pm May-first week in June; Sun-Thurs 10am-9pm, Fri-Sat 10am-11pm (10am-midnight on July 4) second week in June-first week in Sept; weekends 10am-10pm second week in Sept-last weekend in Oct and first weekend in Mar-first weekend in Apr. Closed late Oct-early Mar.*

Beyond its loop-the-loop roller coaster and two-story carousel, Great America shows off all the warm cliches of American history in 125 separate attractions and games. Bugs Bunny and other cartoon characters parade 200 acres of grounds, which include reproductions of a New Orleans French Quarter street, a New England seaport and a county fair. A theater and a giant-screen movie theater run all day. Admission covers rides and shows.

Mission Santa Clara de Asís
University of Santa Clara, on The Alameda between Santa Clara St. and Franklin St. ☎ (408) 984-4528 🏧 *Open daily.*

Founded in 1777, eighth of the California missions, Santa Clara is now part of the campus of the Jesuit Santa Clara University. Affiliated is the **de Saisset Art Gallery and Museum** *(☎ (408) 984-4528* 🏧 *open Tues-Fri 10am-5pm, Sat-Sun 1-5pm Jan 15-June 15, June 22-Aug 7, Oct 1-Dec 20, closed at other times and bols)*, which has mission artifacts and art exhibitions.

Villa Montalvo
Montalvo Rd., Saratoga, 3½ miles NW of Los Gatos on SR-9, Saratoga-Los Gatos Rd., to Montalvo Rd., then 1 mile sw 🏧 *(but* ◼◼ *weekends). Gardens open 8am-5pm, galleries open Tues-Sun 1-4pm. Closed Mon, major hols.*

Senator James Phelan built Villa Montalvo in 1911 as a private residence and retreat for artists. The art galleries in the house and the 175 acres of superb hillside gardens and woodlands are open to the public.

Winchester Mystery House 🏛
525 S Winchester Blvd., San Jose, directly N of I-280 at first exit W of its junction with SR-17 ☎ (408) 247-2101 (recorded schedule) ◼◼ ✗ *Open 9am-6pm. Closed Dec 25.*

Sara Winchester, Victorian heiress to the Winchester firearms fortune, believed in ghosts and fervently believed that they were out to get her. She sought to confuse them by adding new rooms to her house, making it an ever more baffling maze. Finally it had 160 rooms, 2,000 doors (most led nowhere) and 10,000 windows. There is also a small museum of Winchester firearms.

Wine tours
See map 16.

In recent years California wines have firmly seized a place in the world's top rank, regularly outpointing French classics in competitions. Wine is made all over the state, but the coastal valleys lead in quality and scenic appeal, making them a natural tour destination. Winery visiting is a popular California pursuit, and the industry is well used to visitors. Amenities range from simple cellar tours to restaurants, museums and elaborate tasting rooms. Cellar-door sales are nearly always offered. Ample signposts guide visitors, and maps and other literature can be had from the **Wine Institute** *(165 Post St., San Francisco 94108 ☎ (415) 986-0878).*

N of San Francisco, the Sonoma and Napa Valleys have the greatest concentration of quality wineries. S of the Bay area are San Benito and Monterey counties, while halfway to Los Angeles are the vineyards of San Luis Obispo and Santa Barbara. Wines of all styles are made, with a relatively new arrival being the Franco-American ventures into sparkling wine with Champagne expertise and California grapes. Several sparkling wine cellars are listed below.

Napa Valley
The pacesetter for a century in wine quality and now, due to scenic beauty and proximity to the Bay area, the prime wine-visiting destination. There are 150 wineries, ranging from the tiny to the giant. All the larger ones welcome all-comers, but many small

163

concerns ask for a prior appointment. Among those readily visited, and known for quality wine, are **Beaulieu**, **Berenger**, **Chateau Bouchaine**, **Clos du Val**, **Clos Regase** (where the architecture, too, deserves inspection), **Domaine Chandon**, **Domaine Mumm** (both Champagne-inspired and -owned sparkling wine cellars), **Freemark Abbey**, **Heitz Cellars**, **Inglenook**, **Charles Krug**, **Robert Mondavi Winery**, **Rutherford Hill**, **Sterling** and **Vichon**.

Sonoma County

This is w of the Napa, with a cooler climate and closer to the ocean. It is far less organized both topographically and for visiting. Several sub-districts and sub-valleys confuse the geography. Russian River is the largest wine district, with some 60 cellars along or near the freeway between Santa Rosa and Mendocino County 30 miles N.

Cellars readily visited are Buena Vista, **Chateau St Jean**, **Chateau Souverain**, **Clos du Bois**, **Dry Creek**, **Gloria Ferrer** (sparkling wine), **Hop Kiln**, **Kenwood**, **Korbel** (sparkling wines), **Mark West**, **Piper-Sonoma** (sparkling wines), **Simi** and **Rodney Strong**.

San Luis Obispo

The county's capital is the center of one wine district, and more vineyards cluster around Paso Robles to the N. Both are on US-101. Cellars readily visited include **Corbett Canyon**, **Martin Bros** and **Maison Deutz** (sparkling wines).

Ideas for children

Los Angeles, San Francisco and neighboring areas offer visiting children hundreds of opportunities to exhaust their pent-up energies in instructive play. This list notes only the most extraordinary possibilities. Fuller listings of each entry may be found in individual *Sights and places of interest* listings.

Animal parks and zoos

In California, as in much of the rest of the world, increasing emphasis is being placed on designing zoos that put animals into the best possible reconstructions of their native habitats. San Diego is far ahead of the rest in this effort.

Los Angeles Zoo   See *LA Sights*, under *Griffith Park*
San Diego Zoo   See *San Diego* in *LA Environs*, under *Balboa Park*
San Francisco Zoological Gardens   See *SF Sights*
Wild Animal Park   See *San Diego* in *LA Environs*

Books

Children's Book and Music Center   See *LA Shopping*, under *Specialty shops*

Great beaches

California's open ocean beaches seldom allow parents with small children to relax, primarily because of heavy surf. However, some ocean and many bay beaches are ideal for tots and youngsters. Those listed here have tranquil, warm water; most have sand fine enough for castle building.

Doheny State Beach   See *Orange County* in *LA Environs*
Mission Bay   See *San Diego* in *LA Environs*
Santa Barbara Beach   See *Santa Barbara* in *LA Environs*
Silver Strand State Park   See *San Diego* in *LA Environs*

Marine mammal shows

Marine mammal shows lifted much from the old-fashioned circus and put it into permanent surroundings of great style.

Monterey Bay Aquarium   See *Monterey Peninsula* in *SF Environs*
Sea World   See *San Diego* in *LA Environs*

Natural science museums and wildlife refuges
These differ from zoos in having fewer animals and more explanatory displays. The list also includes aquariums.
Coyote Point Museum   See *San Francisco Peninsula* in *SF Environs*
Living Desert   See *Palm Springs* in *LA Environs*
The Living Sea   See *Long Beach* in *LA Environs*, under *RMS Queen Mary*
Scripps Aquarium   See *San Diego* in *LA Environs*
Steinhart Aquarium   See *SF Sights*, under *California Academy of Sciences*
LA County Museum of Natural History   See *LA Sights*, under *Exposition Park*
The Old West
California grew up with Indian wars, the Gold Rush and suchlike Hollywood myths. Some lively souvenirs of the real thing still exist.
Gene Autry Western Heritage Museum   See *LA Sights*
Fort Point   See *SF Sights*
Levi Strauss History Room   See *SF Sights*
Wells Fargo History Room   See *SF Sights*
Science museums
In California's high-technology society, touchable science exhibits for children rank near the top of approved playgrounds with parents and youngsters alike.
California Museum of Science and Industry   See *LA Sights*, under *Exposition Park*
Discovery Room   See *SF Sights*, under *California Academy of Sciences*
The Exploratorium   See *SF Sights*
Reuben H. Fleet Space Theater and Science Center   See *San Diego* in *LA Environs*, under *Balboa Park*
Lawrence Hall of Science   See *Berkeley* in *SF Environs*, under *University of California campus*
Theme and amusement parks
Since Walt Disney first blended thrill rides into more appealing and instructive environments than the carnival or fairground, theme parks have blossomed around the country but notably in California. These are the major ones.
Disneyland   See *Orange County* in *LA Environs*
Great America   See *Santa Clara Valley* in *SF Environs*
Knott's Berry Farm   See *Orange County* in *LA Environs*
Six Flags Magic Mountain   See *LA Sights*
Tours of the entertainment industries
What with the the movies and TV, California has its fair share of industries requiring unusual equipment and skills. Many of these offer tours of their operations. A few are noisy and active enough enterprises to engross children. Two examples:
NBC Television Studio   See *LA Sights*
Universal Studios   See *LA Sights*
Transportation museums
Although contemporary California lives by automobile and airplane, it has museums in celebration of railroads and sailing ships as well as its current favorites.
Aero-Space Museum   See *San Diego* in *LA Environs*, under *Balboa Park*
Cable Car Barn   See *SF Sights*
San Diego Maritime Museum   See *San Diego* in *LA Environs*, under *The Harbor*
San Francisco Maritime Museum   See *SF Sights*
Travel Town   See *LA Sights*, under *Griffith Park*

Index

Bold page numbers refer to main entries. Ordinary *italic* page numbers denote illustrations and plans. Entries and page numbers in larger **sans serif italic** refer only to the British edition: for *Basic information* (pages 7-16), some index entries not in this special typeface may not apply to the British edition.

Index

Index

Index

Z
Zoos, 164
 Balboa National Park

(San Diego), 45
Los Angeles, 52, 53
San Diego, 103-4, 105

San Francisco
Zoological Gardens,
119, 131

Los Angeles street gazetteer

A substantial selection of streets mentioned in the text and labeled on the maps is listed below, with map and page references. As in the main index, page references for the British edition are printed in *sans serif italics*.

Gazetteers

San Francisco street gazetteer

See the introductory note to the *Los Angeles street gazetteer*, page 173.

Numbered streets

3rd St., 117, 136, 154; Map **13**D4

5th St., 130, 149; Map **13**D4

6th Ave., 128; Map **10**E3

8th Ave., 124, 133; Map **10**E3

11th St., 148; Map **12**E3

14th St., 144; Map **12**E2

16th St., 115, 148, 154; Map **12**F3

20th St., 130; Map **9**D4

A

Adler St., 125; Map **13**C4

Arguello Blvd., 119, 128, 132; Maps **10**E3, **11**D4

B

Baker St., 130; Map **12**B2

Battery St., 142, 148, 152; Map **13**B-C4

Bay St., 137, 154; Map **12**B3

Beach St., 131, 136, 152; Map **12**B3

Broadway, 121, 122, 140, 145, 148, 149, 152; Map **13**C4

Bush St., *15*, 138, 141, 143, 144, 152, 153; Map **13**C4

C

California St., *15*, 116, 117, 121, 124, 128, 133, 136, 138, 141, 142, 145, 147, 149, 151, 153; Map **12-13**C3-4

Carl St., 148; Map **11**F4

Chestnut St., 130, 148; Map **12**B2-3

Clement St., 119, 140, 146, 148, 150, 153, 154, 155; Map **10**D2-3

Columbus Ave., 17, 23, 121, 132, 133, 146, 147, 149, 154; Map **13**B-C4

Cosmo Pl., 145; Map **12**C3

Cyril Magnin St., 137; Map **13**D4

D

Dolores St., 129; Map **12**F2

E

Eddy St., 137; Map **12**D3

Ellis St., 123, 143; Map **13**D4

Embarcadero Center, *15*, 121, 129, 137, 142, 145, 149, 152; Map **13**C5

F

Filbert St., 126, 146; Map **13**B4

Fillmore St., 120, 140, 145, 150, 153; Map **12**B-C2

Franklin St., 120, 129; Map **12**C3

Front St., 144, 154; Map **13**C4

Fulton St., 124, 128, 129, 133, 147; Maps **10**E3, **12**D3

G

Geary Blvd., 116, 119, 120, 123, 130, 143, 146, 150, 153, 155; Maps **10**D2, **12**D3

Geary St., 123, 136, 137, 140, 146, 147, 151; Maps **10**D3, **12-13**D3-4

Geneva Ave., Daly City, 126; Map **9**F4

Ghirardelli Sq., 119, 142, 143, 152; Map **12**B3

Gold St., 129; Map **13**C4

Golden Gate Bridge, 127; Map **10**A2

Gough St., *15*, 123, 130; Map **12**D3

Grant Ave., 118, 119, 141, 143, 146, 151, 152, 153, 154; Map **13**C4

Great Highway, 128, 155; Map **10**E3

Green St., 140, 146, 147; Map **13**B4

Grove St., 149, 150, 153, 154; Map **12**D3

H

Haight St., 148, 153; Map **11**E5

Hayes St., 142; Map **12**D3

Howard St., 129; Map **13**D4

Hyde St., 123, 126, 131, 146, 147, 152, 155; Map **12**B3

J

Jackson Sq., 122, 129;

Map **13**C4

Jackson St., *15*, 129; Map **13**C4

K

Kearny St., 122, 125, 151, 152, 154; Map **13**C4

Kennedy Dr., 128, 155; Map **10**E3

L

Laguna St., 142, 151, 155; Map **12**B2

Lake St., 119, 132; Map **11**D4

Larkin St., 129, 131, 145, 153, 154; Map **12**D3

Leavenworth St., 126, 152; Map **12**B3

Lincoln Ave., 128; Map **10**E3

Lincoln Blvd., 127, 155; Map **10**A3

Lombard St., 121, 126, 134, 139, 144, 148; Maps **11**B5, **12**B2-3, **13**B4

Lyon St., 126, 130; Maps **11**B5, **12**B2

M

McAllister St., 125, 131; Map **12**D3

Maiden Lane, 143, 151, 152, 153, 154; Map **13**D4

Marina Blvd., 126, 155; Map **12**B2

Mariposa St., 124; Map **13**F5

Market St., *15*, 115, 117, 121, 122, 123, 124, 130, 138, 139, 146, 151, 154; Map **13**D4

Mason St., 122, 136, 142, 148, 149, 151, 153; Maps **12**B2, **13**C-D4

Merchant St., 140; Map **13**C4

Mission St., 118, 121, 130, 148, 154; Map **13**D4

Montgomery St., *15*, 121, 122, 129, 132, 133, 141, 151; Map **13**C4

N

Natoma St., 148; Map **13**D4

Nob Hill, 137; Map **13**C4

North Point St., 141, 144, 152, 154; Map **12**B3

Gazetteers

176

LOS ANGELES &
SAN FRANCISCO

LEGEND

Area Maps

0   10   20   30   40   50 MILES

Superhighway (with access point)

Main Road-Four Lane Highway

Other Main Road

Secondary Road

Minor Road

Scenic Route

Interstate Highway

U.S. Highway

State Highway

Ferry

Railway

Airport

Airfield

State Boundary

National Park Boundary

Place of Interest

Good Beach

Forested Area

Adjoining Page No.

City Maps

Major Place of Interest

Other Important Building

Built-up Area

Park

Cemetery

Railway

Municipal Railway Station

Cable Car Routes

Hospital

Post Office

One Way Street

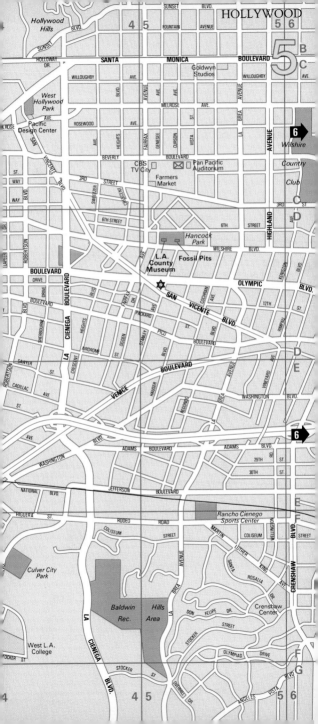

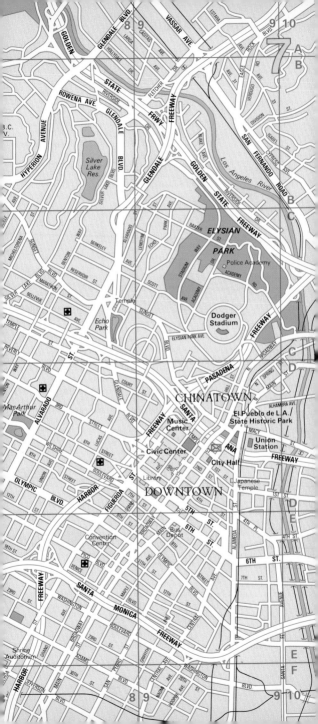

SAN FRANCISCO

0   0.5   1 mile

GOLDEN GATE

Golden Gate Bridge (Toll)

FORT POINT NAT. HIST. SITE

Golden Gate National Rec. Area

PACIFIC OCEAN

Bakers Beach

PALACE OF FINE ARTS

National Cemetery

PRESIDIO

Lincoln Blvd.

Tunnel

Mountain Lake

Lands End

SEACLIFF

El Camino del Mar

PALACE OF THE LEGION OF HONOR

California St.

Arguello Blvd.

Sacr.

RICHMOND

Clement St.

Geary Blvd.

30th   25th

Presidio Blvd.

ROSSI PLAYGROUND & SWIMMING POOL

UNI SAN FRANC

Seal Rocks

Pt. Lobos Ave.

Balboa Ave.

Funston Blvd.

CONSERVATORY

BEACH CHALET

DUTCH WINDMILL

BUFFALO ENCLOSURE

PORTALS OF THE PAST

DE YOUNG MUSEUM

KENNEDY DR.

Great Hwy.

J. F. Kennedy Dr.

GOLDEN GATE PARK

Stow Lake

Middle Dr.

South Dr.

ACADEMY OF SCIENCES

KEZAR STADIUM

Stadium

HALL OF FLOWERS

Golden Gate National Rec. Area

Lincoln Way

Judah St.

10th

Stanyan St.

UNIV. OF CALIF. MEDICAL CENTER

45th   40th   34th   30th

SUNSET

Noriega St.

19th

Grand View Park

Ave.

Laguna Honda

Clarendon

Sunset Reservoir

Sunset Hts. Park

FOREST HILL

Dewey Blvd.

McCoppin Square

Taraval St.

Portola Dr.

Playa

Ave.   Ave.   Ave.

Vicente St.

WEST PORTAL STA.

Mt. Davidson Park

PARKSIDE

Pipe Lake Park

Sigmund Stern Gro.

Sloat Blvd.

CHILDRENS STORYBOOK LAND

SAN FRANCISCO ZOO

Sloat Blvd.

Monterey

WEST OF

GL

Lake Merced Blvd.

Mercer

STONESTOWN SHOPPING CENTER

Ave.

CITY COLLEGE OF SAN FRANCISC

Skyline Blvd.

STONESTOWN

SAN FRANCISCO STATE UNIVERSITY

Serra

Junipero

19th

Ocean Ave.

TWIN PEAKS

Lake Merced

John Muir Dr.

Font Blvd.

Ocean View Playground

Alem

Brotherhood Way

Southern

Mission

WESTLAKE

Daly Blvd.

DALY CITY STN.

DALY CITY

Hillside Bl.

Mission St.

Thornton Beach State Park

John

A **B** **C** **D** **E** **F**

1 **2** **3**

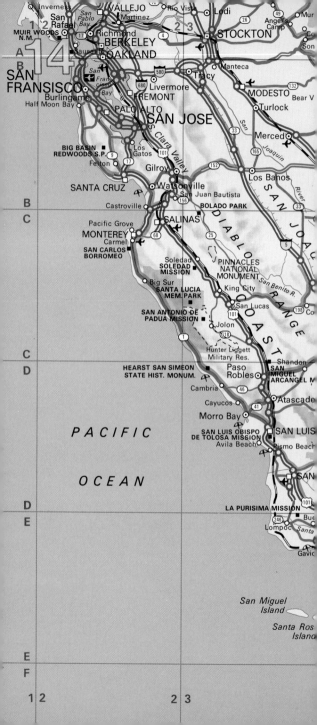